MW01484397

EMPATHY IN POLITICS AND LEADERSHIP

EMPATHY IN POLITICS AND LEADERSHIP

The Key to Transforming Our World

CLAIRE YORKE

YALE UNIVERSITY PRESS
NEW HAVEN AND LONDON

For information about this and other Yale University Press publications, please contact:
U.S. Office: sales.press@yale.edu yalebooks.com
Europe Office: sales@yaleup.co.uk yalebooks.co.uk

Set in Minion Pro by IDSUK (DataConnection) Ltd

Printed and bound in the UK using 100% renewable electricity at CPI Group (UK) Ltd

Library of Congress Control Number: 2025939827
A catalogue record for this book is available from the British Library.
Authorized Representative in the EU: Easy Access System Europe, Mustamäe tee 50, 10621 Tallinn, Estonia, gpsr.requests@easproject.com

ISBN 978-0-300-25960-5

10 9 8 7 6 5 4 3 2 1

To those who believe in the power of change and those who make it possible.

And to Mia and Kai, and future generations, in the hope that they might see the benefits of genuine political transformation.

Contents

Preface

How do we find our way back to each other? And how do we revitalise democracies that feel tired and broken?

These questions have animated me for years: both as an academic working on empathy and emotions, and as a citizen who grew up in the United Kingdom. The Brexit referendum in 2016 exposed the scale of divisions in our country, and revealed that the differences between us regarding our ideas of who we are, and who we want to be, were far greater than we had realised. Many of us had taken it for granted that – while imperfect – our membership in Europe, and all the rights and freedoms it accorded us, worked. But that feeling – as the No vote revealed – was not universal. While, as a Remain voter and passionate European, the result was personally heartbreaking, it highlighted a larger reality – our politics were not working for everyone, and no party seemed truly willing to have the hard conversations about what was needed to make it better.

When Donald Trump came to power that same year in the United States, against all the odds, it reiterated the disconnect between what many who lived and breathed politics thought was right and assumed was needed, and the reality of what so many people were really feeling. I spent the summer of 2016, before the election, on both coasts of America, and was struck by how much support there was for the Republican candidate. People liked his refreshing candour, his desire to break a broken system, and his refusal to play by the rules. This disconnect was hardly visible from Washington DC, where I was doing research for several weeks. Politicians were not connecting with those distant voters or speaking to their concerns and their experiences. So, while the result was a shock, it was not surprising. These patterns of disconnect are not unique to the United Kingdom or the United States, but are replicated in different forms around the world.

A few years later, I was back in the US, this time living in New Haven as a postdoctoral fellow at Yale University. When the pandemic hit in early 2020, there appeared to be another shift in politics. After several years of growing anger and frustration at politics, and deeper polarisation between Remainers and Leavers in the UK, Republicans and Democrats in the US, and similar divisions between the left and right across many countries, for the first six months (at least) it felt as if we were reminded of the importance of connection and had been offered an opportunity to make radical changes. The pandemic transcended political, national, economic, and religious backgrounds, and, while it hit some communities far harder than others, it touched the lives of everyone.

Inspired by political and community leaders who embodied empathy and made it central to their response, and with manifold examples of how friends and neighbours came together, and supported each other – at a distance, following official advice – we saw the power of our communities and had a brief glimpse that change might be possible.

I was invited to write this book in that summer of 2020. Against the context of the pandemic, it was initially intended to be a hopeful account about how, in the midst of the chaos and uncertainty of the time, empathy might prove to be the key to transform our societies for the better. Yet that would have been too easy, and the initial promise of hope was too short-lived.

PREFACE

For as well as revealing its potential, the pandemic demonstrated the challenges of empathy in politics. A year on from the start of the crisis, people became numb to the stories and individuals behind the horrifying death tolls. Some took advantage of the crisis for personal gain. Others withdrew further from the mainstream, finding solace and explanations for what was happening in alternative sources of information. Compassion and empathy fatigue set in.

The strong men who had proven ill-equipped to handle the initial crisis remained popular. Some won new elections, or, like Donald Trump, were historically re-elected years later, while leaders who had been praised for their empathy lost their seats or resigned due to the pressures of their time in office.

It was a period that revealed that empathy mattered, and that connection was something we valued and would miss if it was absent, but also that empathy is more delicate, precarious and difficult than catchy slogans about its power suggest.

This book aims to capture this complexity and these tensions. Empathy remains a critical attribute for political transformation, and for addressing the divisions and disconnects that have defined recent years, but it cannot bring change on its own. This book therefore offers a more comprehensive account of what is truly needed for empathy-centred change, how it could occur, and the obstacles to be overcome. It is informed by academic research, interviews, and experience in politics and policy.

I have seen the challenges of politics first-hand. In an office in Westminster, fresh out of a Master's degree, I was lucky to work for a frontbench politician for several years. He was an innate strategist who cared deeply for people and the constituents he served and would share with exuberance his frustrations with the status quo. He – like so many of the people I encountered across all the political parties – was motivated by ideals of social justice, equity, and creating opportunities for more people. He worked closely with politicians on all sides of the House, who would regularly pop by our office to speak with him, enjoy his sense of humour, and seek his advice.

It was here that I saw how much empathy features in politics and serves as part of the fuel for so many who enter our country's legislative bodies. Yet it is often stunted, inconsistent, and misdirected. Where it is present it soon encounters the frictions and realities of the machinery of politics. There is an unavoidable imperative to make compromises and sacrifices to win votes, not only with the electorate but also on the floor of the House. Few are rewarded for their care, and there are insufficient incentives to change this situation. In the current system, empathy stands little chance of yielding lasting change.

Working across political affiliations in my next role, at a non-partisan think tank, I was further exposed to the tensions that exist between empathy, politics, and policymaking in international affairs. So many of the people I met and worked alongside had a passion for change in the world and wanted to help those who are most vulnerable. They were committed to finding solutions to today's challenges, yet such aspirations repeatedly encountered the limits of politics and operated within systems and structures of power that constrained or undervalued our human inclinations to care and empathise with others to create better outcomes. There were recurrent obstacles: overly narrow ways of framing events, an inability to reflect on the causes of problems and our own role in them, and misplaced assumptions about what sustainable success looks like that impeded more creative approaches and, as a result, greater empathy.

These experiences informed my doctoral research at King's College London on the contours and value of empathy in international relations, research that has led me to now teach empathy and its role in strategy, diplomacy, politics, and security. Throughout this period, my thinking has been shaped by the big political debates and the disconnects of the past few years, as well as by my observations and conversations with countless people about what it is they want from our politics and what concerns them.

In such circumstances, when I tell people I research empathy in politics and leadership, they often are either surprised that you might find any, or curious to know how we can have more of it. Yet I have found it is neither the case that it is completely absent, nor as simple as injecting more. Across the political spectrum we know empathy matters, and we value it as an idea, but our task becomes far harder when we try to translate it into something tangible and real.

I have seen first-hand how empathy elicits very different responses, and how easily it can encounter resistance, especially when teaching people about its role in security, strategy, and diplomacy. Far from being put off, however, I believe we should lean into that discomfort and the complexities of the concept, as that is where we learn how to do it better. And we do need to do it better, because, done well and with intention, it is a way to re-energise politics, strengthen our democracies, and yield more inclusive, creative, and sustainable solutions.

Over the course of writing this book, I have lived and worked in the United States, the United Kingdom, Denmark, and now Australia. These different countries have shaped my worldview, and my beliefs, not only about what is possible, but also about what is needed, and what can be learned from others. Yet while these countries are distinct in their strengths and their values, in their political systems and the domestic issues they face, they all share many of the same challenges. To varying degrees, the growing disconnect from politics and mistrust of politicians and political institutions feels universal and rising. The failure of the traditional left and right to deliver a clear vision for change, and to speak to the real day-to-day issues affecting ordinary people, has left voters feeling like political nomads, or attracted to the farther reaches of the spectrum, where answers and neat solutions appear more readily available. What is more, in political decision-making chambers, and our own homes and communities, the tone and tenor of political discourse has become more tense, and more polarised. It is harder to discuss the views of others in a manner that is respectful and considered without resorting to stereo-types, anger, or moralising. Common ground feels more elusive, and less desirable as a political option. This needs to change. We need better politics, that delivers for the people, and for our future. This book offers a vision of what that might look like if we were to centre empathy and put people at the heart of politics.

Creating such change is a collective endeavour, and so this book is for a general readership. It is for those frustrated with the status quo and tired of broken politics and empty promises. It is also for those who believe that we can do better but want ideas and a foundation for their hope that it is possible. It is especially for those who want to be part of making a difference, and who are ready to lean into the power of community and active citizenry in whatever form that takes. And it is for those, like my younger self, who think politics does not concern them, or happens elsewhere. We cannot afford to be passive in contributing to the future of our societies, or our collective well-being. Healthy democracies depend on vibrant civil societies, and engaged electorates, but sometimes it helps to find points of entry and participation. As such, this book combines academic work with practical case studies and the insights and experiences of experts around the world to offer tangible examples of the potential for change, but also pragmatic awareness of the hard work still ahead.

In writing such a book it is impossible to avoid one's own politics. While I may lean left of centre, the values I hold dear – equality, fair-ness, justice, social well-being, and welfare – are not the sole preserve of the left. Many people I know with different politics share similar desires for a better future for the people they love, opportunities for personal and community growth, the right to rewarding employ-ment, a decent education, good housing, clean water, and security. We may have alternative ideas about how we get there, what compro-mises and steps it will take, and who should bear the burden of change. Yet we all want to feel empowered in our own lives, and have a degree of agency over our choices, even as we should also accept that being part of any community involves certain rights and responsibilities for the common good. This is the beauty of democratic societies. We have a rich diversity of ideas and experiences that makes us greater than the sum of our parts. The key is to find areas of commonality and embrace opportunities for dialogue, without descending into dehumanising language, vitriol, and contempt.

I am not naïve enough to think that change will be easily realised, yet I am reassured knowing that I am not alone in my belief that it is possible. As much as I share in the despair of the current moment, and the seemingly never-ending stream of bad news and new frustrations, I maintain a hopeful account of politics, partly inherited from my grandfather. He would sit at our dinner table and animatedly, and passionately, discuss the importance of politics to enhance the quality of people's lives, to give them opportunities previously denied, and to create from the sum of our individual experiences something far greater. As a headteacher he had seen first-hand the benefits of universal education in lifting people up and helping them find their purpose, and as a scholar of history he understood that change in society so often appears to rest on the confluence of key moments in time, and a vision, and concerted effort to break with the status quo. He and my grandmother, a nurse and similarly inspiring figure, had an unwavering faith in the intrinsic good of most people, and in the power of community. Well into their late eighties, they were active fundraisers, charity organisers, and community activists, taking part and showing up to make small changes in the everyday for their friends and neighbourhood. Such efforts add up, and when we look for them, we find that they are not isolated occurrences.

In every country I have lived in, and across schools, universities, the workplace, and in the community, irrespective of political choices and affiliations, I have consistently found that most people care for others and take care of others, not because it is expected or because it will enhance their status, but because they believe it is the right thing to do, and because they can. Certainly, there will always be outliers:

those who put themselves first and seek their own selfish gains at others' expense. However, we should see them as the exception, not the norm. So many of the people in these pages, and those I love and with whom I work and engage, balance their frustration at the deficiencies of our current politics with a pragmatic and proactive sense of optimism about what is possible, and a desire for change. There is hope in this energy and promise in its application. That is what we now need to harness.

Acknowledgements

Whenever I start reading a new book, I seek out the acknowledgements page early. It is there you see something of the journey an author has been on, and the people who have made it possible – sustaining an author's energy, ideas, and motivation, and critically offering invaluable support and input. No book is a solitary endeavour, and as this book has been several years in the making, I owe huge thanks to so many people who have been a part of that process.

Firstly, thank you to Yale University Press for commissioning this work and generously supporting it. Special thanks are due to my editor, Joanna Godfrey, for believing in this project from the start, and for her guidance, patience, and encouragement as it took shape. Thank you as well to Sophie Richmond for the thorough copy-editing, and to Rachael Lonsdale, Frazer Martin, Chloe Foster, Rachel Hunter, James Williams, Stuart Weir, Sara Magness, and the whole brilliant Yale team for seeing this through and for all you've done to turn this from page to print.

To my anonymous reviewers, who gave me invaluable and welcome advice on an earlier draft, in a way that was both kind and constructive. Neither were the feared Reviewer Two, and I am very grateful for their time and efforts in improving the book. And to my friends and colleagues who have read drafts and offered me valuable input and feedback, you have made this better, and clearer, thank you! Any errors or shortcomings are, of course, all my own.

I am incredibly grateful for the many people around the world who gave me their time, their insights, and their wisdom through the interviews for this book. These are the people who make politics a space of hope and possibility, who look at ways of doing things differently, and embody the idea that we can do more to create better societies and transform our systems. Thank you. I hope I have done justice to your expertise and experiences.

During three years in Parliament, I worked alongside so many brilliant friends and colleagues across all parties. In the example they set, and the aspirations they sought to realise, they have, perhaps unknowingly, sustained my optimism about the potential of politics to make a difference. I am especially grateful to Sir Nick Harvey, Yvonne Keer, Anthony Tucker-Jones, and our many amazing interns for my time there, as well as to Sarah Teather and Matthew Sanders and the team for giving a fresh graduate a chance and getting me hooked on politics.

At Chatham House, I was again fortunate to go to work each day among so many talented friends and colleagues. They enhanced my love of international politics and deepened my unwavering sense of hope about the potential for positive change. Special thanks are due to the International Security Research Department team.

Similarly, at King's College in London, I worked alongside so many brilliant academics and friends who critiqued and refined my thinking, pushed me to go a bit further, and offered a rewarding and enduring academic community. I am particularly grateful for the guidance of Professor Jack Spence and Dr Neville Bolt who supported my thinking on this concept and saw me through the PhD process.

I began writing this book at Yale University in 2020 where I was fortunate to have been a Henry A. Kissinger Postdoctoral Fellow, which gave me much-needed time and space to explore new projects after my PhD. There I was lucky to be surrounded by a talented and dynamic group of peers and staff. Special thanks are due to the brilliant academic team at the Jackson School of International Affairs, International Security Studies (ISS), and the Brady-Johnson Program, including Professor Paul Kennedy, Professor Arne Westad, Dr Michael Brenes, Professor Beverly Gage, and the late Professor Nuno Monteiro. I am grateful for the great cohort of post- and pre-doctoral fellows who shared the experience, provided a vibrant environment, and opened new ways of thinking. Some of my closest friendships were forged during this period.

In 2020, after America and before Denmark, I found myself without a base, the pandemic momentarily giving me a year to consider options and recover. Thank you to my cousin Katie, and Emma Sky, who each lent me their homes when I needed a base in London to begin writing this. Thank you also to Aglae Pizzone and her family for lending me their home in Odense for several months when I first moved there. Every time I have moved to a new country, I have been overwhelmed by the generosity and kindness of the people I meet who make it easier to settle overseas; thank you to everyone who has welcomed me and smoothed that process of settling in.

Tusind tak to the incredible team and my friends and colleagues at Syddansk Universitet in Odense. I am very grateful to the European Union for awarding me a Marie Skłodowska-Curie Fellowship that allowed me to study there and conduct my research, some of which informs this book. Denmark has a special place in my heart, and those two years taught me so much about the beauty of the country, work–life balance, hygge, and the art of fostering community at a societal level. Special thanks to Sten Rynning for morning coffees and book-writing chats, the brilliant War Studies team, and all my friends.

Now living in Australia, I am immensely grateful to everyone who has made me feel so welcome. Thank you to all those who have been a part of this journey and have made me feel so at home. A special thank you to my amazing colleagues and the team at Deakin

ACKNOWLEDGEMENTS

University and the Australian War College, who have been so supportive and patient as I finalised this book. And to the course members who remind me why I love teaching and consistently push me to deepen my understanding of what empathy means in practice, and the challenges and opportunities it poses.

To my many wonderful and inspiring friends around the world, who have heard me talk about this for so long, who are patient with me when I disappear to write, and who champion me from afar and make the process far less lonely. I do not get to see you nearly enough, but your friendship makes my world immeasurably richer.

The same is also true for my amazing extended family – the Yorkes and Richards – and the network of family friends who have always been there for me and my family. My grandparents on both sides have been particularly instrumental in shaping my approach to life, to people, and to politics. I have benefited from their support and only wish they could have seen the finished product, as I am sure there would have been lively debates to accompany it.

Naaman, thank you, for your kindness, your wisdom, your sense of fun, and your ability to ask the critical questions and get to the heart of a matter in a way that always centres care. You and Loki saw me over the finish line, ensuring I had tea, potato wedges, and wine whenever needed, and helping me maintain a sense of balance in the final push. Thank you for celebrating every step. You have shown me that sometimes love arrives when you least expect it and expands your world. I am very grateful as well for the wonderful Kranz family who have made me feel so welcome.

Finally, to my parents, Helen and John, and my sister Elaine, brother-in-law Luke, and magical niece, Mia. None of this would have been possible without you. You have supported my wild ideas and international moves and have been a constant source of encouragement and unconditional love. A thank you will never quite capture how much you mean to me, but I hope you can see your influence across these pages.

Introduction

Empathy is a concept that elicits an array of reactions. For some it is inspiring, offering a vision that celebrates our shared humanity and our differences, providing a path to greater connection and meaning within society. For others it is a source of frustration, a bug in the system that gets in the way of what matters most, manipulating our politics. For the more ambivalent, it can be seen as unnecessary or irrelevant, with little role in a politics they believe should be rooted in rational interests and the pursuit of power.

On the American podcast *The Joe Rogan Experience*, early in 2025, Elon Musk, one of the world's richest men, contended that empathy was 'the fundamental weakness of western civilisation'.[1] It was not, he argued, a criticism of empathy as a concept, as he recognised the benefits of caring for people and civilisation as a whole, but he feared empathy was being exploited by politicians and used against people's interests, leading to resources and initiatives being directed to 'liberal' priorities. Citing Canadian academic Gad Saad, he warned that it risked being 'suicidal',[2] leading to an excess of misplaced care that could overwhelm us.

Such negative comments on empathy are more than a passing critique or concern for a concept misused. On X (formerly Twitter) in mid-February 2025, Musk shared a meme referring to people on essential benefits as the 'parasite class',[3] using language that dehumanises people in vulnerable and precarious situations and implying there was a hierarchy of worthiness. His views on empathy are part of a concerted political agenda and a philosophy for how to reform government and redirect resources, rooted in a belief in the power of data, first principles, and the need to disrupt in order to create something better from scratch.[4] As his biographer Walter Isaacson noted several years ago, Musk's love of video games, especially civilisation-building ones like *Polytopia*, taught him that 'empathy is not an asset'.[5]

At the time of his podcast remarks, Musk was putting his ideas into action, making stringent cuts across the American federal government in his former role leading the Department of Government Efficiency (DOGE) for President Donald Trump. Ideas of connection, emotion, and shared humanity do not fit easily with such an efficiency-driven approach. In a matter of weeks, the administration and DOGE announced sweeping changes to social security benefits, the end of diversity, equity, and inclusion (DEI) initiatives, thousands of federal job losses, and critical cuts to grants and funding to institutions in America and overseas, including the US Agency for International Development (USAID). Millions of people in America and overseas found themselves in precarious positions, suddenly out of work, or lacking vital funding. This absence of empathy in how policy priorities are set and decisions are made has far-reaching and detrimental implications, at home and abroad.

Musk is not the only critic. There are growing voices in politics, especially among the American evangelical right, who consider it toxic,[6] a sin,[7] and dangerous to Christian values – in contrast to the more traditional roots of the religion.[8] Empathy, they argue is manipulating people to care about the wrong things and encouraging support of progressive ideals such as the right to love who you want, or to choose what you do with your body. Such views, it could be argued, are not entirely devoid of empathy; instead, in a polarised political environment, they reflect a form of 'parochial empathy',[9] directed to their own community, as part of a belief that some people are more deserving of empathy than others.

While cynicism about the revolutionary and transformative power of any concept is healthy, and necessary, the idea that empathy is a weakness in our politics and the source of contemporary problems is a misreading of empathy, its role, and its potential.

Indeed, far from being a hindrance to effective politics, empathy is a key to its transformation. In this book I argue that empathy is essential for healthy, robust, and effective democratic systems, and for vibrant societies where we celebrate diverse backgrounds and experiences, where more people can flourish, and where we are able to collaborate to address the challenges we face.

However, empathy is no panacea. It is embedded in power structures and asymmetrical relations that have to be observed and untangled in order to be changed.[10] It is not expedient. It does not help you get from A to B faster, nor does it yield neatly parcelled solutions. It is messy and complex, demanding and difficult. It requires courage, patience, a long-term investment in change, and a willingness to self-reflect and accommodate difference. Yet it is exactly what we need to navigate the present moment.

Around the world, politics is increasingly characterised by heightened divisions, a surplus of short-termism, and a lack of visionary, long-term leadership. In response to a series of crises, successive politicians continue to paper over the cracks with eye-catching short-term initiatives yet little of depth or substance. They have been swayed by the loudest voices but have failed to address the root causes of growing inequality, rising poverty, and the precarity far too many people face in accessing vital healthcare, education, welfare, and opportunities. There needs to be another way that can bridge the divides, connect us with each other, redefine what matters and what is important, and deliver urgently on what society really needs. Empathy is a route to that change.

This is therefore a book about why empathy is so important, and how it can transform politics, but it is also an exploration of why empathy is so hard to put into practice, and it offers a vision for how we can do better. For, even as we value it, we struggle with the demands empathy makes on us for understanding, compromise, and the accommodation of difference. If we want to create change it is not just about extolling its power or highlighting its potential: we have to know how to put it into action and rethink the ecosystem in which it is so needed.

DEFINING EMPATHY

I define empathy as an attempt to understand the experiences, perspectives, interests, beliefs, motivations, and feelings of another. It can never be completely accurate or definitive, as we will never truly know how the world looks from another vantage point, but in the process of seeking to understand others, the effort itself matters.

It is a process, a practice, an ethos, and a mindset. It offers both a lens to expand our aperture and view the world differently, and a tool to change it. Empathy is, in the words of Rebecca Solnit, 'an act of imagination'.[11] And it can be seen in the form of words, actions, and behaviours. In how we speak both to and about others, in how we connect and relate to others, and how we treat them with dignity and respect.

At heart empathy is relational, a process of cultivating connection to others and seeking to understand their experiences and perspectives. It is therefore iterative. It encourages us to be self-reflective and consider how we are experienced by those with whom we interact and engage, and the impact we have on them, so we can adapt accordingly. Our identity and sense of self are formed in relation to and difference from others; they are intertwined and inseparable.[12] As such, empathy involves genuine listening, and developing the curiosity, imagination, and humility to understand another. In the process

4

it reaffirms our differences.[13] Yet by seeing the world through the eyes of different people and communities, we can gain insight into other perspectives and ways of being, which can help us find spaces of commonality or ways forward.

Empathy is important because it confers recognition on people.[14] Tapping into very human needs, it says, 'I see you, I hear you, you matter.' It is therefore a powerful force in our sense of belonging, which can be both a demand and a need.[15] By failing to see people, to understand them as they see themselves, 'nonrecognition or misrecognition can inflict harm, can be a form of oppression, imprisoning someone in a false, distorted, and reduced mode of being'.[16]

Empathy is often divided into emotional and cognitive forms. Emotional empathy refers to the way you physically feel the experiences – such as the pain, joy, or anxiety – of another, as an embodied response. It is a sense of connection and deep understanding of what another may be going through, even if such insight can never be perfectly accurate. It is part of our internal wiring as humans, a trait shared with many in the animal kingdom. Biologists such as Frans de Waal have demonstrated, for example, how chimpanzees, bonobos, and rats respond to others, alleviating them of pain, or helping them to access food.[17]

Cognitive empathy involves a more deliberate and conscious process of seeking to understand the perspectives, experiences, and position of another. It can be more detached and rationalised: a mental journey of imagination and understanding. Such a form may be more calculated, designed to tap into how different people think and their perspectives, but it can also contribute to crafting more considered and intentional communications and relationships with others.

Far from being a neat binary, however, emotional and cognitive empathy are interconnected. For even in cognitive empathy, it is essential to understand the emotional dynamics at play, both in oneself and in the other person or group of people.

Empathy offers us a lens to understand the construction of meaning and significance in our lives. A central part of Verstehen, a concept made popular by sociologist Max Weber, empathy points to how reality is constructed through social interactions, through the meaning we give to events, ideas, circumstances, and identities.[18] Our worlds are of our own creation, and so empathy offers a way to understand the substance and worth different people give to ideas, values, principles, and ways of being and seeing the world. It is therefore a critical attribute for navigating the current political space.

Far from being weak or soft, empathy can be hard, and deeply uncomfortable. Empathising with others compels you to confront different perspectives and experiences, some of which may not sit easily with your own assumptions and sense of the world, and some of which you may actively disagree with or dislike. It compels a level of emotional literacy and maturity to sit with, and process, the uncertainty and discomfort it can provoke.[19] Empathy is therefore dependent on courage and emotional resilience.

Even though the concepts are similar and often conflated, empathy is distinct from sympathy and compassion. Sympathy involves an expression of pity, or sorrow, for another's situation. We can see it when leaders express sorrow or sadness for a national tragedy. Yet it often has a more distant quality: it is something that we feel for the suffering of another, but we do not necessarily partake in the suffering itself. Consequently, it can sometimes be seen as patronising or condescending; an expression of relief that we are not victim to similar misfortunes, or a pitying of the fate of another from a position of privilege or comfort.[20]

Compassion is more pro-social, evoking ideas of connection, kindness, and care for others. It involves a sense of obligation to respond to the situation of another, an ethical duty to alleviate pain or suffering. However, it is more overtly pro-social, connected to an ethics of care or empathic concern. It is an essential concept for good politics, as it centres the most vulnerable people in society, and encourages efforts to alleviate suffering.[21]

Jennifer Nadel co-founded Compassion in Politics with Matt Hawkins in 2018. Their organisation advocates for more compassion to create better politics. They work with politicians from across all parties, as well as policymakers, grassroots organisations, and other likeminded individuals in their call for change. Their vision is for the kind of politics that serves people better and prioritises their well-being, delivering on social justice, through a political system rooted in principles of integrity, empathy, and fairness.[22] I asked her what distinguishes empathy from compassion. For her, 'empathy is a necessary prerequisite for compassion', as compassion is rooted in empathy, but compassion goes further and is 'about taking action based on our understanding'. Critically, she argues, it 'can help re-assert the moral courage of politicians', giving them a cause and an impetus to act. Empathy does not compel action and can have positive and negative connotations. Yet empathy can help provide a more nuanced understanding of what action is needed, and how suffering can be addressed.[23]

Empathy certainly aids compassion and sympathy, and ideally it makes us more inclined to help others, but it is not essential. It can be, as philosopher Martha Nussbaum argues, morally neutral, an 'imaginative reconstruction of another person's experience, without any particular evaluation of that experience'.[24] It has contours and harder edges. A leader mobilising their country for war when faced with threats of violence from another needs neither compassion nor sympathy for their adversary. It is incredibly hard, if not impossible, to muster such feelings for someone who seeks to use violence and aggression against you and your people. Imagine President Zelenskyy asking the Ukrainian people to understand the Russians who are advancing on their cities and destroying their livelihoods. It is hard to envision, and politically difficult to sustain. However, empathy can help those in power to better understand their adversaries, the context of the situation, and their opponents' motivations in order to fight and defend themselves more effectively.[25]

Applied in this way, empathy can inform strategic and policy objectives. Strategic empathy is the idea that empathy is an asset for more effective strategy as it assists better understanding of those for whom, or against whom, you are designing policy.[26] It is less associated with kindness and more detached. In this form, empathy provides data and insight about how different people experience the world to shape policy choices and priorities. The 'strategic' prefix reduces the softer connotations of the word to make the concept more palatable and accessible for decision-makers, especially on defence and foreign policy where it is most used. Former US General H.R. McMaster has spoken repeatedly of its value in understanding America's adversaries, such as Iran and China.[27] And it is not a new concept. During the Cold War, political psychologist Ralph K. White made similar calls for American leaders to understand the Soviet Union better, and to avoid projecting stereotypes and false images to avoid conflict.[28] Used effectively in these critical political contexts, it can yield deeper levels of understanding and facilitate relations to provide more insights and contribute to better outcomes in more pragmatic ways.

At the more manipulative end, it can be used to exploit others or to exclude them. Indeed, some leaders and political actors use empathy to connect with their intended audience at the expense of others. It can exacerbate in-group versus out-group divisions, cultivating a strong sense of connection to those that we consider to be like us, and diminishing our capacity to see commonality in others.

Some of these forms of empathy can feel misplaced, treading a fine line between empathy and something else – especially for those who view empathy as intrinsically about kindness or virtue. Yet there is a distinction to be made between empathy as a way of doing politics, and empathy as an end in itself, as we will explore throughout the chapters of this book. By understanding the complexity and tensions within the concept, we are better able to determine its role and realise its potential, as well as accept and seek to overcome its limits.

EMPATHY, POLITICS, AND LEADERSHIP

Empathy's potential for transformation is the focus of a burgeoning body of work. People are extolling its value in enhancing the quality of our relationships and fostering greater appreciation of the strengths that lie in our differences. As a personal ethos, it can help us be a little bit kinder, more connected and engaged with our loved ones and our communities.[29] In businesses it is associated with more emotionally literate leadership and management practices that put employees, not profit, first.[30] As an essential tool of education, empathy can help students to open their minds and see the world through different eyes.[31] It can help foster greater resilience and a capacity for connection. In innovation and design it can help everyone, from service providers to town planners, governments, and global brands, to find solutions to problems with people in mind.[32] And it can be a central feature of emerging smart tech and artificial intelligence – with benefits and disadvantages – creating more responsive and attuned technologies.[33]

However, its role in politics has often been overlooked. When people talk about empathy's capacity to transform politics, we typically focus on the quality of our leaders,[34] and their ability to inspire us and guide us to embrace our better angels. But this rests far too much weight on any one person's shoulders. We are all fallible and inconstant, and we need more sustainable approaches. More than just empathetic individuals we need empathetic systems and ways of doing politics to create more lasting change. Empathy is a part of the process of deliberative democracy, of how politics is done and what it values.[35] It can be found in civil society, and in how citizens come together and connect, as well as in the forces and causes mobilising grassroots activism and protest. Healthy societies need these systems and structures of governance as much as they need the activists and agents pushing for change.

Politics is about how we live together, how we navigate shared problems, and create healthy, vibrant societies where people can flourish. It is inescapable, woven into the everyday fabric of our society. Empathy is something we should not leave just to our elected leaders. It should be something we each strive to utilise to create a better kind of politics and societies that are more secure, cohesive, and vibrant.

To understand empathy's role in politics, therefore, we should view it through the lens of an ecosystem, networked, interconnected, and incorporated and valued at all levels. It should be in the character and values of those who lead, in the infrastructures and systems of governance and politics, in the culture of how politics is done, in how we are represented, the stories we tell, and those that are shared by the media.

Approached in a more holistic way, empathy can encourage us to think more creatively about the problems we face, and as Jamil Zaki argues, 'by thinking different, we can choose to feel differently'.[36] If we can understand better how people feel, and why, and interrogate not only the sources of distress, trauma, insecurity, fear, but also hope, connection, and pride, such insights provide a richer picture into the state of society. Curiosity around new approaches, and alternative lenses for interpreting our current situation, can open up new avenues and offer innovative solutions to respond better to the needs and interests of society.

Empathy is key to such transformation because it is pro-social, what Roman Krznaric defines as a vehicle for social change.[37] It encourages altruism and awareness of the lives of others and our role in shaping them. It is, in the words of academic Neta Crawford, 'likely one of, if not the most important, routes to peace and justice'.[38] As it centres people, and encourages listening and dialogue to understand the needs, interests, and motivations of others, it is an essential ingredient for social and organisational change, and can contribute to more inclusive, equitable, civil, and just societies.[39] Done with intention, empathy offers the means to overcome divisions and find the common ties that unite us.[40] It is connected to trust, offering paths for restoring the connection between politics and the people, and increasing the necessary engagement for healthy democracies.

Nevertheless, even though empathy may be good for our politics, it must be voluntary, not mandated. If people are forced to care or shamed for being considered unempathetic it is self-defeating. We have to see the value of empathy despite the obstacles or resistance to it.

Precisely because empathy can be used so widely and have an array of applications, it can mean different things. I argue that for leaders and citizens alike, empathy in a political context can be a way of:

- connecting – by building relations and community;
- communicating – helping people to engage more effectively with others in dialogue, and convey understanding and care;
- thinking and learning – an ethos and mindset, that recognises the importance of listening and being attuned to how different people experience the world;
- practising – part of how politics is done, and a tool to design better and more sensitive policies;
- being – how we as individuals value others and relate to them with dignity, respect, and understanding;
- appearing – a more performative and image-based approach, that focuses on empathy's positive connotations for one's public image or reflects norms of expected behaviour in politics, albeit sometimes without the substance in action;
- envisioning the future – as an integral part of strategy and planning.

In this way, empathy can be a means of politics – a way of conducting politics, of communicating, understanding, and getting things done – as well as the end of politics. There is an important distinction between these two modes. Most effective politicians understand the power of empathy as a means. It is how they win votes, connect with an electorate, and build relations. Local activists and civic leaders similarly use empathy to cultivate community, to connect with others, and arouse support around pressing issues. Empathy as an end, however, is a vision for how politics should be. It is centred on the importance of healthy, pluralistic democracies that value debate and dialogue and difference. It involves putting people at the heart of our politics, and political institutions, strengthening the link between the individual and private, and the political and collective.[41] It means rethinking the way we do politics, opening it up, making it more inclusive, and centring well-being and a wider array of metrics beyond economic growth and national interests.

This book looks at both types of empathy. We need the means to improve the everyday, to reinforce the value of relationships and connection in the way we do politics, but for a more ambitious and sustainable vision, we also have to think more deeply and critically about the ends we want to achieve. How we do politics, how we think about each other, how we envision and create the societies where we can thrive and feel like we belong – what does success mean in such a context?

In considering these elements of empathy there is a further dimension. Politics tests empathy. Precisely because empathy is so valued as a moral attribute and mark of good character, there is a risk that it can be insincere, used to garner votes and win a popularity contest, but not to make lasting change. I therefore make a distinction between performative and sincere or genuine empathy. Both serve a purpose. Performative empathy is not intrinsically bad or morally lacking. It is an integral part of politics – of displaying understanding and care to a broad and disparate audience of people whom politicians do not know personally. Yet, without substance and action to back it up, such empathy can appear hollow. I contend that, ultimately, it is genuine empathy – empathy that is integrated into how we imagine and design political outcomes and learn to live together in our differences – that is what we should be striving for if we want to make lasting change.

Transforming politics is intrinsically difficult. Change normally occurs slowly and then in an instant, requiring both patience and rapid adaptability. It is a space of tough decisions, compromises, and inevitable disappointments. Whereas in small teams and businesses empathy can aid closer interpersonal relationships, assist in team-building, and cultivate healthier organisational cultures, in politics, leaders typically have sizeable and diverse audiences and the complexity of political preferences and identities to manage. In a country of 2 million or 200 million, or a community of 50 or 5,000, even the most inclusive of leaders will have opponents and critics. It is impossible to satisfy everyone. Yet small changes can have a significant impact, and we as citizens have a critical part to play.

Indeed, by viewing politics as an ecosystem, where the diverse elements are interconnected and exist in a symbiotic relationship with each other, it may also be easier to rally hope in the possibility of transformation, and recognise our role in aiding it. Antonin Lacelle-Webster, an expert and postdoctoral fellow in hope in deliberative democracies based at Yale University, articulates how hope is something that is shared and collaborative. For if we invest hope in an individual – a charismatic leader – we will invariably be disappointed. Instead, hope is collective, it is created through relations with others.[42] Understanding how we think of politics and accord it value is essential to revitalise these relations and energise a sense of what could be possible. Then, rather than passively hoping for change, we can claim our own agency and make small changes in our immediate circles that have larger ripple effects and wider cumulative implications.

By centring empathy, this book offers a different vision of politics and leadership, while also exploring the many ways in which it plays a role. It brings together diverse case studies from around the world, and examines some of those who exemplify empathic leadership, as well as those who have used empathy to sow division, to reveal empathy's role in politics at all levels. Admittedly, one of the limitations is that by taking such an international approach the book does not go into the specifics of any one country in depth, instead highlighting how empathy has been important in diverse contexts and cultures to extract lessons and evidence of how it worked and why it mattered.

In the process, the concept itself can be hard to pin down. Identifying and measuring empathy is variable and subjective. Despite the comfort we find in absolutes, and in neat black-and-white answers, when we engage with how people construct meaning, what they value, what they have experienced and perceive, there are few universal truths. Such ambiguity is unavoidable. The most interesting things in life, and in politics, happen in the grey space.

Here empathy is approached qualitatively, analysed in discourses, actions and behaviours, the signs and signals of public and political life, and the nature and quality of relationships. Discourses encapsulate all forms of public expression in written or spoken form by political figures and by the media and commentators. The meaning and significance of the actions and behaviours of leaders and other figures in politics are inferred and interpreted, judged according to criteria that include efforts to understand the experiences of others, to see things from different perspectives, and attempts to foster connection and relate to others.[43] The criteria also incorporates perceptions of integrity, sincerity, and credibility; levels of public trust and support in leadership; the ability of leaders to read events and the public mood, and their receptivity to change; personal humility and the ability to accept and admit error; efforts to speak to all of society and acknowledge differences in opinion and experience.

AN EMPATHETIC ECOSYSTEM

This idea of the ecosystem is reflected in the structure of the book. Chapter 1 begins by digging deeper into what empathy means for politics in the current context, the framework in which we should understand it, and why it is so needed now. It examines how empathy incurs costs, and challenges the idea that it is the preserve of any one part of the political spectrum, offering a path to lean into more collective ways of creating change.

Chapter 2 then turns to the importance of leadership, and the qualities that inspire and motivate us to embrace change, as well as how context can shape a leader's capacity to act, and the qualities we value. It also examines some of the tensions inherent in empathy and expands on the difference between the sincere and performative forms.

The role of leaders and political figures is carried into Chapter 3, which is about crises, and why empathy is essential to navigate the uncertainty and insecurity they present. The concept came to the fore during the pandemic, amid a series of political shocks and crises. This chapter looks at how such periods can test empathy, but also why it matters so much to reassure citizens, manage uncertainty, and foster greater resilience.

Power is an integral feature of politics, capable of causing harm or yielding transformation. Chapter 4 looks at how more populist leaders use a form of empathy to great effect, indicating to their supporters that they are the only ones who are listening and protecting their interests. The chapter also encourages a reconsideration of power, where it resides, and why. Empathy helps us to understand experiences of power and powerlessness, and what we choose to do with them. In the process it advocates a shift from power *over*, to power *with*, and calls for empathy to be at the heart of policymaking, to contribute to more iterative and citizen-centric approaches.

As political transformation requires new ideas and more creative stories, Chapter 5 digs into how these help define who we think we are, and their power to bring us together and overcome divides. Richer stories and ideas that centre people and community over profit or gain offer a path to a more vibrant and healthy society, and a means to guide new ways of thinking about the challenges we face.

Turning to the systems and structures of our politics, and how they shape political outcomes and the quality of leadership, Chapter 6 focuses on how we can improve the political ecosystem, rectify bad behaviour, improve training and conditions, and increase ways in which citizens can contribute to more tolerant and inclusive civic cultures.

Women may have been praised for their natural capacity for empathy and compassion during the pandemic, and the growing number of women in positions of power in recent years in countries such as Finland, Denmark, and Taiwan is seen as integral to valuing more empathic leadership styles.[44] Yet women do not have a monopoly on empathy, and a gendered view of such traits can do a disservice to all genders. Chapter 7 explores gender, the myths associated with it, and the importance of inclusivity and representation in politics. It highlights the challenges women face, the misogyny and prejudice that hinder greater representation, and the importance of fairness and equity. However, it also recognises that empathy-centric politics has to address the critical and growing experiences of marginalisation and disconnection among men.[45]

The media has a key role in connecting us to politics, and in telling better stories that can bridge divides and offer more hopeful accounts of human behaviour. Chapter 8 considers the media as an integral part of our democracies, and looks at how social media has brought new dynamics to the media landscape. It explores how politicians use the media to convey a certain image, or to engage with audiences. And, returning to the importance of telling richer stories, the chapter argues that we need to invest more in local media, to connect us more with our communities and help hold politicians to account.

Expanding on the importance of communities, Chapter 9 looks at how empathy is already flourishing across societies but is often hidden from view. In local politics and civil society in particular, people are already incorporating empathy into their work to transform how cities are run, creating communities that are more cohesive and inclusive, and building deeper citizen engagement and participation in politics. Connecting politicians and leaders with the people, it highlights how participatory democracy and citizens' assemblies can contribute to effective change.

Politics may look bleak right now, but our present circumstances offer a chance for a reckoning with what is going wrong, and where our assumptions and priorities are misplaced. Chapter 10 reflects on sources of hope, such as the opportunities that accompany crises and the potential for innovation they offer. It contends that there are benefits to be found in expanding the circles of our concern to make politics more inclusive and thinking more creatively about the challenges we face and the solutions we have available.

Finally, because it can sometimes be hard to translate the idea of empathy into something tangible and real in the everyday, after the Conclusion, I offer 'A Plan for Action': a guide to putting some of these ideas into practice and making changes in our lives, our communities, and our countries.

We need bolder, more creative ideas that do not just aim to go bigger in an attempt to catch headlines but go deeper, critiquing and challenging the prevailing assumptions of politics, power, and prosperity. We need a politics that gets to the heart of what people and societies need to thrive, and to live a 'good life'. A politics that offers a vision people believe in, and in which we feel we belong. Integral to that, what most people need, and want, is basic dignity. To be seen, to be heard, to know that they matter. This is not only about making people feel good but is essential to building cohesion in society and developing the resilience required to withstand the inevitable challenges that the future holds. From climate change, rising conflicts and resource scarcity to the rise of technology, population displacement, growing polarisation, and rapid social change, there are multiple storms ahead. We can only meet these challenges if we work together, if we lean into community, and our shared humanity, to transform our circumstances and create a different kind of politics.

1

Empathy and Politics

Politics is an imperfect, human science. Precisely because it is about people, it is messy and complex. It infuses every part of our lives: from decisions around international action on climate change, to national action on health and education, to the books local councils decide you are allowed to read in school. It is inescapable. Politics can be defined as an arena – a parliament, a legislature – or a process, a way of getting things done.[1] It involves 'a promise', between politicians and citizens,[2] that politicians will operate with citizens' best interests in mind, and for the good of the country. Indeed, what is the point of politics if not to improve our lives?

In his works, Aristotle speaks of politics as a means to create a virtuous society in which all citizens should be engaged as part of the political community.[3] However, it often does not work as effectively as it should.

Politics can be a source of belonging and of constructing cohesive societies that can navigate change. Or it can equally be used as a means of alienation and exclusion. As former Austrian politician Matthias Strolz observes: 'Politics is the place where we decide how we want to live together.'[4] In democracies this means embracing plurality, and the diversity of voices and interests within a political system. Yet, democracy contains within it implicit tensions. To be effective it is dependent on debate, dialogue, understanding, and the ability to make 'legitimate, binding collective decisions'.[5]

We are often insufficiently equipped to navigate the differences between us. In order to do so, therefore, we first have to understand the current context, the origins of the problems we face, and the dynamics at play. Second, we need to consider the obstacles to change, and the costs and limitations that empathy can involve. Third, we need to view change as a collective effort, not dependent on any one person or group, but on shared engagement and ideas of what kind of society we want to live in, and why that matters. Finally, we have to overcome the ways divisive politics blocks progress and stifles vital dialogue across parties. Empathy is not a unique trait of right or left, and we have to lean into seeing the humanity of the other side.

THE CURRENT CONTEXT

At the international level, the context is defined by growing insecurity and uncertainty. Conflict and aggression between countries is rising, calling into question the stability of global order and the values of democracy and freedom. And climate change is a collective existential challenge that requires not just effective leadership to yield sustainable and rapid solutions, but also whole-of-society approaches. This is hard to achieve.

In our current politics we are too often operating in systems that value zero-sum notions of success. In an adversarial political environment, where parties want to win at all costs, there is far less space for the dialogue and engagement required to understand the bigger picture or make concessions.

Moreover, democracy itself is more fragile. In 2023 Freedom House offered a dispiriting view of the state of democracy. Not only was democracy in decline, but the gap between those countries that are free and those that had deteriorated was at its narrowest in seventeen years.[6] There are growing curtailments on individual rights and freedoms. Protests are being banned or restricted in many Western democracies, with protests in support of Palestinians or climate action regularly being shut down or moved on in cities across Europe and America. The Economist Intelligence Unit's 2024 Democracy Index notes that although political participation has improved globally since 2008, the biggest deteriorations have been in civil liberties and electoral processes and pluralism.[7] A similarly negative view was offered by Transparency International's Corruption Perceptions Index of 180 countries, which showed corruption is rising.[8] Even among advanced economies, it is increasing. And while it may strengthen the hold of political leaders on power, it weakens the fabric of society itself, undermining trust and limiting engagement to particular groups.

To compound the problem, there is a shortage of courageous and visionary leadership: leaders who can put people first and navigate societies through crises with a calm head. This deficit leaves a vacuum easily filled by those with ready-made solutions and quick fixes. Too many politicians respond to passing moods, echoing and mirroring the trends of society and offering quick short-term fixes without looking beyond them and offering longer-term solutions. There needs to be a more sustainable view of what we need, and efforts to inculcate greater resilience within society, not only in terms of our infrastructure and our social foundations – such as healthcare, schools, and welfare – but also in terms of how societies feel, and in the levels of trust in politics, in institutions, and in each other. There needs to be a greater focus on strengthening our capacity to withstand crises without losing ourselves or what we value. A critical part of the solution lies in cultivating communities and a deeper sense of belonging. Yet this is hard.

At a national level there are significant problems that limit the ability of political leaders to effect lasting change or address international challenges. Crucially, there is near-universal low trust in our politicians, who typically score at or near the bottom of trustworthiness ratings.[9] This lack of trust shapes how people feel about the systems that serve them, and the politicians who represent them, making it harder to convince people of the possibility of change and the efforts required to realise it. This can lead to disconnection from the political process and apathy. As citizens, it is not enough if we only have a say and engage in the political direction of our countries at elections. Data repeatedly shows that continuous active engagement correlates with trust, in our politicians and our institutions.[10]

Within societies there is growing inequality. The pandemic put many of these challenges in stark relief. The gap between the richest and the poorest in society is widening and this has significant political repercussions. The contrast is particularly visible on social media, and in the celebration of billionaires while many are losing jobs or struggling to reach the end of the month before their pay cheque runs out. Such disparities in wealth corrode the fabric of healthy societies and generate resentment and frustration. Yet few politicians are willing to address the problem, instead tinkering around the edges without confronting the importance of equity and justice in our countries' economic policies, and the asymmetric burden it currently imposes on people. There needs to be a more honest conversation about wealth, how it is distributed, what is 'earned', and what is fair. Capitalism in its current form, without sufficient restraints and controls, does not work effectively for people or the planet. It is not just or ethical but exacerbates inequalities and contributes to divisions. Rather than working in the service of our democracies, it seems to be driving them, with big money and business interests shaping political agendas and determining priorities instead of working in support of them.[11] Furthermore, it is rapacious, with the constant desire to produce and create profit exceeding what is viable, sustainable, or – critically – beneficial for society and our environment. A key part of this involves moving away from models of success rooted in growth mindsets and GDP (gross domestic product) that may capture the overall wealth of a country but hide the daily reality of economic inequality.

One reason for the growing appeal and strength of populist leaders is that many of them speak to fundamental issues of economic security, housing, jobs, and food prices. While their opponents are calling out their character flaws and the dangers of a rise of populism, these leaders are highlighting the falling living standards and growing precarity more and more people are experiencing. These leaders are effective at political storytelling, able to express an understanding of the scale of the problems people are facing, and point to how politics is not working for people in a way that feels more direct and genuine than some of the more mainstream parties.

Moreover, we are more isolated and disconnected from our communities than before. Social media, technology, and the allure of our online worlds, with their veneer of validity, are partly responsible, but this is also on us and what we value. And it is dependent on how society is structured in terms of having the time, resources, and opportunities to foster connection. Long hours, low pay, exhaustion, and structural inequalities make it hard for people. Arguably, wealth can also be isolating, removing you from the everyday realities of others, albeit without the visceral fear of not being able to pay the rent or feed your children.

In May 2023 the US Surgeon General Dr Vivek Murthy categorised loneliness as an epidemic. It was not only that we are more isolated and marginalised than before, less connected to our communities, but an extensive tour of the United States had shown him that it has significant implications for our personal and societal health. His data suggested that loneliness incurred a '29% increased risk of heart disease, a 32% increased risk of stroke, and a 50% increased risk of developing dementia for older adults'.[12] Even more, it led to a 60% greater risk of dying early, and heightened problems with mental health and depression. He identified the tonic: social connection, community, and belonging:

Given the significant health consequences of loneliness and isolation, we must prioritize building social connection the same way we have prioritized other critical public health issues such as tobacco, obesity, and substance use disorders. Together, we can build a country that's healthier, more resilient, less lonely, and more connected.[13]

This goes beyond health-centred solutions: it requires a rethink of how we do politics, and how we cultivate connection.

Part of the challenge is our inability to see others in our society as equals. Across society, divisions have grown between those who disagree.[14] The United States is among the most polarised of democratic states, but it is not alone.[15] This involves both ideological polarisation – where division lines are based on political preferences and values – and affective polarisation – where they are due to feelings of distrust and dislike for those with different views.[16] Political leaders can stoke such sentiments, giving justification for people's grievances and turning them against their neighbours. These divisions are not entirely due to an absence of empathy, however, as empathy itself can contribute to polarisation as people turn towards their 'in-group' and identify those who do not belong.[17] Nor are such divisions new. Throughout history such tensions are a constant theme of politics, often in more violent ways. However, to counter the more negative current trends and divisiveness in politics, we need to get better at the art of conversation, and at listening to different perspectives and treating people with dignity in public discourse. This is more challenging when we are more isolated and disconnected from each other and from our communities than is healthy. Instead of curiosity, we are becoming more entrenched in our way of viewing the world. We lack the emotional language and literacy to encounter discomfort, and to process difference.

Among Americans, for example, there is a dismal view of the state of politics, with many feeling it is divisive, corrupt, polarised, and chaotic.[18] People are mixing less frequently with those who have different backgrounds and experiences, meaning they have less exposure to alternative ways of thinking, and are less likely to see others as their equals.

Politics and democracy itself need to be re-energised. Our political systems are typically not equitable. Some people seem to matter more, to have more power and louder voices.[19] Although there has been significant progress in increasing diversity in politics, legislative chambers still do not fully represent the diversity and demographics of the societies they serve, nor accord them equal value.

Nevertheless, even with the very real problems and challenges of our current moment, it is not all bleak. People are becoming more active. They want to share their voice, and they want to contribute to a different kind of politics. At the local level they are engaging in community building and leaning into being more active citizens. They are participating in protests, expressing their democratic rights and calling people in power to account. Such efforts may be slow, and encounter repression and stonewalling, but they have an impact and are a vital part of healthy democratic systems.

THE COSTS AND PRICE OF TRANSFORMATION

Such change does not come without costs and significant discomfort. And for many people in the current political climate, it seems hard to empathise with the other side. Empathy is a quality that often quickly dissipates at times of conflict or heightened tensions.

At a fundamental and personal level, empathy is deeply uncomfortable. This makes us reluctant to embrace its full potential. We like our own certainties: to feel our worldview is right, just, and true, and that others are wrong, or misguided. Empathy forces us to confront how different the world can be for others. It is not only about grasping the pain and hardships that others experience, but also the logics that guide their beliefs, the assumptions that feel at odds with our own. In being reminded of another's 'otherness', we become aware of our own, and this can challenge our sense of self.

Academic Naomi Head outlines some of empathy's costs – 'epistemological, cognitive, emotional, material, and embodied' – which involves costs to our identities, our sense of community, our thoughts, feelings, and sense of self.[20] This is especially true in times of conflict, where it is politically difficult, and even dangerous, for leaders to advocate empathy with an enemy. When leaders engage with adversaries, the analogy of Neville Chamberlain appeasing Adolf Hitler in 1938 is typically invoked – deriding the weakness in engaging with and offering concessions to aggressors. However, it is not just leaders who incur costs. It can be a lot to ask of the public to think differently about someone, or a group of people, towards whom they have previously felt animosity. It requires a dramatic shift in the whole of society, with the inevitable frictions that accompany it.

Yet, trying to understand the views of others, to see if there are opportunities to avoid conflict, or find grounds for cooperation, does not mean condoning them.

Even so, there are a number of barriers to empathy. Political psychologist Ralph K. White identified a series of factors that can impede it, including the reduction of complex situations to simple narratives, and binaries of black-and-white solutions. When our politics rests on deceptively neat answers, it is harder to see the nuance and complexity required for empathy to be effective.[21] Roman Krznaric identifies four blocks: prejudice, authority, distance, and denial.[22] We can choose not to see things or allow them to be obscured by our own assumptions and biases. Our proximity to events, or our desire to maintain a level of deniability can also make it harder to access empathy.

In his provocative book *Against Empathy*, Yale psychologist Paul Bloom argues that empathy's role in crafting powerful human stories can create hierarchies of concern that can distract us from a wider array of pressing issues.[23] By caring about the story of just one child with a terminal illness, there's a risk we miss hundreds of other children in urgent need of care, distorting policy choices and resourcing priorities. He argues instead for 'rational compassion' – an approach still rooted in care, but involving what he argues is a more detached and objective consideration of societal well-being.[24] Another academic, Fritz Breithaupt, similarly highlights the darker sides of the concept. Even while recognising that empathy is an integral part of being human, he notes that its application is not always positive, and sometimes can lead to 'self-loss', binary black-and-white thinking, or even vampiric empathy, which benefits the empathiser but not the recipient.[25] Empathy is a complex and multifaceted concept.

Moreover, as much as it may hold the potential for change, it also presents genuine challenges. Critically, empathy can perpetuate political power imbalances. If empathy is extended from someone with more power, to those with less, without due consideration of one's position, or a desire to change it, it can appear patronising or condescending, further exacerbating difference and hierarchies. Carolyn Pedwell points out how our focus on empathy can leave us failing to question its limits: 'empathy can distance as much as it connects, exclude as much as it humanises, fix as much as it trans-forms, and oppress as much as it frees'.[26] It can set the parameters of care, and delineate who is deserving of it. Yet all concepts can have multiple applications. Power can be used to lift people up or to suppress them. Security can mean initiatives to foster inclusion, cohesion, and community, or legitimise the introduction of walls, gates, and surveillance cameras. Empathy is no different.

There are further obstacles to change. The sense that our current mode of doing politics is crumbling can hold within it what American scholar and cultural theorist Lauren Berlant describes as a 'cruel opti-mism':[27] where a hope for a better life can be accompanied by a sense of comfort derived from the 'impasse' which stalls change.

Equally, apathy – a sense that nothing will make a difference and action is futile – can present sources of friction and frustration that get in the way of empathy. Apathy is not necessarily rooted in people not caring or being passive, but can be a product of caring too much but seeing too little change. Empathy and compassion fatigue can occur when there are overwhelming problems on multiple fronts and you have insufficient energy or resources to address them.[28] The belief that nothing can be done, and that the systems we have in place are unchangeable and 'as good as it gets', fosters disillusionment in politics and hinders the engagement required for something new. Once apathy sets in, it can lead to inertia and disengagement, making change harder. It also stifles curiosity – 'What's the point?' – and breeds a sense of futility, limiting our desire and capacity to imagine and create better.

CHANGE IS A COLLECTIVE ENDEAVOUR

Empathy in politics involves a level of abstraction. It is not just about empathy at an interpersonal level, or within your closest community. As a citizen, if you are asked to empathise with the problems facing school children who are going without lunchtime meals, with nurses who are working excessively long hours with low pay and few breaks, with industry workers who want better work-place conditions, or with foreign populations who require urgent resources to address famine or flood, this is an invitation to care about people you don't know, and to see your interests and well-being, and those of society, as tied up with theirs. This is a central feature of politics. Politicians and prominent figures invite people to care about certain causes – unemployment, housing, pensions – in order to facilitate the use of resources, budgetary allocations, or permit a change in priorities to address or alleviate the issue. In this way, as C. Daniel Batson and others explore, empathy for the collective good can be connected to social dilemmas.[29] Where is the balance between self-interest and collective interest and where are the thresholds? Working this out requires negotiation and accommodation in the public space.

The friction between care and self-interest is one reason why empathy is difficult to cultivate and why it can be unpopular in a political environment where scarcity is abundant. With finite resources, and a sense of frustration with the capacity of politics to bring genuine change, it can feel more appealing and more necessary for people and politicians alike to protect one's own interests instead of embracing the common good. And moving to a politics rooted in empathy will not be cost free. It will incur a short-term expense, even if there is a potential long-term gain. How, then, do we incentivise empathy in society? How do we change mindsets? One way may be by protecting inclusion, representation, diversity, and tolerance through the law and consistently upholding them. Yet even those rights that currently exist encounter resistance and are being dismantled in some countries. Since President Trump's election in the United States, DEI initiatives are being rolled back. This has international implications, as global companies like Goldman Sachs, Walmart, and McDonalds seek to ensure good favour with the administration by following suit. Empathy therefore has to be rooted in both a logical argument and clear vision of how and why it matters for us all in our everyday lives, as well as through a more collective story that creates an emotional connection to its benefits.

There needs to be greater public consciousness about how our lives and well-being are dependent on the strength of our societies and each other.[30] We cannot afford a zero-sum approach to politics but instead should centre our shared humanity and each person's intrinsic dignity. Such a concept is central to many national constitutions.[31] And, although dignity can be a 'squishy, subjective notion',[32] it emphasises the intrinsic worth of everyone and therefore accords value and recognition to all in society.[33] Recognising the dignity of all can also help prevent the dehumanisation of (some) others, which inhibits empathy. This aspiration starts, in part, with how we talk about those with whom we disagree, without belittling, humiliating, or dismissing them, and instead recognising their intrinsic humanity.

It is especially valuable for political leaders to do this, modelling the capacity for decency and respect in public office and political spaces. Investing in genuinely listening to different points of view and cultivating constructive dialogues that help all sides feel seen and heard can contribute to this shift. It is a work in progress.

However, science shows that empathy is something that can get stronger and better through practice.[34] It can be enhanced through training and is teachable.[35] Our capacity to become more empathetic is partly dependent on what Carol Dweck calls a 'growth mindset',[36] meaning we have a willingness to learn, grow, and improve. Yet it can be variable, and context dependent, so as Jamil Zaki argues, our empathy can be turned up and down, like a volume control.[37]

As an ethos and a practice of relating to and engaging with others, centred at the heart of political spaces, empathy connects people within society and facilitates the dialogue between political leaders and citizens. As a collective dynamic, it has a strong social dimension.[38] With the greater sense of awareness it brings, empathy should encourage people in positions of power to reflect on and understand how other people experience the world, and the impact that policy choices have on people's everyday lives. By expanding the political space, giving voice to more people, and taking into account more perspectives, empathy can contribute to vital efforts to engender more equity and social justice in society.[39]

The concept of empathy has ethical and moral significance. By understanding difference, and experiencing the world as others do, it compels us to reflect on our own identities and values, and who we want to be, and how our actions, behaviours, and choices have an impact on others.[40] In politics it prompts the question: What do we owe each other? It is therefore integral to a healthy and effective social contract,[41] offering a mechanism through which to manage the relationship that exists between the state, the people, and the institutions and organisations that comprise our society. It determines our rights but also our responsibilities, and emphasises the collective effort and investment required for vibrant, prosperous, and highly functional societies. The quest for more empathy offers a useful motivating question: How can we understand each other better and help one another more effectively to bring about constructive political change? To which should be added: What do we owe to our future? And how can empathy be more embedded and sustainable, so it is not just a passing phase?

In South Africa, the concept of *Ubuntu* captures the sense of interconnectedness of community. It is not only a word in the Zulu and Xhosa languages but also a philosophy. It centres our common humanity and is reflected in the Zulu phrase '*Umuntu ngumuntu ngabantu*', meaning, 'A person is a person through other persons.'[42] It emphasises the idea of according people respect and dignity, and promotes peaceful coexistence, dialogue, and harmony in our interactions. Shared prosperity is better than individual gain. It was an idea that underpinned the Truth and Reconciliation Commission of South Africa after Apartheid. Similarly, *Sawubona*, another Zulu word, means 'I see you' and carries the idea of recognising the intrinsic dignity and worth of others.

Collective ideas of empathy, connection, and belonging are animated, in part, by our emotions, and how we feel about our experiences, our current circumstances, and each other. Too often, in politics and society, there is a privileging of reason, as if we are solely thinking beings, capable of detached objectivity. We are encouraged to be careful of excesses of emotions and repeatedly lack the language and expressions to articulate and interpret what we feel and its significance. However, extremes of reason can be just as harmful as extremes of passion. They can lead to cost–benefit analyses and rigid metrics of success where complex human experiences are reduced to profit margins, efficiencies, or targets, without due consideration for how people feel, and how that shapes the quality of our well-being, or our capacity to thrive.

Emotions are an unavoidable and essential part of human life. They determine what we value, and offer insights into what works or what doesn't;[43] they also mobilise us to act. As Martha Nussbaum describes, they can 'have large-scale consequences for the nation's progress toward its goals', reinvigorating a sense of national identity and belonging, or creating and strengthening new divisions and amplifying tensions.[44]

Our politics is often less about what is most in our rational interest, than what we *feel* to be important. People in more precarious economic and social circumstances will often vote for parties who propose policies that disadvantage them at a rational level – tax cuts for the rich, cuts to welfare and benefits, or privatised healthcare – because other policies these parties offer speak to how they feel about the direction of their country, to their fears and hopes, or to their sense of identity and values.

Our societies and social interactions are guided by emotions, collective feelings, and shared investments in pride, anger, joy, grief, or anxiety. Indeed, 'some of the most profound forms of empathy are built on the shared experience of pain, anxiety, and loss'.[45] They often prompt us to bond over a shared experience and lead to opportunities for the creation of shared meaning.

They can have a 'sticky' or contagious quality,[46] especially when they are intense. We can catch emotions, internalising the public mood and responding to the vagaries of current events and popular opinion. These processes can emerge organically from within society, to some extent, though deeply influenced by all forms of media; they can also be guided by leaders who can shape our response to circumstances. Anyone who goes to live music, festivals, or sports events knows the contagious feeling of belonging and shared emotion in the moment of an epic song, a dramatic win, or humiliating loss. Emotions circulate and resonate with people in different ways, shaping how they perceive and interpret events. As a result, they can help 'shape political agency', and the sense of power or connection people have with ideas, and their ability to influence events or enact change.[47]

Politicians can influence how we feel and legitimise empathy as a collective response. They can equally shut it down, disparage it, and make it part of a narrative of weakness or submission to an 'other'. This is why what people in politics say and do is so important: how they talk about people, the values they champion and those they diminish. Through their actions and communications, they can determine and model what is permissible and what is possible. This shapes what we feel we can and should do. Likewise, when they extend care, they create greater space for it in society.

Yet it is also not a one-way street, or a top-down process. In healthy democracies, civil society and the media equally provide scope and latitude for leaders to adapt, to be braver and more courageous, and to offer a vision knowing they are on firm ground. Politicians operate within an 'Overton window', or the boundaries of what is possible, acceptable, and legitimate in political debate.

Civil society and the media can expand these boundaries, and create space for different approaches. This has been visible in how political debate has changed across Europe towards providing humanitarian responses to the Palestinian people in Gaza and calling for an urgent end to the violence. For Western politicians, the Israeli–Palestinian conflict is all too often a political third rail – one that they are reluctant to touch. However, sustained protests and criticism from citizens and public figures about the silence of governments as the death toll of innocent civilians rises and the living conditions in Gaza deteriorate has led more politicians to speak out about reaching a resolution to the conflict and delivering relief. In Western Europe, new research by YouGov shows that public opinion on Israel's actions has reached the lowest level since 2016. Overall, 63–70% of countries have an unfavourable view, with only 6–16% of publics across the region believing the response to the horrific events of 7 October 2023 are just and proportionate. Such shifts legitimise new political action.[48] Politicians can feel more assured that the numbers are on their side – although, in an ideal world, political convictions should not be dictated by poll numbers.

How, then, do politicians and collectives move from being to transforming? Greater emotional literacy and agility are critical.[49] By being conscious of how we and others feel, and why that is, we can forge stronger feelings of connection, compassion, or empathic concern, and respond more effectively to others. In this way empathy can 'be actively cultivated in an effort to construct more inclusive, non-violent and rehabilitative configurations of community'.[50]

Politics also has to convey an idea of a collective vision and collective good, including the sacrifices and compromises it may take to realise it. Central to that is storytelling.

Politics has always been a process of storytelling. It is a negotiation of how we give meaning to who we are as people, as communities, and as nations. These stories shape what we value, where we direct our attention and our care, and where we invest our political capital and resources. Sometimes these stories are at the expense of one group or another. Sometimes they are too simplistic and exclusive. Part of empathy's power is that it offers us opportunities to tell different stories. Stories that are more inclusive, expansive, and empowering, that speak of hope and connection, not fear and division – that encourage us to think and feel beyond ourselves. To counter the despair and frustration of the current moment, we need to tell better stories about who we are and the aspirations we have for the future. These stories have to capture the scale of the problems, while also offering pathways to fix them. Working collaboratively we have to weave the threads of our diverse experiences together in order to make our politics and our communities richer and more resilient.

EMPATHY ON A SPECTRUM

Each of us has a distinct and innate scope or range of empathy. Depending on factors such as our backgrounds, the circumstances of our upbringing, our socio-economic status, our present circumstances, our sense of self, and our cultural heritage, we may more naturally feel greater empathy for some people over others. These alignments of who and what we care about and empathise with shape our political colours and identities. Those who care most about maintaining traditional family values and a hands-off approach to politics might tend more to the right, whereas those who care most about the environment are more likely to lean more towards the Greens. Those who care passionately about the rights of animals may find common cause with smaller parties that champion such issues. Our spectrum of emotional engagement and care determines what resonates with and motivates us. We can go beyond this, and widen our ambit, but this often needs to be more intentional and considered, taking the time and effort to look beyond our areas of comfort and what we know. That is, ultimately, the purpose of empathy in this space.

Irrespective of their political colours, most politicians I speak to cite empathy as a motivation for pursuing a political career. The majority entered politics because they wanted to make a difference. They care about local issues, they seek to understand the people they represent, and they know the importance of connecting and engaging with the electorate to realise political and policy objectives and gain re-election.

Among them, Janet Rice is one of the founders of the Green Party in Victoria, Australia, and was a senator from 2014 until 2024. Empathy is an important motivating force in her work. She entered politics due to a strong commitment to care and social well-being, and a passion for the environment informed by her background as a climate scientist. She found community in urgent campaigns to protect the environment, such as the 1983 Franklin River Blockade and, despite frustrations with the status quo and the lack of genuine progress in the country, she has found most MPs to be empathic at a personal level. They want to make life better.[51] When speaking about how change occurs in politics, she observes that the debates that most move people in committee meetings and on the floor of the House are those that elicit empathy and care from fellow politicians. These might be stories of a family who are left homeless as a result of financial policies and economic blindspots, or children who have suffered neglect, compelling a change in child protection laws.

Similarly, in the United Kingdom, the Rt Hon Johnny Mercer told me of the centrality of empathy to his work. He is a former military officer and former Conservative politician for Plymouth, Moor View, who lost his seat in the 2024 election. As a serving MP, he would not only meet and greet constituents, but spend time with them – nurses, firefighters, teachers – to understand how they worked, what challenges they faced, and what solutions they wanted to see, irrespective of their political affiliations.[52]

Nevertheless, despite it being common for so many who enter politics, empathy is often seen as a preserve of the left.[53] It has featured more prominently in the language of left-identifying politicians such as Jacinda Ardern, Barack Obama, and Joe Biden, who have heralded its value. It is found in ideas of the welfare state, or raising the minimum wage, or expanding civil rights.

Some research appears to support this. Studies done in Israel, the US, and Germany on the differences between liberals and conservatives revealed that, on average, liberals – those more associated with the left – tend to have a greater tendency towards empathy, want to feel it more, and are more keen to help others. And both liberals and conservatives feel more empathy towards their own in-group.[54] However, such neat binaries can be problematic. Much can depend on the context, and whether people of different political persuasions see those they should empathise with as part of their in-group or not. People of faith, for example, may feel more deeply for others of their faith on certain matters, irrespective of their political leanings.[55]

Those who identify with the right of the political spectrum argue that they also care. In 2002, George W. Bush launched an initiative to put care at the heart of his Republican platform. He wanted to move away from 'big government' and 'indifferent government', and encourage the American people to be citizens, not spectators.

I call my philosophy and approach compassionate conservatism. It is compassionate to actively help our fellow citizens in need. It is conservative to insist on responsibility and results. And with this hopeful approach, we will make a real difference in people's lives.[56]

The initiative did not fare well; if it was well intended it was short-lived, attracting criticism that it was a marketing tool, designed to provide a kinder veneer for several pet projects and issues. And its approach to investing in welfare initiatives, such as helping the unemployed and investing in education, put off the more financially minded Republicans.[57]

Yet, many years later, President Bush continued to stand by his conviction that compassion was not incompatible with conservativism. Indeed, he wanted to push back against ideas that conservatives were 'heartless'. It is, he argued, a conservative and compassionate approach to ensure families have more money to spend, that children are properly educated, and workers needed to be supported if they were being displaced by changes in the workplace.[58]

Under Prime Minister David Cameron, the Conservative Party in the UK adopted a similar approach, giving it a British flavour. For Cameron, the launch of compassionate conservativism was rooted in the importance of trust, inclusion, and the empowerment of people. It was accompanied by ideas of a 'Big Society' that would develop civic engagement and give people more agency. In a report for Policy Exchange, a right-leaning think tank with strong ties to the Conservative Party based in London, Jesse Norman and Janan Ganesh championed the approach. They argued that it was what was needed to gain a better understanding of British society, and what it could become, and thus create 'radical, effective and wide-ranging new policies'.[59] Ideas of care, compassion, and empathy are not tied to any one political colour, though they may translate into different types of politics depending on where, and for whom, such care is directed.

A former UK Government special advisor who worked under David Cameron, Alastair Masser, confirmed the sincerity of this commitment to care. Yet he noted how it was striking that the more conservative parties feel the need to claim the mantle of compassion and understanding, to counter perceptions of them being the 'nasty' party or the 'uncaring' rich. In contrast, the left normally has to fight stereotypes that its care is naïve, misplaced, or weak.[60]

What the left frequently missed, he said, was that they often approach a problem with similar priorities but different solutions:

> Look at trains in the United Kingdom, one side wants to nationalise the railway, the other wants to privatise it. Yet if we actually sat down and talked about it, we would find that we can agree on the desire and intention behind our policy positions – we want trains that run on time, are affordable, and comfortable.[61]

It is a critical starting point for dialogue, but one we miss when we focus on our political colours instead of the issues at hand. Too often we get angry at how someone votes – just because they are a Tory or a Social Democrat – before we get curious about who they are, and what motivates them.

For his opponents, President Donald Trump is hardly considered an empathic leader: he mocks disabled people,[62] makes derogatory and demeaning comments about women, and regularly insults political and media opponents. Yet many of his supporters see him as a figure who takes them seriously, listens to their concerns, and gives them a voice in a system where they feel unseen, unheard, and disregarded. He speaks in everyday language and says what he thinks – something many people I spoke with in rural America in the run-up to the 2016 election liked about him. They were frustrated at the ubiquity of glossy media-ready politicians who did not listen to them or understand their reality, offering only slick soundbites instead of real change.[63] This speaks to the disconnect of politics from the people. Many people thought Trump lied, that he was abrasive and difficult; they were not blind to it, but they felt other politicians were the same in their own way. Unlike them, however, he did not make them feel inferior, and they felt he took them and their concerns seriously.

Indeed, many figures on the right argue that it is the left that fails to understand the current frustrations and grievances of people who feel that the growing inequalities and insecurity they are experiencing are the product of a lack of care from the 'political elite' who are detached and uninterested in their reality.

Indeed, the political left can be equally guilty of invalidating others who view the world differently. The idea that they are motivated by care or better values, while their opponents make decisions based on a lack of education or understanding of government or are motivated by greed or self-interest, limits the ability of the left to engage with those who disagree. They can look patronising or superior, and this stance creates blind spots that deny our shared humanity, regardless of how we might feel about each other's politics. Empathy can exist even if it does not align with our own politics, or if it is not directed towards the groups we empathise with or support, whichever side of the political spectrum we are on.

There can be a contentious moralism in associating one's own politics with greater empathy – it signals a perception of virtue and care in opposition to another. It can make us feel good, but also casts a judgement on others, especially as the traditional notions of left and right have changed and our politics are more fluid. Rather than us being identified by any one party, our politics are increasingly governed by the issues that matter most to us. In this way, left and right might overlap on topics like healthcare, economic policy, or foreign policy, even whilst they come from different perspectives. We can see this in the mistrust of vaccines: some on the right – like US Secretary of Health Robert F. Kennedy Jr – consider vaccines to be harmful and argue against policies that make them mandatory, while on the left, wellness gurus and 'influencers' – who, one may assume, might have more social-democratic economic leanings – are similarly concerned about vaccines' impact on health.

Denying the capacity of others to care – especially those who are political opponents – can be detrimental to building the dialogue needed for change. It risks demeaning their sense of their moral code and worth. It implies they are heartless, or unkind, and obscures the complexity and nuance of all our politics. Instead we should all try to engage with people on the basis of the arguments, and avoid ad hominem attacks.

How our empathy manifests, and where it is directed, may differ, but it is something we can harness more effectively across the political dividing lines if we talk about the issues – taxes, transport, access to healthcare, gas prices – rather than the identities and ideologies of those involved. As part of this, by focusing on what people are *for* – rather than against – we can find areas of commonality and connection. Peter Coleman, a professor of psychology and education in New York, has done a series of experiments with people on contentious issues like abortion, and found that once people have time to speak to those on the other side of the divide, and to see their reasoning and that they care, while this may not change minds, it does reduce some of the animosity and facilitates finding more constructive ways forward.[64] It also ensures a focus on the problem and creates initiatives to find collaborative solutions, with give and take involved from all sides.

Empathy recognises that we will not always agree, and will always have our differences, but asserts that our strength also lies in those differences. In the current polarised environment, this feels hard to countenance. We do not want to accommodate extremism – on any side. Nor should we. But to find a way beyond the current extremes, we have to get better at meeting in the middle – at finding the common ground between the moderates on both sides and listening to one another as equals with dignity and respect. This means focusing less on how voting preferences shape empathy, or which political colour can most accurately claim the mantle of care, but engaging more in essential conversations about what are the priorities for society, and how you conduct yourself when encountering difference.

*

Instead of ascribing empathy to any one group, therefore, it is helpful to see that these different sides of the political spectrum may all use empathy as a political means. It is an asset in the art of connection, of fostering relationships, and building bridges between divides. But we must also care about the ends. For truly empathetic politics and leadership, empathy should be an ethos and a practical approach that centres care, creates more inclusive spaces, and bolsters pluralistic and participatory democracy.

Despite the obstacles, there are many causes for optimism. There is a genuine appetite among people for change, for more involvement in democratic decision-making, and a desire to contribute to shaping the future.

In the face of multiple competing political crises, with some political leaders drawing dividing lines and arguing for a return to past glories, there is space for an alternative, more hopeful vision. One that celebrates what we share and articulates how we can coexist and thrive together. More than wishful thinking or laudable ideals, we need a clear path to get there and examples that show it is possible to create a more inclusive, representative, and engaged political space. This is why effective leaders are so important. They should energise and inspire us, turning apathy to hope and galvanising action and engagement.

2

The Art of Leadership

Mia Mottley, Prime Minister of Barbados, speaks often about the significance of empathy, compassion, respect, and dignity for politics. In 2018, when she addressed the United Nations on climate change shortly after becoming leader, she called for new approaches to rectify the serious failings in this respect, especially towards the 'Global South' and more vulnerable states. 'I say simply that we cannot plan our affairs or that of our people on the basis of luck. It must be on the basis of policy and decisive action but above all else on the basis of caring and empathy.'[1]

At home, she conveys a similar ethos, championing golden rules about how people in society should look after one another. She is one of many leaders to evoke empathy as a key part of their leadership ethos and guiding values, and as a tool to navigate global challenges such as climate change and economic inequality.

Former president of Ireland, Mary Robinson is another such leader. During her time in office, from 1990 to 1997, empathy was visible in her approach to others and to the divisions of the country. Now, as a member of The Elders, an independent group of global leaders founded by Nelson Mandela in 2007 to promote peace, justice, and human rights, Robinson speaks often of the importance of empathy, not only 'in family, in community, in country, at so many different levels', but also as a means to address 'the gross inequalities that raise issues of justice'.[2] It is a route to collective action, and people coming together to effect change. In the process, she recognises how such an approach requires one to be comfortable with being unpopular, especially as a lawyer championing issues that may not serve those in power, such as human rights.

There is greater appetite for such leadership. It makes us feel more connected, more seen and cared for by those in positions of power. Following the pandemic, multiple surveys and articles revealed that people increasingly wanted empathy from their leaders, championing its value in workplaces, relationships, and society.[3]

At the same time, however, a common default at times of uncertainty and insecurity, can be to look for the strong leader. Those who articulate the problems, give voice to the grievances, offer easy answers, and identify themselves as the solution. The familiar idea that the strong leader is the most effective is a myth, albeit a pervasive one.[4] While they may exert a firm hold on power, they make their countries poorer. They show little trust in society, or the media, eroding both and stoking divisions, undermining the values of democratic pluralism. Their approach yields heightened insecurity, fear, restrictions on freedoms, and the growth of vested interests and wealth in the hands of a few at the expense of the many.

For those who seek to push back against such leadership it can be too easy to play the same game. To mirror and echo back the divisions, instrumentalising and amplifying them as a way of gaining and maintaining power. Instead, we need leaders to act as lighthouses, offering steadfastness and dependability to navigate the chaos, while providing a light and sense of direction to guide us to better shores.[5] This is dependent on the strength of character and moral courage of a leader and their capacity not to be swayed by every small event, as well as our sense of connection and trust in their vision.

This is where empathy is an asset. It can be an attribute of leadership, a character trait and virtue that signals a leader's connection to the people and their moral qualities. It can also be a way of leading, putting people first and centring care, inclusion, and societal well-being. It is a tool and skill to navigate crises, to reassure citizens and provide understanding at testing periods. Yet it is a versatile and multifaceted concept. In politics, it can be seen as a weakness, a naïve response to complex and challenging problems, especially when dealing with matters of security and national identity. But it puts people first, and centres a better kind of politics, even when it is not expedient or easy.

THE TRANSFORMATIONAL LEADER

Political leaders hold a variety of roles and responsibilities. They are the representatives of a people and responsible for governing on their behalf. There is a critical distinction between those who merely have authority to govern, and those who inspire us to be more than we thought, and to be active and engaged members of the political community. James MacGregor Burns wrote of the difference between transactional and transformational leadership. Whereas transactional leaders base their politics on the exchange of goods, power, and needs, meeting the basic requirements of the electorate in exchange for support, transformational leaders are 'more potent'.[6]

Certainly, disruptive leaders can be transformational, leaving a country dramatically different from the one they inherited when they took office. They can embody strength and determination, be immoral and corrupt, and have the capacity to drastically alter politics. Yet they do not enrich the country or instil a greater sense of belonging, community, and cohesion. They weaken democracy and faith in the power of democratic institutions to represent the people and support them in their daily lives. Such an argument admittedly reflects a normative judgement: that leadership should serve the people, not those closest to the leader, and that those in power should enrich society and expand the opportunities available to citizens.

Leaders should excite and inspire us, empowering our best instincts. This demands of them 'courage and character',[7] and the ability to navigate their unique circumstances with equanimity. Such leaders have vision[8] and can even be revolutionary,[9] offering radically different ways to coexist in society.

Such a leader 'seeks to satisfy higher needs and engages the full person of the follower' in a relationship that elevates both, converting followers to leaders and leaders to 'moral agents'.[10] It is a mutual relationship and interaction, that inspires collective action and social change. 'The transformational leader emphasizes what you can do for your country; the transactional leader, on what your country can do for you.'[11] They inspire civic engagement and share power more widely within society.

In part they do this through the strength of their own character and their example – including their higher moral qualities.[12] Nelson Mandela's experiences gave him moral authority. It is hard not to respect a man who has spent over twenty-seven years as a political prisoner, and who emerges from his confinement more compassionate and committed to a positive vision of the type of country and society that he believes the people can create. Nelson Mandela's mastery of his emotions, and his magnanimity towards his former captors and the Afrikaner government served as a source of inspiration around the world and offered an example for others to follow. Despite the hardships he had endured, when he took office as South Africa's president on 10 May 1994, days after the end of Apartheid rule in the country, Nelson Mandela sought to mediate between a desire for peace among the people, and those who wanted to see justice or revenge.[13] Through force of will, and with a unique story of triumph over adversity, he demonstrated that another way was possible, showing the power of alternative approaches rooted in empathy, unity, and cooperation.

Such leaders understand the importance of how people feel, and how to 'touch citizens' hearts and to inspire, deliberately, strong emotions directed at the common work before them'.[14] This was visible with Ukrainian President Volodymyr Zelenskyy, whose bravery inspired collective action, creating a strong sense of common fate and a clear vision for how his country would navigate adversity and withstand conflict.

In the first few days of Russia's invasion of Ukraine, in February 2022, expectations of the Ukrainian president were low. He was a celebrity politician with limited experience, more famous for playing a high-school teacher-turned-politician in the TV satire *Servant of the People* than being one. As President Vladimir Putin began his assault on Ukraine, people assumed Zelenskyy and his family would take the first flight out of the country, as offered to him by American forces. From the outset, the size of Russia's armed forces compared to Ukraine's looked to be unbeatable. With a military force of around 900,000 active forces against Ukraine's 196,000, the odds were not in his favour.[15] Zelenskyy's fate, if he stayed, was expected to be short and sealed. And yet, he remained.

From his office, dressed in combat fatigues and a simple army t-shirt, he spoke to the people about the significance of the moment and his steadfast commitment to them and their country. Later, he shared videos online of himself walking around Kyiv with his team. He would tour hospitals and get to know the patients, share dinner with soldiers – many of whom had been civilians just a few days earlier – and meet with the citizens who were pushing back against the Russian aggression. He listened to their stories, heard their hopes and fears, and thanked them for their efforts. His message was clear: he was going nowhere, and they were all in this together: 'I need ammunition, not a ride.'[16] He put empathy into action, signalling shared purpose, connection, and experience with the people. In so doing he defied the odds, demonstrating a powerful example of the strength and value of leadership and courage in a crisis.

There is immense power in such acts of bravery. It boosted morale among the Ukrainian people. Zelenskyy was struggling politically before the conflict, but his approval ratings went from 31% to 90%,[17] and prominent critics who had questioned his leadership now revised their opinions.[18] His commitment to his country gave a common purpose and intention. It led many ordinary people to enlist, or to find ways to fight back and support the country on the frontlines, and in their towns, cities, and online.

It was in these very early days of the conflict that he also spoke to the Russian people. In Russian, his native tongue, he emphasised their shared history, their common bonds, and how this conflict would affect all sides.[19] Even though his speech was unlikely to be seen in Russia, it spoke to the futility of the conflict and the potential for a different future. It was these actions, and his courage and tenacity in standing up to Putin's expansionist ambitions, that proved inspirational. Internationally, he received widespread acclaim from allies and NATO countries. In December 2022, he was *Time* magazine's 'Person of the Year', in recognition of the force and impact of his leadership.[20]

True leaders elevate and empower the people.[21] They help them realise their full potential, giving them agency and trust to make the necessary changes. Importantly, they lead with them, as well as for them. Effective leadership builds bridges and collaboration rather than assuming one hero or 'great' man or woman can fix everything. None of the challenges we face can be addressed by any one person or country alone. We need leaders who can work with others, who are able to build consensus and cooperation, seek advice from experts, and learn and adapt as they see the implications of their political ideas turned into reality. This applies within their parties, their cabinets and governments, and in wider society.

Ego can be a critical hurdle to such leadership. It centres self over others, can compel self-interested behaviour, and make people susceptible to over-react to perceived slights. When politicians feel vulnerable, or attacked, they can often shy away from the healthy confrontation and the contestation of ideas that can make them better. It can lead them to surround themselves with supporters and 'yes'-sayers who will not give the kind and honest, albeit often hard-to-hear, truth they may need. The capacity of leaders and the qualities that define their role are therefore also shaped by the people they have around them, ensuring they do not become disconnected or isolated from the people they serve, or the issues they have to address.

Effective leaders have to balance accessibility with authority – being seen not as imprinted by the last person who spoke to them, but open to hearing different perspectives. They must be reachable, especially for those in their party. Sir Nick Harvey, former Liberal Democrat politician, defence minister, and a close friend of former party leader, Royal Marine and diplomat Lord Paddy Ashdown, reflected on how the latter used to love to test out his ideas. Paddy would often invite his close friends and party allies to debate with him – at the time of his leadership there were forty-six MPs in the party – and be proved wrong. He wanted people to critique his plans, demonstrating an intellectual humility that was rarely perturbed by challenges from others to his own thoughts and ideas.[22]

However, as much as national leaders may shape the trajectory of a country, our lives are also deeply influenced and inspired by other leaders who transcend borders and champion vital political issues. These figures draw attention to inequalities, campaign for better well-being, or create opportunities for those the current system leaves behind. Such people have the power to change the conversation or mobilise action in support of a more hopeful vision of possibility.

Among them, Malala Yousafzai is a powerful Pakistani activist and leader with global reach. She was born in Swat Valley, where her father was a teacher who ran a local girls' school. When she was just 11 the Taliban took control of the region and put severe restrictions on the rights of women and girls. Passionate about her right to an education, she began to speak out for the rights of girls to have the same educational opportunities as their male counterparts. This made her a target. In October 2012, while she was on the way home from school, a masked man boarded the school bus and shot her in the head. Flown to the United Kingdom for lifesaving medical care, she woke up ten days later, requiring further extensive surgeries and rehabilitation to recover from the attack. Despite the threats against her, she has continued her campaign and set up a fund with her father to support girls' access to education and opportunities. In 2014, aged 17, she became the youngest ever Nobel Peace Prize Laureate.[23]

Her work has sparked vital conversations and action on education around the world, especially for girls, and inspired millions. Her leadership and authority comes not only from the conviction of her advocacy and its relevance to millions around the world who are denied a good education, but also from how she champions the cause, and her courage, tenacity, and endurance in the face of adversity and threat.

Similarly, Denis Mukwege, a gynaecologist and humanitarian from the Democratic Republic of Congo (DRC), is famed for his care and support for women who are survivors of sexual violence. In 1999 he established Panzi Hospital in Bukavu in the DRC, initially to help offer maternity services in a region with high maternal mortality rates. Mukwege has spoken about how its purpose quickly changed after treating women who had experienced horrific sexual violence during conflict in the country.[24] Since that time, Mukwege and his team have treated over 80,000 women and girls, providing invaluable support, and they have campaigned to reduce the stigma and shame associated with sexual violence and rape. His mission has been to encourage a deeper understanding of sexual violence as a weapon of war, and its consequences, both to generate more empathy and understanding for survivors, and to find ways to prevent it.[25] He has also been awarded a Nobel Prize for his efforts and continued commitment to humanity, helping the issue receive wider attention.

Beyond the prominent figures and the celebrities, some of the most influential people are those in our local communities. They are just as important. These people dedicate their lives to creating participatory spaces and community. They take part in local politics because they want to improve the quality of life for people in their area, volunteering time to those in need, and sparking innovations from the ground up. An expansive definition of political leadership reveals that great leaders are not only in the highest offices or in charge of governments. They are closer to home. And once we start looking, there is genuine hope to be found in the sheer number of people driving positive change, sharing their vision for how we can be better, and creating solutions to the problems we face away from the spotlight and outside of conventional party politics or electoral systems.[26]

EMPATHY IN LEADERSHIP

Empathy is a prominent quality in effective leadership. But it does not have one form. It is dependent on individuals, their role, their audience, the circumstances, and their strengths and values. In his work on applying empathy to organisational leadership, Michael Ventura speaks of seven archetypes and how the concept manifests in different ways according to personality types and skill sets. There is the Sage, the Inquirer, the Convener, the Alchemist, the Confidant, the Seeker, and the Cultivator. Some people are better able to listen, others to bring people together in ways that feel organic and safe. Some nurture others, while others are pushed by their curiosity to ask the deep and difficult questions.[27] In politics too, empathy is distinct to the individual's means of expressing and conveying it. It may also have different functions and roles.

Returning to the seven criteria outlined in the introduction, empathy can be used as a means of connection, communication, thinking and learning, as part of political practice, a way of being, a way of appearing, or for conveying a vision for the future. Taking each in turn we can see the value it brings and the attributes.

First, it can be a means of connection and relating to people. Good politicians are accessible and relatable. Even if we do not always agree with their politics, we can recognise their innate abilities to connect and represent people. Australian leader Bob Hawke has been rated the second-best prime minister in the country's history (second only to the wartime PM John Curtin).[28] He successfully drove a modernisation of Australia's economy in the 1970s and was a talented handler of Cabinet. But he was also well liked by the electorate and enjoyed meeting with them. He is famed for achieving a record beer skol – drinking a yard of ale in eleven seconds – and, despite having received a Rhodes Scholarship to Oxford, he carefully cultivated what Australians call 'ocker chic'. He constructed a sense of being a 'man of the people', and a larrikin[29] – identifying with normal Australians and not a select elite.[30] He also offered a vision of how, by 'sticking together', the country could be stronger and more dynamic.[31]

Second, it can be a means to communicate and convey care.[32] People who met President Bill Clinton, even those more cynical about his charms, would come away speaking of how personable and magnetic he was, how they felt very seen and were impressed by his presence. There was a strong charisma. Such a quality was evident during his election campaign. In a famous town hall debate in 1992, Bill Clinton joined the incumbent Republican President George H.W. Bush, and independent Ross Perot, to speak about their vision. In the context of the financial crisis at the time, a woman in the audience asked the three men whether they were truly able to solve America's problems when they had no direct experience of the challenges ordinary Americans were facing. Answering first, George H.W. Bush struggled with his response. He could not understand the question, nor see why his distance from poverty might make it hard for him to meet the needs of millions of Americans. Indeed, he turned it around and invited the audience to empathise with him and the challenge of his role and position.

In contrast, when it came to his turn, Bill Clinton reiterated the question, checking that he had understood the woman correctly. Then he spoke from his personal experience. He knew those who were struggling, who had lost their jobs and livelihoods, and were facing bankruptcy. He had grown up with them. They were in his town. Going beyond demonstrating understanding, he provided an explanation and an account of the problems in the system that were causing so much suffering. Too many people were being left behind and the government had failed to invest enough in communities, healthcare, welfare, and education.[33] It was a powerful performance that influenced the campaign. He won that election.

In the political space empathy involves a personal ability to connect with others, to relate to them and communicate in such a way that they feel they matter, and that you understand them. It is a central part of effective political communication, along with the power to move and mobilise people with words.[34]

Third, empathy as a way of thinking is visible in how President Obama centred it so often in his writings and his works. It was a fundamental ethos in his politics and his intellectual philosophy. We see it too in how New Zealand Prime Minister Jacinda Ardern asserted it as a central feature of her leadership ethos. Pushing back against those who viewed it as naïve or a weakness, she countered: 'It takes strength to show empathy.'[35] It requires courage to use empathy to confront issues head on and not shy away from what might be difficult or uncomfortable. And it takes courage and humility to understand the limitations and blind spots of one's own worldview. Such courage, matched with competence, can command respect.

Fourth, empathy can be integrated into political practice, a way of building inclusion into one's leadership and politics that encourages diversity of thought and experience. This can be part of political practice in coalition governments, where different parties must work collaboratively to understand and manage their distinct political agendas to deliver a shared mandate. It is also an element of participatory democracy, such as citizens' assemblies (featured in Chapter 9), and emphasises the value of understanding the needs of different people to shape more inclusive politics and enhance citizen engagement by cultivating deeper awareness of democratic practices.

Yet empathy can be part of a more intentional effort to model reconciliation and build bridges after periods of conflict or disunity. The sixteenth President of the United States, Abraham Lincoln, who served from 1861 until his assassination in 1865, was one of those leaders who made it a part of his approach. Praised for his ability to unite people after the violent civil war that had divided the country, his Team of Rivals was a unique cabinet that brought together figures from across the political spectrum and sought to heal the nation.[36] Such initiatives and examples of bipartisanship and cooperation happen far too rarely.

Fifth, empathy can be a way of being. A leader's character and commitment to their ideals can make them a compelling and inspiring figure at home and abroad. In Uruguay José Mujica, known familiarly as 'Pepe', was president between 2010 and March 2015. The international press would refer to him occasionally as the world's poorest president, the most radical,[37] and a philosopher president.[38] He was famed for his humility, his empathy, and his enduring commitment to the socialist ideals that had fuelled the political activism and violence of his youth.

At a time of instability and inequality in Uruguay during the 1960s and early 1970s, he had been a member of the Tupamaros guerrilla group – a violent, armed, Marxist group who were part of a revolutionary uprising against successive governments that they considered to be inefficient and incapable of addressing the deep socio-economic crisis in the country, and who, especially under the leadership of the Colorado Party and President Jorge Pacheco Areco, cracked down more strongly on unions and student groups. As a result of his actions and beliefs, Mujica spent around thirteen years in solitary confinement. Like Nelson Mandela, he was forced into a period of self-reflection and contemplation about his ideas, and what makes good politics, and the steps required to address the challenges of his country. In the documentary film *El Pepe: A Supreme Life*, he attributes to these experiences the making of his character and approach to leadership. Had he not had such time in isolation, he noted, he would have been 'more futile, more frivolous, shallower', 'more success-driven, more short-sighted, more aggressive'.[39]

As president, he drove an old sky-blue VW Beetle, with no motorcade, and lived in a humble house on a farm with his wife. He would do walkabouts around local towns with few of the security and protection measures of other presidents. Each month he would give away between 70% and 90% of his salary to support the country's poorest and invest in housing schemes, such as Plan Juntos, which ensures those in the poorest areas have housing – especially as these areas have the highest proportion of children and single mothers in need of help. However, his legacy is mixed. While he may have been inspiring in his care, he did not necessarily achieve transformation in the country. Some big plans fell short and lacked investment.[40] The danger of the ideal of a 'saviour' leader is that no person can ever truly live up to the hype.[41]

Sixth, because empathy connotes moral qualities and virtues, it can be an integral part of a leader's image – of how they want to appear and hence, seventh, convey their political ethos, values, and vision of the future to the electorate.

We saw this in the American presidential elections in 2020. As he walked on stage to claim victory, the large screen behind Joe Biden read: 'The people have chosen empathy'.[42] Greeting the buoyant and cheering crowd in Wilmington, Delaware, the president-elect spoke of the importance of unity, of healing the divisions within society, and of repairing the damage of the pandemic, and the growing insecurity and inequality in the country. 'It's time to put away the harsh rhetoric, lower the temperature, see each other again, listen to each other again and to make progress. We have to stop treating our opponents as our enemies.'[43]

Biden's plan for transformation would be marked, he said, by 'compassion, empathy, and concern'.[44] As the 'empathy' candidate,[45] the concept had been a central feature of his election campaign. His ability to connect with people from all walks of life was the core message of his campaign videos: he was not an elite politician, just an 'Average Joe'. They shared stories of his friendships with the Amtrak conductors on his weekly commute,[46] his work across the political divides, his efforts to overcome a stutter (as well as his support for a young boy who was struggling with one),[47] and his own family story and experiences with tragedy and grief. He would recount the mantra, long instilled by his mother, that had helped him navigate politics: 'Joey, no one is better than you. Everyone is your equal, and everyone is equal to you.'[48] It was not the first time he had drawn on empathy, both as a value in his leadership, and as a civic virtue. It was considered a tonic after the previous four years, which had been marked by heightened discord and division under President Trump, and by his failings in handling the pandemic.

Ideally, empathy should be a part of leadership that seeks to transform politics, that offers ways to re-energise democracy, and to expand the range of voices and experiences reflected in the political sphere. By modelling understanding, tolerance, balance, and care, by showing what is possible and communicating clearly and effectively about the purpose and benefits of greater empathy, leaders can create legitimate space for it. Yet it can also have performative value.

A PERFORMANCE OR A SINCERE CONNECTION?

Some leaders want to be seen as empathic because this has positive connotations of being kind, caring, and interested in others. An empathic leader appears to be one of the 'people', who listens and engages. As such, empathy will often feature in political speeches and initiatives or be promoted as a part of someone's image.

This makes sense as their career is dependent on elections where they have to make the case that they are the candidate who best understands and represents you, and that they are listening to your concerns and are aligned with your needs, even though you have never met.

Precisely because it is an important means to signal care and understanding there is a risk that empathy can be performative, that is, a way of doing politics, not backed up by substance. Bill Clinton's claim to 'feel the pain' of the American people, and to know first-hand the impact of the financial recession in 1992, was hailed as a successful aspect of his presidential election campaign because it felt spontaneous and natural. Yet, when over-managed it can feel banal and insincere.

In February 2018, the White House held a listening session for survivors of school shootings. At the meeting President Donald Trump was photographed holding a White House notecard with hand-written prompts encouraging him to convey empathy to his audience.

1) What would you most want me to know about your experience?
2) What can we do to help you feel safe?
   ... (covered by his fingers)
3) I hear you

These are just and important questions, but how genuine can they be if they have to be spelt out? Newspapers and media outlets pointed to the notes as evidence of Trump's empathy deficit:[49] proof of a president who had to have his care scripted. But, perhaps, maybe what matters more to people is that, whether or not it is genuine, Trump at least *showed* care. In certain contexts – after a tragedy, at times of upheaval – empathy may be part of the norms and standards we expect politicians in the public space to uphold; adhering to these may be important to meet, irrespective of their sincerity.

The same issue of performance and substance can apply when empathy is used by the left. If political rhetoric is disproportionately full of hope and kindness and 'positive vibes' but fails to get to the meat of the issues people are facing, such words are hollow, and the public can feel that. Such language points to a disconnect between those in elected office, with the privileges that brings, and the electorate and their concerns. There has to be a balance, where the left is not afraid of observing where the system has failed, and is failing, ordinary people – and where their assumptions about 'free markets', or globalisation, have not translated into the reality they intended. They have to be open and humble enough to recognise where their assumptions have blinded them and brought unintended consequences.

There is a danger that, because of the rhetorical and political power of empathy in building connection with audiences, and its connotations of care, empathy becomes so ubiquitous that its value is diluted. If all politicians use the language of empathy and understanding without taking action with practical effect, people may become more cynical. The public may see through it, and doubt its meaning, aware that it is a perfunctory expectation of communication and not a genuine expression of care. Integrity in actions, rhetoric and substance are critical to give empathy transformational power.

Yet it can be hard to judge. Our perceptions of what is sincere and what is fake depends on where we stand. On the attributes we value, our political leanings, and the ways in which certain character types such as 'the charmer', 'the clown', 'the policy wonk' or 'the straight talker' have disappointed or served us in the past. Research suggests it can depend, in part, on whether we see a link of commonality with such figures, irrespective of their politics.[50] This might be through shared identities, experiences, or emotions. It gives us a point of relation and connection that allows us to infer something of their character and values – real or not.

Apart from figures like Elon Musk and members of the Christian evangelical right who are leading the recent anti-empathy backlash, few wish to be seen as unempathetic, especially with the implications that one is unkind, lacking humanity, and intolerant. Even President Richard M. Nixon, a man rarely praised for his kindness, wrote motivational notes encouraging himself to be more compassionate. One, on 6 February 1969, was a list of resolutions for how he should be: 'Compassionate, Bold, New, Courageous ... Zest for the job (not lonely but awesome)'. Then in early January 1970 he wrote again: 'Hard work – Imagination – Compassion – Leadership – Understanding of young – Intellectual expansion ...'[51] He also spoke openly about the importance of understanding others in international relations. While looking through his files for my doctoral dissertation, I came across his personal small, embossed, leather-covered notebook, no bigger than my hand, which featured a mantra: 'Kindness is more valuable than dollars.'[52] Perhaps it was a just a catchy quote, or something he'd heard that he wished to think more about. However, as the son of Quakers, it is not inconceivable that he understood and valued its importance, even if he could not translate the words into actions. He wanted to be perceived as compassionate, understanding, and creative, as well as having the virtues of strength and courage. He aspired to be a great statesman, alongside his own heroes of history: General Charles de Gaulle of France, and Prime Minister Winston Churchill of the UK.[53] Even though such an image does not align with his common public persona, it was something he was acutely aware of in crafting his public face.

There are more unlikely examples. At his trial for war crimes in The Hague in 2012, including his role in the Srebrenica genocide in 1995, the former Bosnian leader Radovan Karadžić invoked his sense of his own empathy in making his case: 'Everybody who knows me knows I am not an autocrat, I am not aggressive, I am not intolerant. ... On the contrary, I am a mild man, a tolerant man with great capacity to understand others.'[54] He was given a life sentence. Reinforcing an earlier point: not everything is empathy just because the word is used, or the efforts performed.

But there are ways to judge whether a leader, a politician, or any member of society is demonstrating or using genuine empathy or just performing it. The criteria include:

- Do they care about people and treat them with dignity? Do they put them first above their own self-interest?
- Do they appear to listen to different perspectives?
- Do they communicate understanding and demonstrate care, consideration, and connection?
- Can they handle challenges and criticism with equanimity?
- Are they curious to learn about how different people see the world?
- Do they reflect on their assumptions, their decisions, and their mistakes?
- Do they speak to people across divides?
- Do they take time to meet people, or do they keep themselves removed from citizens and people in their communities?
- Do they make decisions for a wide constituency or a select, close group of people aligned with their own political interests?
- Do they reach out to, and engage with, those who are more vulnerable or less privileged than them?

Such a list is indicative. Given the range of topics and issues politicians cover, and their own interests and priorities, there may be variations in style and intensity. Empathy may not be constant. Instead, people's capacity for empathy and its role in politics should be judged by how much talk of empathy aligns with their actions, and the integrity they exhibit in speaking of their understanding and following through with actions that align.

In this way, demonstrating empathy and using it to connect with audiences in a public setting should be not just a means of politics, but an end. For politicians, it should reflect care for the people they represent, respect of their inherent dignity, and a commitment to a more inclusive empathy-centred politics.

Nevertheless, empathy is an imperfect, complex attribute. Even for those leaders who are commonly associated with the quality in the media and academic literature, such as Jacinda Ardern in New

Zealand, or Barack Obama in the United States, there are limits and inconsistencies in their approach. They are as fallible as any human, and their empathy can be inconsistent or conflict with other priorities or interests. As a result, all leaders should be accorded a certain amount of grace.

*

Great leaders are defined by their strength of character, the virtues and values they exhibit at times of crisis and uncertainty, and the vision they offer that change is possible and achievable. Effective leadership provides the impetus and confidence that galvanises people to action. Yet it is far too scarce. There are not enough leaders who put people, over politics, first. Who look out for the many and not just the few.

However, the capacity of people for empathy, and the potential of it to yield change, are never down to one individual alone. What matters is that there are structures, ecosystems, and cultures where such traits are valued and celebrated so change can occur.

3

Navigating Crises

On 15 March 2019, in Christchurch, New Zealand, a lone gunman opened fire at two mosques during Friday prayer, killing over fifty worshippers and injuring many more. The first attack, at al Noor Mosque was live-streamed on Facebook. The perpetrator had been radicalised by far-right websites, online forums, and social media expressing hate for Muslim communities. In a broader international context, it was the latest in a growing number of attacks inspired by right-wing extremist ideologies. The Global Terrorism Index of 2019 reported a 320% increase in such attacks in a five-year period.[1] The perpetrators of such violent acts, although often acting alone, typically found community and common cause with others online. Their manifestos and ideologies included themes such as a dislike of Islam, a fear of immigrants and refugees, and misogyny.

Although reaction to terrorist attacks in other countries had focused on the attackers, their background, and their intentions, sharing assumptions about their rationale and motivations, Prime Minister Jacinda Ardern refused to say the name of the perpetrator of the Christchurch attacks. If terrorists committed their acts to gain attention for their ideology and to shape the political debate, she argued, then she would not give them that satisfaction. Instead, the message was one of cohesion within the country. Ardern was praised internationally for her empathy and compassion in response.[2] In her public speeches she emphasised the power of communities and demonstrated support and care for the Muslim population that had been targeted. In one of the most widely distributed images of the day, she was seen in the mosque, dressed in black, with her hair covered by a scarf, consoling worshippers.

Going beyond gesture politics, and in an effort to address the problem, a few days later she announced a series of initiatives to reduce the proliferation of guns and online radicalisation. Working with French President Emmanuel Macron and Canadian Prime Minister Justin Trudeau, she led a global initiative, the Christchurch Call.[3] She combined understanding with action and commitment to change.

Her approach was organic to her, and her style of leadership, not engineered by a communications team or spin doctor. It marked a shift from a dominant rhetoric of threat that had prevailed since 9/11 2001, shunning the language of security to emphasise the importance of the people affected and the strength of communal relationships. While some critics may have felt it did not engage with deeper conversations around extremism and security and would have preferred a harder line, her response demonstrated there was another way to address the harms of terrorism and violence without adding more fear and insecurity. Resilience was to be found in community and connection. Such expressions of empathy and care can be powerful. Ardern's words set the tone and framed subsequent discussions, leaning in to supporting the victims of the attacks and signalling the priorities of the response. It offers lessons for how crises are managed, and how leaders can set the tone for the public response.

Crises are intense, sometimes prolonged, periods of stress, uncertainty, and elevated risks. They have a high impact that can lead to dramatic shifts in societies, often leaving them deeply changed. They include pandemics, terrorist attacks, economic recessions, natural disasters such as tsunamis, hurricanes, and floods, as well as humanitarian crises and famines. They are demanding of both leaders and people, testing their resilience, cohesion, and social trust, while requiring people to come together.

At times of disaster, empathy is truly tested. Do we panic and lash out? Do we lose sight of our humanity? Or do we double down on community and support each other? In such moments, we tend to turn towards our closest groups, to find comfort and safety among those with whom we most identify – our families, friends, community. This can lead to heightened empathy among an 'in-group', sometimes at the expense of an 'out-group'.[4] Political leaders can stoke this in-group versus out-group sentiment, strengthening their political base and offering seemingly simple answers to complex problems, while contributing to broader divisions and tensions between groups. Alternatively, disasters hold opportunities for political leaders to respond differently, to break a pattern and offer an alternative vision for how to overcome collective challenges and provide a roadmap for change.

Crises rarely exist in neatly bracketed periods of time. Good leaders know that plans can be disrupted in an instant by matters beyond their control or expectations. However, they offer hope for how to overcome the worst of times and cultivate a sense of belonging and common bond to bring people together in a collective and communal response.

For this reason, at such times, empathy is key. And it takes on a range of forms and functions: offering understanding and reassurance, demonstrating care, or providing insights to guide better decision-making. However, although it can be a tonic for the insecurity and uncertainty that crises bring, it comes with costs, and its effectiveness is not guaranteed. Furthermore, rather than being a stand-alone attribute, empathy is strengthened and made real through leaders demonstrating integrity, trust, courage, and a broader vision of how we not only endure challenges but can find ways to take strength from them.

A TONIC FOR FEAR AND INSECURITY

When the world came to a halt in March 2020, it felt like a turning point. While the Covid-19 virus had been identified in Wuhan, China, in late 2019, by the spring of the following year it was a global concern.

Lombardy, in northern Italy, was at the forefront of the initial wave of Covid-19 in Europe. As the virus spread over the first few weeks, the media was full of distressing images of healthcare professionals in full protective gear in hospitals that were overwhelmed with patients exhibiting a range of symptoms. Fatalities increased at an alarming and horrifying rate, and pictures showed bodies lined up, wrapped in makeshift shrouds and white sheets because there was no room in local morgues.

As the scale of the crisis grew, the Italian government introduced a series of increasingly strict measures to limit exposure to the virus and those who may have been in contact with it. They set the tone for the policies followed by many other countries. Life could not continue as normal, and drastic change was required in the daily habits we so often take for granted. Many other countries followed suit.

Around the world, as countries went into lockdown, people were encouraged to work from home, schools and universities were closed and education was moved online. Travel slowed and those crossing borders often had to quarantine themselves at home or in hotels (often at their own cost). Out and about, masks created further physical barriers to human connection.

In these early days of the pandemic, across many countries, society rallied. Faced with an unknown virus, which was taking an unprecedented toll, people came together even as they stayed apart. Nurses, doctors, teachers, delivery workers, supermarket staff continued working to maintain essential frontline services. Neighbours brought food to those who were the most vulnerable. In countries with strict lockdowns, people made sacrifices and compromises, and endured extended periods of isolation, to keep others safe. As hard as it was as a collective experience, the pandemic demonstrated, once again, the power and potential of empathy and compassion in society. When times are difficult, people tend to connect and collaborate to help others.[5]

The crisis compelled empathy, compassion, and swift decisive action from political leaders, who had to look after citizens and ensure that critical services worked during an unexpected and unpredictable event. Political leaders had to match information and evidence that justified the introduction of unique measures to stem the spread of the virus with calm and understanding of the unprecedented demands being made on people. From capitals across the world, leaders gave regular briefings alongside scientific and medical experts, with extensive graphs and charts to illustrate the number of deaths and hospitalisations, and fluctuations in the virus.

In New Zealand, Prime Minister Jacinda Ardern was one of many leaders who chose care in the face of crisis and once again received international praise for her approach and her empathy.[6] She deftly demonstrated the power of the human touch and connection. Acting swiftly and decisively in March 2020, she closed borders and locked the country down. Strict quarantine policies meant few could enter the country, and those who did had to stay in a hotel and be tested until given the all-clear. Her speeches were honest about the challenges but recognised the burden the policies placed on people, ensuring people felt they were seen and their concerns understood.

In Taiwan, President Tsai Ing-wen (蔡英文) was known as the Covid Crusher for acting swiftly to minimise the harm. Equipped with extensive experience of other respiratory diseases such as SARS (Severe Acute Respiratory Syndrome) that had affected the country previously in 2003, and with national infrastructure already well versed in responding to pandemics and health crises,[7] she mobilised science to make the case, while also creating a strong sense of common purpose, aligned with cultural norms of unity and collective good over individual interests.[8] She helped people to pull together in the early phases, although future waves of the virus, which had been partly delayed by the initial efforts to contain its spread, would test the country.

In Barbados, Prime Minister Mia Mottley also spoke regularly to the people.[9] Through her communications she recognised the challenges but emphasised the importance of people coming together and creating shared meaning through the crisis. By believing in the capacity of the people for change, she helped signal her trust in the community. Announcing a phased reopening on 29 April 2020, she gave a detailed account of the different measures, the costs and inconveniences that would be involved, and the implications:

> Above all, we must treat each other with high levels of empathy and kindness. This, I swear, is a winnable fight, but its winnability is based on our commitment to change our behaviour in a way we have never done before. It's hard for me, and I know it's hard for you, but just as I can do it, I know you can do it; and when we do it together, we can say that we have succeeded as one.[10]

Empathy recurred as a central theme in many countries, as leaders sought to create common bonds and demonstrate their connection with citizens and encourage a collaborative effort across society.

However, the period presented a number of challenges for leadership and empathy. Empathy becomes harder when large numbers of people are involved. We are less likely to feel a connection with the suffering of others once people become statistics rather than stories. In part this is a product of 'compassion collapse' and being overwhelmed: huge disasters become too much to process and so we become numb or distance ourselves.[11] Tensions between care and personal interests were exacerbated during the crisis by the impact of ongoing restrictions, which cost people certain personal freedoms; deprived of contact with loved ones and social interactions, and with financial and job losses, people's daily lives became harder to sustain.

The pandemic not only highlighted the meanings of care and collective responsibility, but also revealed the costs that can accompany it. The elderly and those in vulnerable positions (such as those on low incomes, in casual jobs, or with chronic illnesses) were most affected, and often most isolated – forced to avoid family, friends, and public spaces where they might be exposed to the virus. More widely, the impact of enforced isolation on many people led to higher levels of mental health challenges, with depression and anxiety rising during that period.

Leaders and people in positions of power have to be able to alleviate that anxiety. They simultaneously have to demonstrate care *for* people at a difficult time while encouraging people *to* care. They have to make the case that certain policies, and especially restrictions and deprivations that are required to navigate a crisis, have legitimate objectives. And, they have to be able to adapt and modify their approach when evidence reveals what is and is not working.

Analysis done in Denmark by a number of political scientists demonstrated that while lockdowns were effective at preventing the spread of the virus in the short term, if used as the only mechanism for managing the virus, with no end sight, they had far more detrimental longer-term consequences on mental health and well-being.[12] The cost–benefit analysis revealed that people needed connection and social contact, even if this increased the potential for further transmission. Successive lockdowns were causing loneliness and social alienation, and fuelling anger, anxiety, and frustration with governments. It is for leaders, therefore, to use empathy to understand what is needed, to read the public mood, and to balance the trade-offs and compromises involved in different courses of action.

Crises also offer opportunities for leaders to take charge, to resolve conflicts and chart a new course. This was evident in the 1990s, during the Northern Ireland peace process. The process was designed to address a prolonged and intractable conflict which was marked by violence in Northern Ireland and frequent terror attacks in mainland Britain, including the bombings at the Conservative Party conference in Brighton in October 1984 and the Warrington bombings in February 1993. The Troubles lasted from the late 1960s to the late 1990s and led to the deaths of over 3,500 people. Empathy played a critical role among politicians involved in the process as they sought an end to this violence. On all sides there had been an extensive investment of time and personal energy establishing effective working relations between the parties, through formal and informal channels. George Mitchell, the American negotiator, was famed for his ability to listen to all sides of the conflict, and has spoken of the power of listening, dialogue, empathy, and understanding to navigate the agreement.[13] The resolution of such conflicts requires this effort, to build relationships with people across the divides, seeking to truly understand where they are coming from, and what they seek, and cultivating trust and credibility as a mediator.

Although the peace process had been going on for many years, across several governments, the talks had halted. In one important moment, in January 1998, British Secretary of State for Ireland and Labour MP Dr Marjorie (Mo) Mowlam took the bold decision to go into Maze Prison near Belfast to speak separately to Loyalist and Republican prisoners. Her decision was considered either 'mad or brave' in the context of the peace negotiations,[14] as well as a risk to her political career. Going to the H-Blocks, where in 1981 Republican prisoners had staged hunger strikes that led to ten of them dying,[15] she spent nearly two hours speaking with the prisoners, listening to their concerns and experiences.

Mowlam's own style of leadership made such a move possible. When she was appointed to the role, she had remarked to a journalist that her approach was based on 'sensitivity in some senses, but at the same time, a directness and an openness which may help the process too . . . all I can do is bring people together'.[16] She was known for her charisma, and her warm, breezy nature. During walkabouts in Belfast, she greeted local people informally and with good humour, believing it was an important way to connect with others. Reflecting on the people she met, she shared with journalists her assumption that there was an inherent decency among most people, a view that helped her connect and relate so well with people across the divide.

Nevertheless, a number of prominent figures were openly critical of Mo Mowlam's move, claiming it undermined the process. For the prisoners, her meeting was instrumental in getting them to the negotiating table.[17] It signalled a willingness to seek agreement and progress, contributing to trust-building measures, and showing intent. And while Mowlam was aware that some had taken offence to her approach, she believed the 'only way [to] make progress to permanent peace in Northern Ireland is by taking a proactive stance and talking to reach the broadest possible agreement'.[18] Her risk paid off.

However, she was not the only leader who was working to heal the divisions, nor was empathy alone responsible for progress. Her efforts were part of broader initiatives on all sides, and there were important political considerations that made the intensification of efforts to bring peace possible. Labour had won a huge political majority in the House of Commons in 1997 (with a majority of around 179 seats), which gave them more leeway and the opportunity to act. In Northern Ireland, too, Sinn Féin had greater influence in shaping the terms of political discourse and progress, with more united leadership and a more coherent communication strategy articulating the implications and costs of agreement.[19] This political latitude meant the main actors were slightly less vulnerable to attacks from their opponents and were both put on a more stable domestic footing. Such calculations were vital when making such a significant political shift, ensuring a level of stability and reassurance in political relations with the other side, and in creating a more legitimate space for new stories and identities of those affected to emerge. With a more amenable domestic context – even though opposition remained – those involved could move negotiations more from the private to the public space and begin to normalise the intended change in relations.

It is an uncomfortable and inconvenient reality, that only through all parties gaining confidence in the talks and the process could the different sides find a way through and both address the grievances and injustices, and reconcile their aspirations for the country. It took leadership from all sides to help make it happen.

The Good Friday Agreement was signed a few months later, on 10 April 1998, signalling a new relationship and constructive steps towards peace. As part of the agreement, a number of prisoners were released, a move that was controversial and difficult for those who had lost loved ones to the violence of the period, but seen as a necessary step by those in power for the country's future.

This is the task of good leaders: to take calculated risks in pursuit of a greater objective – such as peace or unity – even if it makes them unpopular or harms their own career. There are always trade-offs and compromises, and it takes a strong, committed, and visionary figure to navigate the difficult, yet often necessary, path to a solution.

THE COST OF EMPATHY AND ITS ABSENCE

Empathy is often expected in a crisis. It is a norm of response at times of tragedy. Therefore, when empathy is lacking, it can cause unintended harms to citizens, both in the moment and in the aftermath.

The global economic crisis in 2008 was a systemic-level disaster. The impact of the crisis has had long-term reverberations, economically, socially, culturally, and politically. Part of the current frustrations with capitalism, and with mainstream politics, can be traced back to this period. Indeed, there is a valid argument that the rapid growth in interest in empathy's potential over the past twenty years comes from dissatisfaction with the failure of the markets leading to people looking for more care-centred approaches.[20]

It began with the collapse of the US housing market, with falling house prices and people unable to pay their loans. But it had been brewing for many years, due to unethical financial practices, overextended lending, overconfidence in the markets, and regulations that were too lax, lacking necessary regulations and oversight. The bankruptcy of Lehmann Brothers in the United States in September 2008 prompted a dramatic and catastrophic collapse of the international financial system. Governments in the UK, US, Ireland, and elsewhere nationalised their banks, or offered significant bailouts, in an attempt to mitigate the harms. As the ripple effects of the crisis spread, other countries were hit: Germany, Italy, Sweden, and the Netherlands, which had all invested in these American funds. Around the world employment opportunities disappeared as the job market shrank and millions became redundant. People lost their homes, or the chance of owning their own home. Savings evaporated, and people faced severe financial uncertainty. By the end of 2009 around 205 million people around the world were jobless, 27 million more than in 2007.[21]

The effects of the financial crisis were felt acutely by large sections of societies around the world, especially – but not exclusively – the young, the working class, and the most vulnerable. Often it was the most advanced economies that were hit the hardest due to their interconnectedness with the international financial system and the markets. Young people, fresh out of school, faced diminished job prospects. In all countries affected, as levels of unemployment increased and with growing economic precarity, the demand of food banks and welfare rose, and not just for the poorest in society.

But for politicians and the media, this did not appear to be the primary concern. The stability and recovery of the banking sector was paramount. Although this is understandable, given its centrality to every part of our lives, it appeared to many that financial institutions were privileged over people's needs. Huge sums were doled out to banks as part of widespread bailouts while the most vulnerable in society faced the loss of jobs and livelihoods, and eviction from or dispossession of their homes. Many politicians did not sufficiently reassure populations nor do enough to alleviate the problems. Opportunities to make fundamental changes to the economic system and the regulatory system as a result of the crisis, including reducing the vulnerabilities that contributed to the collapse of the markets, and holding people accountable for the crisis, were missed. This had an impact on trust in politicians and the banking sector.

At times of economic crisis, people look to leaders for reassurance about their jobs, the security of their homes, mortgages, savings, energy prices, and well-being. Just as presidential candidate Bill Clinton expressed his understanding for the pain and struggles of the people in Arkansas and across America when asked about the economic crisis in 1992,[22] people want to feel that those in positions of power understand the consequences and impact of the crisis not only in the moment, but also its implications for their everyday lives. They are looking for empathy from a political class all too often removed from the majority of people. Those who occupy the highest offices typically come from the most privileged backgrounds. There are frequently high costs and barriers to entry, and they are often protected from the worst impacts of economic crises. They are therefore largely disconnected from the difficult realities and experiences of those with less security and privilege.

This was seen after the pandemic, when, far from politicians focusing on bringing in greater equity and focus on well-being, thousands lost their jobs while the fortunes of the world's wealthiest increased. Recent figures by Oxfam show that the majority of the world's wealth is currently held by just a few billionaires.[23] There was a missed chance to do things differently, and to combine care and vision for a reset.

An absence of empathy, especially during crises, can be politically costly. On 23 August 2005, a tropical depression over the Bahamas brewed rapidly to become Storm Katrina. As it swept across the Gulf of Mexico, it gained in intensity, and by the time it made landfall in southeast Louisiana, it was a Category Three hurricane with deadly speeds of up to 140 mph recorded. As it moved across the states, it devasted the communities in its path. In New Orleans, where wind

speeds reached 100 mph, the levees designed to protect the population from floods broke, leaving 80% of the city underwater, and 95%
in some districts. Although many people had evacuated the city, thousands had stayed, many of them unable to leave due to being too sick,
too poor, or lacking transport. Before the storm, New Orleans already
had a high level of poverty, with research suggesting over 40% of
people were living below the poverty line or in vulnerable positions.[24]
Katrina compounded these problems. Around 1,833 people died.

As the floodwaters rose, harrowing images emerged of the bodies
of drowned victims, and people who had lost their homes and livelihoods. In stark contrast, President George W. Bush was on vacation,
with media reports showing him casually playing guitar with country
singer Mark Wills at a naval base in San Diego – an image at odds
with the gravity of the moment and the distressing photos of Katrina's
victims circulating around the world. Compounding the problem, in
his first address – days after the hurricane had wreaked its damage –
the president's speech lacked compassion or understanding, offering
only practical efforts and solutions, without sufficient emotional
acknowledgement of the toll the disaster had taken, or its scale.[25]

Bush faced extensive criticism for this delayed and insufficient
response. When he finally travelled to the region, a photographer
captured an image that was widely shared in the media of the president looking out of the window of Air Force One at the devastation
of the hurricane. He was criticised for being 'detached and uncaring';[26]
he was up there, high above the people, rather than on the ground,
speaking to those who had suffered the devasting impact and who
were now trying to make sense of what had happened and rebuild
their lives. It was an image Bush would later concede was ill-advised.[27]
Criticisms of Bush and the rescue effort were exacerbated by perceptions of racial prejudice and socio-economic divides. The victims of
the hurricane were predominantly, albeit not exclusively, Black
Americans on lower incomes. According to the Pew Research Center
in 2005, 67% of Americans felt the president could have done more,

with significant differences along racial lines in perceptions of his response.[28]

His administration never really recovered from the perception that the federal government had not cared enough, had taken too long to respond, and had been insufficiently prepared. They underestimated how much 'being there' matters, for it shows concern, moral solidarity, and a genuine commitment to the people.[29] In the gap left by the government, civil society organisations and community leaders stepped in to give support.

Here the performance of empathy was also an expected norm. Even though it is important that empathy appears to come from the heart, how a leader is seen to act in such circumstances matters, whether or not they actual feel and practise empathy. There should have been genuine empathy for the tragedy, of course, but there were also social conventions and an expectation that this empathy should be highly visible. Leaders have to be able to convey – through images, actions, and their public persona – that they care and that they are empathic.

Nevertheless, even while empathy may be valued in our leaders, it can involve heavy personal and professional sacrifices as well as emotional, psychological, and political costs. A few years after the worst of the pandemic, many of those who guided their countries through the crisis are no longer in office. Leaders including Jacinda Ardern of New Zealand, Sanna Marin of Finland, Nicola Sturgeon of Scotland, and Mark McGowan, the premier of Western Australia, resigned citing tiredness.[30] For some, despite the initial surge of support for their empathic policies and personal touch, the crisis tested their popularity. A fine balancing line emerged between care, strength, and ideas of freedom and security. Empathy alone is not enough to be a good leader, nor is it guaranteed to have consistent outcomes. This further adds to the impression that the concept can be inconsistent and variable.

Indeed, because empathy is complex and not constant, as much as it may be integral to change, it is not always welcome. At times of heightened fear or anxiety people do not always want to see politicians express empathy or understanding for those who may be perceived as a threat. In these circumstances, it becomes harder for those leaders who seek to talk to terrorists or end conflict, as we are reluctant to understand those who have caused harm. A leader who exhibits empathy in this kind of context risks offending people, or being seen as weak, especially at the pointier end of politics. In his book *Talking to Terrorists*, Jonathan Powell, a former senior British civil servant, diplomat, and a key negotiator in the Northern Ireland peace process during the 1990s, wrote of the distaste people expressed about talking to the Irish Republican Army, until they realised there would be no other way to resolve the conflict. It can be seen as a moral failure, especially in the public space, where people can view such efforts to understand terrorist actions or to reason with terrorist groups as an acceptance of the violence. Consequently, politicians and diplomats often have to pursue a process of dialogue behind closed doors until the relationships and dynamics of a negotiation can withstand public scrutiny and offer a path forward.[31]

In 2015, as the refugee crisis was growing across Europe, with people seeking security and safety from conflicts in countries including in Syria, Iraq, Libya, and Afghanistan, Chancellor Angela Merkel made the decision to open Germany's borders and welcome them. Countries along the Mediterranean were struggling to cope with the influx of people. Some were openly hostile, with Hungary building a wall to prevent refugees entering. Other countries were overwhelmed by the numbers and were turning them away. In August 2015, seventy-one people were found dead in the back of a lorry in Austria.[32] The Chancellor had already signalled her support for tolerance, inclusion, and understanding. In her New Year's message the previous year, she had encouraged people to reject racism and Islamophobia,[33] and she was repeatedly critical of those who protested against refugees and sought to close the doors. As the crisis intensified, in mid-August she visited shelters where asylum seekers were gathered following a string of attacks, demonstrating care. This was matched by efforts to override the Dublin Regulation and let refugees register in Germany, even if it was not the first country in which they had arrived.[34] At that time, the number of asylum seekers entering and staying in Germany had risen from 202,645 in 2014, to 476,510 in 2015; it would go on to reach 745,155 in 2016.[35]

At her press conference on 31 August 2015, Merkel invoked empathy as the means to solve the crisis, highlighting how little people knew of the anxiety and exhaustion that accompanies fleeing for one's life with one's family.[36] She appealed to her European counterparts, arguing that this was a test for the Union: 'If Europe fails on the question of refugees, if this close link with universal civil rights is broken, then it won't be the Europe we wished for.'[37] Opening the door to refugees, and granting them the right to build a home in Europe was, for Merkel, a moral imperative.

Initially, her response was praised as an act of moral courage and strength. Just a few days after her press conference, on 2 September, a Syrian toddler, Alan Kurdi, was photographed, face down on a beach in Turkey, one of thousands of people who had lost their lives seeking safety. The image of the drowned child went viral, putting a human face to the scale of crisis and prompting a wave of compassion from citizens and politicians alike in many countries in Europe.[38] In Germany the term '*Wilkommenskultur*' (welcome culture) was widely used in the media, as people helped refugees settle into the country. This welcoming attitude reached its peak in November 2015.

Yet such sentiments were short-lived. Following the ISIS (Islamic State of Iraq and Syria) terrorist attacks in Paris in November 2015, and a spate of sexual assaults in Germany during New Year's Eve, criticism of Merkel's policy quickly grew both from outside and inside her party, and across Europe. Her empathy and emotionality were seen as a failing, causing her to misjudge the wider security context.[39] Her determination that 'we can do it' would later be seen as problematic.[40] Even if empathy was a laudable part of a moral motivation, it met with political opposition, and fears about the longer-term implications of such a move for German society and regional security.[41]

There is also a counterpoint to consider here that those who objected to Merkel's policy might raise. Resistance to expressions of empathy and compassion, as in Germany, may not be due to a lack of empathy, but due to a proportion of the population feeling that empathy is directed towards the wrong people. There may be a perception that such care comes at the expense of their own interests, their livelihoods and well-being. This highlights, again, the concept's potential subjectivity, depending on our own vantage point and values.

PART OF A LARGER EQUATION

Crises require decisive action in very short time frames. Decisions have to be made in contexts where events change rapidly and unpredictably, where the stakes and the costs are high. It is impossible for leaders to be able to consider every different perspective – they typically represent thousands or millions of people – or to take into account all experiences. They have to work with the information available, and, when critical crises suddenly emerge, such information can be scarce. They cannot afford inaction.

When President John F. Kennedy was navigating the Cuban Missile Crisis in 1962, he had a luxury few contemporary politicians can enjoy – relative time and space to think. The thirteen-day stand-off with the Soviet Union followed an escalation of tensions regarding the placement of Soviet nuclear weapons on Cuba, and the construction of missile sites. It was the closest the two powers had come to a nuclear confrontation. On the recommendations of his close advisors, President Kennedy engaged in a series of public and private communications with the Soviet leader, Nikita Khrushchev. Some messages were delivered indirectly, as former Secretary of Defense

Robert McNamara explains in his memoir, with Khrushchev simultaneously sending more conciliatory private messages to the US president, followed shortly after by more bombastic public messages of Soviet posturing to the American people. Faced with these public and private messages from the Soviet leader, Kennedy could take his time, seek guidance, and consider his options.[42] He was under no imperative to respond immediately, ensuring he could consider the longer-term implications of his actions. Despite advice that military action against Cuba and the Soviets would be the only solution, he chose to invest in diplomatic channels and give them more time to yield a different outcome. Responding to the private message over the public one, he was able to diffuse the crisis, and, through diplomatic means and agreements regarding the basing of Soviet missiles in Cuba and American ones by the Black Sea, the sources of tension could be addressed. Such time, space, and privacy to make such a decision is difficult to envisage today.

One of the biggest challenges these days is that the pace of news media, the ready stream of updates and opinions, can constrict the space and time needed for reflection and consideration. The problem has only become worse with the ubiquity of social media. The imperative now is for politicians and political leaders to respond, to speak, to avoid a silence that others might fill. As British journalist Nik Gowing wrote in 'Skyful of Lies' and Black Swans in 2009, there is a tyranny of information.[43]

Effective, transparent, and clear communication is therefore critical, ensuring leaders can articulate the decision-making process, and convey the tensions between the choices made, and the considerations and compromises. If politicians can foster 'connection, engagement, and interaction', this creates a relationship between the people and the state 'that can help mitigate the impact of a crisis'.[44] As the pandemic revealed, gaps in the narrative and ineffective communication can lead to spaces that others can fill with alternative explanations and theories. During this period, prominent media figures and influencers shared news about the dangers of vaccines and conspiracy theories grew. This becomes more all the more pressing in a 24/7 news cycle and with the ubiquity of social media, which creates the imperative to respond almost instantaneously.

While empathy has political power, if it is to have substance and credibility in communications it has to be matched with integrity. It is not enough to say you understand and care for the people or that you are there for them if your actions betray you. During the pandemic, British Prime Minister Boris Johnson deployed empathy rhetorically, expressing understanding for the sacrifices people were making, and the hardship and constraints government policy had imposed in trying to mitigate the effects of a deadly and unknown virus. At regular briefings, he would be joined by senior scientists and experts who provided fact-based data and information to support the choices made. Such an approach was important, yet it proved to be empty words, and was undermined by incongruous behaviour as reports emerged of recurrent parties, group drinks in the office, and social gatherings at 10 Downing Street at odds with the strictures and restrictions imposed on the people. This showed a lack of respect for the sacrifices that were being made by the population as a whole.

How can you truly understand what people are going through if you do not adhere to the rules you make? Such actions provoke a loss of trust in political leaders and officials, and anger that there is one rule for the people and another for those in charge. These feelings are not isolated to one administration or leader but have a longer-term corrosive impact on relations between leaders and the people. The loss of trust that follows can be hard to rebuild, revealing the longer-term harms of ineffective leadership.

In contrast, successful leadership requires those in positions of power and authority to be not only emotionally literate and articulate but also able to regulate the feelings and thoughts that inevitably arise when dealing with intense and demanding events. This applies to their personal emotions, those of the people around them, and those of the wider public. Leaders have to be emotionally agile,[45] and simultaneously capable of managing themselves and how society feels.[46] Good leadership is about constructive mindsets and ways of thinking, as well as how to behave and communicate.

Humility is an asset. Leaders have to be able to self-reflect, admit errors, and seek advice. It involves self-empathy and awareness. The global consultancy McKinsey recognised this when it included empathy as one of five core traits of effective leadership.[47] It emphasised that empathy should not only be directed to others, but is also, notably, about being open to *accept* it from others, acknowledging the importance of self-care and well-being for those managing crises. Yet this capacity to learn from mistakes and truly own them is rare. It is hard to find many examples of leaders who do this well, even though it is one way to rebuild trust and connection with disaffected populations.

If leaders are overwhelmed by the intensity of their own emotions, such as anger, fear, or a sense of injustice, this can cloud effective responses. Short-term intensities instigate long-term consequences. The anger and fear behind President George W. Bush's response to the horrific attacks on 9/11, initiating the 'war on terror', while to some extent justified, set in motion a series of events around the world with far-reaching, violent, and catastrophic consequences for millions of people. It securitised the debate, and resulted in an enormous military operation, with a dominant, albeit inaccurate, narrative that Islam was a primary problem. This framing had detrimental impacts on Muslim communities around the world, and led to divisions and mistrust among communities. As Jacinda Ardern's approach to Christchurch demonstrated, there was another way.

Some leaders have that capacity to tap into the subtle but perceptible changes in how people feel and the tone of society. Despite polls and data that purport to capture shifts in public moods, such as YouGov's mood tracker,[48] this skill is based on intuition and perception. It involves curiosity: How are people experiencing this moment?

How might it evolve? What are the sources of emotions such as fear, anxiety, hope, or pride? How might these emotions manifest and play out in how people respond to policy decisions and political reactions? And how can sentiments be transformed to alleviate insecurity and uncertainty? Crisis leadership is therefore not just about demonstrating empathy, or communicating with empathy, but also having the emotional agility and leadership skills to shape how people respond to events in ways that enable more sustainable outcomes in the long term.

During a crisis empathy takes on different but important qualities. Publicly it is a source of connection – a way of conveying to people that they are considered and supported at a time of intense uncertainty and amidst potential dangers. It therefore serves as a form of reassurance that can help to shape the public mood to manage responses. As a tool of leadership, it informs decision-making, offering a breadth of data and insight with which leaders can navigate uncertainty and account for the disparate experiences of events. And, at a personal level, empathy helps to signal valued virtues of a leader, that they serve the people and are someone of good character. Contrasting with those leaders who put money or personal status above the good of the country, leaders who demonstrate empathy can in this way legitimise their claim to be servants of the people. Under any circumstances, empathy offers a source of connection between political leaders and their audiences.

Yet the value of empathy in the context of crises goes beyond how leaders navigate the immediate period at the eye of the storm. It also should inform how they prepare – as Henry Kissinger advises: 'Wise leaders must pre-empt their challenges before they manifest themselves as crises.'[49] Early warnings of the possibility of pandemics had not been taken sufficiently seriously. In the UK's Strategic Defence and Security Review of 2010, for example, pandemics were listed as one of the top risks to the country.[50] However, as they were considered low probability, despite their high impact, resources and funding were diverted from pandemic preparedness and supplies. When the crisis hit, the government was not ready and so scrambled, and failed, to get ahead of its impact. As we will see in later chapters, empathy and wider connection with the public, as part of more participatory politics, should be built into policy design processes and crisis antici-pation early on. In that way, when crises hit, countries are not depen-dent solely on the capacities and abilities of those in power but have systems and structures in place to provide the vital resilience and response in the immediate term.

Finally, coming out of a crisis, leaders need to manage the trauma, grief, and shock of the experience. They need to reassure society and help process the collective trauma that can continue to shape soci-eties long after crises have ended.[51]

*

At a time of crisis, we look to leaders to provide a calm head, a steady hand, and care for the people they lead. Empathy serves as a vital and mobilising force in this. It says: I am there with you, I understand this is hard because this is hard for me too, and I am doing everything I can to make this better. At a collective level, it offers a source of connection, encouraging people to bond in their experiences and emphasising the power of humanity when times are testing. It also speaks to fears and concerns, offering reassurance that can aid resil-ience and recovery.

Yet empathy alone is not enough. To take people beyond the crisis, effective leadership and politics demand courage, vision, and effi-ciency. Leaders need to show integrity and demonstrate that they can deliver on their promises or at least explain adequately why the present times are hard and demand sacrifices and resilience. They have to convey the power of credible hope and be able to offer a vision of life after the crisis, of the potential for future flourishing beyond mere survival. We saw it with Prime Minister Ardern and her faith in the significance of cohesion and unity to overcome those who sought to divide communities. And we saw it during the Good Friday

Agreement negotiations, in the hope that somewhere beyond the violence, the hurt, and the tensions, there was a solution around which people could connect and rebuild.

Effective leaders use difficult periods as sources of transformation, placing the moment of crisis as a part of a longer narrative arc. For them, hope is tenacious. Their political rhetoric speaks to the inherent courage, resilience, and strength of people and they galvanise action for change and persistence.

However, they also tell a bigger story about us, and how we come together. Crises reveal the power of the helper; the strength of community to unite and support one another. Amid some of the worst experiences, we often see the best of humanity: courage, tenacity, care, resilience, and community. We therefore need to rethink the meaning of power, and where it is found.

4

From Power Over to Power With

Power is an integral and unavoidable feature of politics. It can be seen in the ability of leaders to exert influence, in the spaces where people gather for collective action, and in the use of force, or its threat, to quell challenges and dissent. Power is essential to effect change and make things happen. However, in politics our ideas of power are too often quite restrictive, focusing on its misuse or its ability to dominate, or coerce, rather than its potential to transform and uplift.

Films, books, and television series often reinforce this and convey power as a corrosive force. In the British (and then American) political drama *House of Cards*, Francis Urquhart (Frank Underwood in the US) pursues power at all costs, eliminating those who threaten his position: sometimes literally. He is unscrupulous in his quest – the embodiment of the Machiavellian archetype. In *Yes, Prime Minister*, a 1980s British sitcom, the butt of the jokes is the hapless politicians, motivated by their egos and desire for self-preservation, and dependent on their civil servants. They are concerned more with power than truly governing. Although the Danish series *Borgen* offers a more Nordic twist on the role of power, where institutionally and culturally it is less centralised, the values and aspirations of idealistic Birgitte

Nyborg are gradually influenced and diminished by the nature of the institution and the perceived imperatives of her own political success and survival. In *The West Wing*, which offers a more idealistic vision of how American politics might be if only Martin Sheen were president and leaders had unwavering ideals and the courage to realise them, the cast are consistently navigating the competing demands and trappings of power. Power, it says, is inescapable and ultimately corrupting.

Even for the most moral, incorruptible, and principled individuals, getting to the top and achieving their vision can incur compromises and fragile or questionable allegiances.

There is some evidence that power makes empathy harder. Professor of Psychology Dacher Keltner has studied this for over twenty years. Over the course of his research he noted that the traits that get people into power and enable them to make a difference – connection, compassion, generosity, care – can then reduce once they are in power. It is what he terms a Power Paradox.[1] Those in power are seduced by the trappings and benefits that power can confer, and so paradoxically start to behave in ways that are self-serving and that contravene the qualities that brought them to power in the first place. They become limited in how they think about power and its potential. Susan Fiske and Eric Dépret also observe how those with more power tend to feel less need to gain information about others[2] and are more prone to stereotyping.

Yet empathy in contexts of power is further complicated by the cyclical and constantly changing nature of politics and the pressures of the current political environment. Former French government minister Moises Naim speaks to the disparity between the perception of power someone has, and the reality – and the frustration that accompanies that realisation.[3] Politicians can be led more by electoral cycles than the pursuit of longer-term visions, which makes power feel finite and scarce. And there can be an imperative for leaders to hold onto power, and the system that sustains it, rather than use it as a vehicle for progress. This is what needs to change.

Interrogating our ideas of power, and examining where it resides, how it operates, and what purpose it serves can reveal opportunities not only for qualities like empathy to come to the fore, but also for different ways of thinking about politics and how to create vibrant, thriving, and prosperous societies. This does not mean we ignore the realities of power, or its more pragmatic constraints, but that we question the assumptions that underpin it, and the behaviours and actions of those with power that we reward.

POWER, POPULISM, AND THE RISE OF STRONG MEN

We are seeing the resurgence of traditional concepts of power.[4] The growth of 'strong man' leadership replicates ideas of the importance of centralised and paternal power, and the utility of force and a heavy hand in maintaining a sense of control and security.

In India, speaking from the ramparts of the Red Fort in Delhi, on 15 August 2014, Indian Prime Minister Narendra Modi delivered a powerful speech to mark the country's sixty-eighth year of Independence. He spoke for over an hour without notes and without the safety of bullet-proof glass, breaking the usual conventions. Over the course of his speech he delivered a vision for India rooted in his own upbringing and intimate experience with poverty. He championed more freedoms and rights for women and girls, promised to make government work more effectively, and to bring toilets into people's homes to improve sanitation and cleanliness. It was odd, he noted, for a leader to speak of toilets, but these were important issues that mattered in the everyday reality of the people. Over the course of his career, he has been effective at making the connection with the people, at appearing to speak as one of them. In his election campaign, he emphasised his past as a *chaiwallah* (tea boy) in comparison to the very prestigious political families of his opponents – the Nehru-Gandhi family. He uses techniques such as 'intimacy', 'simplicity', and 'intermediation', translating ideas for the people in a way they could understand and speaking in a more informal way.[5]

Many of these more populist leaders are attractive precisely because they appear to be speaking to people about their concerns. They are showing empathy for their audience. Moreover, they speak to them in ways that resonate emotionally, making them feel seen in ways that other politicians do not. In this way their power is disruptive.

Empathy in such contexts can be instrumentalised to cultivate strong in-groups at the expense of others.[6] Populist leaders use it to convey to their supporters that they understand their concerns about immigration, unemployment, their frustrations with the political elite, and uncertainty amidst changing cultural and gender norms.

Indeed, the power of populist leaders lies partly in how they give voice to those who feel powerless. They recognise their concerns, their fears, their aspirations, and they acknowledge their inherent worth. When Hillary Clinton derided the 'basket of deplorables' who would vote for Donald Trump, she might have been expressing justifiable frustration at his popularity, given his comments on and disrespect for women, migrants, and people with disabilities. However, it also conveyed a sense of disdain for those who voted for Trump, which served to confirm existing feelings that the traditional political elite did not value that section of society or their opinions.

Yet populist leaders do not just speak to those who feel they lack power but also give voice to those whose power is challenged: those who are confronting changes in society where they are being asked to accommodate into their spaces, their workplaces, their homes different ways of being and thinking, and living in the world. While the left is seeking change and a continual march towards progress sometimes seemingly with little concern for the costs, populist leaders remind people of what was good, and what felt safe, however true or untrue that myth might be.

Centrist parties and prominent politicians have failed to address the rising popularity of these populist leaders. In the UK, US, France, and the Netherlands, they tend to focus too much on the leader themselves, making personal attacks on their questionable character without listening to their audience, or offering any substantial changes in their own ideas or vision of what is needed. Populists can argue that attacks on them are proof of the threat they pose to the 'elite', and claim it is part of their efforts to maintain their privileged position. Project 2025, launched by the Heritage Foundation in the United States before President Trump's election, taps into this and utilises ideas of worthiness to galvanise support from its base. Among an array of themes, it critiques perceptions that the political elite do not value 'those who shower in the evening after work, rather than those who shower before' – as a way of identifying the distinction between those who do hard, often manual, jobs and those they see as living lives of relative comfort.[7]

In Europe, attempts to minimise the power of populist movements have led to their language being co-opted by some on the left, especially on immigration and refugees. However, rather than stealing the thunder of populist movements, doing this gives such movements added legitimacy, while making the left look opportunistic. Given their past history and politics, the sudden shift of leaders like Labour Prime Minister Keir Starmer talking about the UK being an 'island of strangers'[8] seems a little too reminiscent of the rhetoric of former Conservative MP Enoch Powell and his anti-immigration 'rivers of blood' speech, about how Britain's white population 'found themselves made strangers in their own country'. It looks more like an effort to prevent other parties like Reform from winning votes as their popularity rises, than being a sincere policy, aligned with deep-rooted political principles.

Responding to the vagaries of smaller parties and perceptions of public opinion rather than truly leading and setting an agenda puts more centrist parties on the back foot. There are significant missed opportunities for policies that combine balanced and pragmatic approaches to the challenges of immigration and domestic public concerns about its impact with greater empathy and humanity. Once again, there is a lack of empathy and a lack of courage.

We share some responsibility for these developments. Antonio Gramsci, an Italian Marxist philosopher who lived at the turn of the twentieth century, has argued that citizens, and members of society, give their consent to be led.[9] This is not just through our votes, but through our acceptance of ideas, ideology, and cultural norms. Such things are often pervasive, taken as accepted wisdom, but they facilitate and legitimise certain forms of power over others, and can limit the sense of our own agency in politics. This is why we must be more active in shaping the kind of societies we want to see, and in wielding the power that we have. We have to be more critical in assessing and evaluating the prevailing norms and assumptions: Who do they serve? Do they support the greater good or do they benefit only a small elite?

Relatedly, philosopher and historian Hannah Arendt wrote powerfully of the 'banality of evil'. Reflecting on the trial of Adolf Eichmann in 1961, as part of efforts to bring the perpetrators of the Holocaust in Germany to justice, she noted that it was too simple to consider evil as the sole preserve of egocentric, cruel, and manipulative individuals, such as Adolf Hitler and other Nazi leaders. Instead, the actions that made it possible were to be found in the everyday actions of apparently normal people who did nothing to prevent the atrocities, who were complicit in the bureaucracies that facilitated their policies, or who turned a blind eye in the street to the injustices and violence against their fellow citizens, including their Jewish, gay, Romany, and disabled neighbours.[10]

So long as we reward or accept those who abuse power, and do not hold them accountable, it will be very difficult for more empathic leadership to flourish, or any other kind of leadership rooted in values of integrity, courage, kindness or competence. Maybe the corrupt or bad leaders get their come-uppance – they lose an election, or stand trial for abusing their position – but in the process, if they are not fully held to account, they can still break or weaken the conventions of a democratic system that is dependent on collective acceptance of certain forms and standards of behaviour.

When talking about leadership, it is therefore essential to consider our own role and the expectations we hold of those in power and the standards we require them to meet. What do we reward? What do we tolerate? What do we value? The dangerous ideas and poor behaviours of those in office are given power if we are not discerning. We can perpetuate power's worst excesses by not holding those who wield it to account. How, then, do we exercise our own power, to effect change, to champion the issues that matter to us and our communities?

This can be difficult where we may feel there is not much choice or if we feel disconnected from our leaders. If politicians are all viewed as the same or gathered in the centre with little separating them, then it can feel futile to choose one over another. There is, therefore, a need to humanise our politicians: to understand more clearly the demands and expectations of the role they perform. Then we may be both more understanding of their inability to deliver on every promise, but also – critically – more able to hold them to account when they do not.

ADDRESSING POWERLESSNESS

Empathy does not assume a singular experience of power. Instead, it invites curiosity about how and where people lack power. In so doing, it should not be condescending, patronising, or pitying of those who are struggling.[11] It should be coactive, and motivated by a desire for justice and equity. Guided by such values, it can lead to better conversations, deeper understanding of the scale of contemporary problems and more creative initiatives.

This comes in multiple forms. The Black Lives Matter protests that began in the United States during 2020 and spread worldwide after the death of George Floyd from a police officer kneeling on his neck drew attention to the disproportionate and asymmetric nature of power in policing and security. It highlighted serious abuses of power and gaps in justice and due process by those in positions of authority. Although this instance was in no way the first, it captured the public attention in a more profound way. Millions came out to march or participate in demonstrations in the US and around the world. It was estimated that over 40% of counties in the US saw protests, and the vast majority of these counties were also predominantly white.[12] It sparked vital discussions and questions to be asked about racism and biases in the police force and other institutions, and shone a necessary spotlight on how so many Black people in America often felt powerless when confronted by some members of the police, and the excessive and far too common use of violence as part of law enforcement efforts.

To rethink power, we have to consider how people feel and experience powerlessness.[13] Powerlessness is when people feel that no matter what they do, or who they vote for, nothing changes: their life circumstances do not improve and no one is invested in, or interested in, their well-being. Far too many people are working in gig economies, or in low-paid jobs where there is a lack of security, poor conditions, and limited prospects for advancement. This is exacerbated by economic systems that deliver record profits for the directors and CEOs in the top roles. In addition, at a time when loneliness has been categorised as an epidemic, people no longer feel the same sense of power in community.

Power does not reside solely with leaders, or those in office. Too often we forget the power and agency we have as citizens. We can deny our labour, boycott goods, protest. Small actions can contribute to global impact. Around the world people are claiming that power. There are historical precedents showing that it works.

The civil rights movement in the United States turned powerlessness into concerted action, through sit-ins, marches, and moral power. Reverend Martin Luther King, a prominent political leader and champion of civil rights, tolerance, non-violence, and under-standing, recognised its potential. His readings and experiences were sharpened by his time as a pastor in Montgomery, Alabama, where he arrived in 1954. Around a year later, inspired by the actions of one woman – Rosa Parks – the bus boycotts began. As he wrote: 'The Negro people of Montgomery, exhausted by the humiliating experi-ences that they had constantly faced on the buses, expressed in a massive act of non-cooperation their determination to be free. They came to see that it was ultimately more honourable to walk the streets in dignity than to ride the buses in humiliation.'[14]

Informed by his experience and time spent on a five-week tour in India as a pilgrimage to Gandhi and ideas of non-violence, King later observed in 1960 how non-violence and moral power removed the violence, hatred, and bitterness.[15] It also compelled both empathy and respect:

The nonviolent approach does not immediately change the heart of the oppressor. It first does something to the hearts and souls of those committed to it. It gives them new self-respect; it calls up resources of strength and courage that they did not know they had. Finally, it reaches the opponent and so stirs his conscience that reconciliation becomes a reality.

In her 'principled defiance' of the strictures that told her to give up her seat to a white person and sit at the back of the bus, Rosa Parks displayed such power.[16] In his speech granting her the Congressional Gold Medal in June 1999, President Bill Clinton spoke of the power she wielded with this quiet defiance and principled commitment to human dignity: 'we know that in a funny way, people who have no position or money and have only the power of their courage and character are always there before the political leaders. We know that.'[17]

Power can be found in small actions that have wider implications, that are part of a more global concerted movement. In Ireland in July

1984, during the period of Apartheid in South Africa, an employee of Dunnes Stores, Mary Manning, refused to sell goods from South Africa as part of a wider global boycott initiative. It had been gaining ground since the late 1950s but with limited effect. Her actions raised the profile of the ongoing injustices in the country and, in 1987, Ireland became the first country in Western Europe to ban goods from South Africa. News of her actions, and those of her colleagues, reached Nelson Mandela – then a prisoner on Robben Island – and Desmond Tutu, who gained solidarity, comfort, and reinforcement from them.

Our ability to wield power requires our own awareness of it. One of the most prominent spaces where people have been claiming their power and amplifying their voice for change using peaceful means is climate change. On 20 August 2018, in protest at the Swedish government's inaction on climate change, 15-year-old Greta Thunberg posted a photo on Instagram of herself alone outside the Swedish Riksdag. She had a large white placard with a slogan written in black capital letters: 'Skolstrejk för Klimatet' (School strike for the climate). On her post she wrote:

Vi barn gör ju oftast inte som ni säger åt oss att göra, vi gör som ni gör. Och eftersom ni vuxna skiter i min framtid, så gör jag det med. Jag skolstrejkar för klimatet fram till valdagen. (We children usually don't do what you tell us to do, we do what you do. And since you adults screw up my future, I'll join in. I'm on school strike for the climate until election day.)

She became an environmental activist after becoming more aware at school of the problems, and frustrated by the lack of action from those in power.

Her actions, and those of countless other young people, have inspired others around the world, empowering people to share their voice. In September 2019, as the United Nations Climate Action Summit began in New York, Greta took to the stage to accuse states of inaction, and of disregarding the futures of so many young people.[18] She is one of thousands of young people who have sought such change, and who are working tirelessly to make a difference. And their actions have sparked valuable conversations, and attention, that become harder for politicians to ignore.

For those who view power as a zero-sum game – a way to dominate and win at the expense of others – the voices of the powerless are relatively inconsequential. But we cannot create healthy democratic systems without cultivating a more inclusive and representative form of power. To support those who want to address our current challenges, and to rebuild and create new systems of governance that give more power to the people, for the people, we need to move to ideas of power *with* rather than power *over*.

FROM POWER OVER TO POWER WITH

Empathy in politics can help us move from these ideas of 'power over' to 'power with'. Rather than power being concentrated at the top of political systems, empathy can offer ways of engaging with others to achieve collective change and objectives. It helps by sharing power's potential, and its costs, as well as its responsibilities.

Power over can be about force and domination, using control or influence to confer asymmetrical advantages. We see this most acutely in authoritarian regimes, which use fear, intimidation, threats of violence, and surveillance to get people to conform to the government's will. In such countries the government's close hold on the media stifles dissent and critique, meaning there is little to no space for opposition or accountability. Such dominant forms of power may be effective at maintaining control in the short term, but they can be counterproductive, and short-sighted. For opponents in such countries, as James Baldwin eloquently noted: 'force does not work the way its advocates think in fact it does. It does not, for example, reveal to the victim the strength of the adversary. On the contrary, it reveals the weakness, even the panic of the adversary and this revelation invests the victim with patience.'[19]

However, power over can also involve the paternalistic centralisation of power, which assumes those in power know best what people need and want. It sets rules and limits, and rigid processes for change that are top-down and bureaucrat-led. It discounts or insufficiently engages with civil society and citizens.

An alternative account is that power is generated through uniting as societies in collective efforts for change. As Hannah Arendt describes, this can be found 'when people gather together and act in concert, which disappears the moment they depart. The force that keeps them together . . . is the force of mutual promise or contract.'[20] There has to be both a shared sense of belonging and community, and a collective investment in a new form of politics. This takes time, effort, and courage to build.

Mary Parker Follett, one of the earliest advocates of 'power with', is a woman deserving of far greater attention. Born in Massachusetts in 1868, to a family of Quakers at a time when women could not vote,[21] receive an education, and own property, she pursued an extensive education and became an influential figure in management and organisational theory, sometimes known as the 'Mother of Modern Management'. She was ahead of her time. As a philosopher, political theorist, management consultant, and social worker, her ideas on the importance of working with the people and building community to support the development of initiatives would not be out of place in contemporary debates. Writing in an era of philosophical debates around social reform, her work embodied the ideas of pragmatic idealism.[22] She imagined we were capable of genuine transformation but recognised the everyday trappings and constraints that made it hard. Although she is often cited in contemporary work on management, she also had a lot to say about politics and societal life.

She considered 'power over' to be pseudo power.[23] It gives the impression of strength but lacks true legitimacy. She argued that people resist it, they dislike being patronised and are reluctant to be led.[24] Power over can make people feel coerced, under-appreciated or unseen. It leads people to feel like a cog in a wheel and denies them agency or dignity.

In contrast, *power with* is 'coactive'. Working with others to 'jointly develop ... power' can unify people, while simultaneously 'allowing for infinite differing'.[25] It aligns neatly with empathy, where power is co-created but does not assume any one side or person is superior. For her, 'interweaving experience creates legitimate power'[26] and helps in finding solutions where all involved can be reflected in the outcomes.

This is especially important given the nature of the challenges we face today. Longer-term threats like climate change, economic insecurity, conflict, and technological change require wider perspectives on power and a more long-term investment from government and leaders across parties and initiatives that engage and empower the people.

At the same time, many people and organisations have a stake in the status quo. It benefits them and their interests. Visionary leaders who want to transform power in its current form therefore have to be able to articulate why and how the status quo does not serve those invested in it and offer a credible and viable alternative. Empty promises and idealistic visions can seem naïve and unrealistic, especially in countries that have experienced recurrent challenges and a breakdown in trust. Progress and change have to be conveyed as attainable and manageable, in incremental and palatable steps.

Such a process cannot be without boundaries. And it is here that empathy presents its harder edges and raises ethical quandaries. How do you, and should you, seek to understand those who willingly choose to use violence to achieve their political objectives? Or those who denigrate and dehumanise their opponents or other members of society? Or who seek to deny the validity or identity of others? Do calls for unity in societies deny the rightful attribution of blame and agency to those who have sought to sow disunity? Or perhaps it is in the process of identifying accountability and collectively seeking new ways, that the divisions can be healed. These are permanent questions for all societies.

Creating power *with* others compels a process of accepting how power has been, and is still being, denied to some or abused by some who hold it. This involves a reckoning with the historical, political, economic, psychological, and emotional implications of such experiences, especially if they have gone on over extended periods of time. What is required is an intentional process of developing consciousness and understanding of oppression, and sources of current and historical injustices. This includes being open and honest about the nature of slavery and its horrific and devastating impact and long-lasting implications; demonstrating awareness of how racism and policies such as segregation and racial biases have disadvantaged people from certain communities; and acknowledging gendered biases and prejudices within society.[27] It includes acknowledging how First Nations people have been overlooked and their history ignored or erased and finding ways to rectify this. There are already many initiatives seeking to address these historical legacies.

Even so, unpacking these alternative experiences can be hard. There can be resistance to such conversations. Some people deeply believe these past experiences were generally good or not as bad as other people claim. More generously, those with power or privilege in society may not have been conscious of their position nor aware of the detrimental impact a system that served them had on others. The stories we tell ourselves about the way things are, and the assumptions and ideas we have about ourselves and each other, can be powerful and appealing. When they are challenged, or when alternative versions of such stories are presented, it can be confronting and unsettling. Countries themselves have powerful national narratives about their strengths, their values, and their proud history. Yet – and this is harder to countenance for those who are attached to such stories – maybe the freedom that a country's founders championed was not a universal experience, as in the case of the US. Or the global influence and power exerted by a country during its age of empire was less beneficent and far more violent and oppressive for millions around the world than its history classes have taught, as for Britain, France, and other colonial powers

Psychologically, emotionally, and intellectually, it can be easier for us to find ways to ignore or play down the implications of such information, rather than finding ways to process and accommodate a richer, more accurate, and more nuanced account of our pasts. Denial can be a protective psychological mechanism, helping us to avoid distress, anxiety, and the processing of difficult emotions. There can also be a reluctance to acknowledge responsibility for past and present actions, and discomfort with ideas of historical guilt incurred from events that took place before we were born. For those who point to the harmful legacies of empire, there are those who counter quickly with its benefits rather than looking at how we process these truths to move forward in a constructive way for all involved. We can and should tell a more nuanced history that does justice to the past whilst also shaping a more accurate and inclusive vision for the future. If we can do this, it can be a means to repair and redress.

There have been visible attempts to do this in Australia, although there is still a long way to go. Between 1995 and 1997, a National Inquiry led by the Human Rights and Equal Opportunity Commission examined the events and implications of the Stolen Generation – a dark period in the country's history where, between 1910 and 1970, Indigenous children were forcibly taken away from their families and put in foster care or institutions, where many experienced physical and sexual abuse. Thousands of families were split during the period, and children were taken away from their native lands as part of an erasure of their culture, language, and heritage.[28] The Inquiry interviewed over 500 people who had been affected, and their testimonies revealed the scale and depth of harm during this period. It was accompanied by a grassroots campaign process that was seen as a people's apology, and in the late 1990s all state and territory parliaments issued an apology for the policies and laws that had made it possible.

Then, on 13 February 2008, after consultation with Indigenous groups about the best approach, Prime Minister Kevin Rudd offered a heartfelt National Apology to Indigenous Australians, and especially those who had been a part of the Stolen Generation. Presented to Parliament in the form of a Motion, he was accompanied by the leader of the Opposition, Brendan Nelson, who was equally committed in his support. It is a powerful statement, acknowledging past wrongs and the enduring legacies they had wrought. It marked a significant turning point in confronting the past and moving towards reconciliation.

In response, Lorraine Peters, an Indigenous Weilwun and Gamilaroi woman, and a survivor of the Stolen Generation, presented both political leaders with a glass coolamon vessel, traditionally made from wood. It was, she remarked, 'a symbol of the hope we place in the new relationship you wish to forge with our people'.[29] Words signal intent, but do not change realities alone. Efforts at deepening reconciliation and telling a more accurate account of the nation's story continue, and initiatives are embedding Indigenous Australian experiences in cultural sites, national storytelling, political institutions and educational curriculums to increase understanding and awareness of the forgotten stories. There is still further to go. However, the act of acknowledging the past was a powerful step forward.[30]

Living in Australia as a British citizen, it is striking how much of the country's history and Britain's role in some of its more violent episodes, including the massacres of Indigenous Australians, is not taught about or really discussed in the United Kingdom. There is scope here too for deeper understanding of the country's historical legacy, and for finding the means to seek redress and recognise the implications.

In this way empathy can be a path to justice. It can expose inequalities, and asymmetries of power and opportunity in the past and present.[31] Through a process of understanding what people are experiencing, or have experienced, and legacies of harm, it can help identify injustices and seek ways to rectify them.

Justice can also balance empathy.[32] The mechanisms of the law, and principles of what is just and ethical, can help to ensure that empathy does not tip too much into the excessive caring for one group over another, as those who are more cautious about empathy's benefits highlight.[33] Empathy is not about giving everything to one group. Instead, it is through justice and the law that legal scholars, policymakers, and citizens can find ways to make fully informed decisions, and balance competing priorities and claims for care from multiple people or groups across societies. It helps to build on, and often challenge, existing tenets in society and the norms and laws that guide it, centred on core principles and ideals of individual rights and freedoms and collective responsibilities and needs. One example where this is visible is tax brackets. Most people wish to pay less, and yet some are more deserving or in need. Justice and the law can help determine who owes what, who needs what, and what people can afford to pay in a manner that – ideally – is fair, equitable, and proportionate.

Many of the most transformative legal reforms – including anti-discrimination legislation, human rights charters, compensatory schemes, and restorative justice models – have emerged from an empathetic understanding of specific groups' lived experience. These laws often seek to redress historical injustices and actively shape social norms and values. Importantly, they are administered by independent judicial systems, which help to ensure that they are applied consistently, impartially, and in accordance with established legal principles. In this way, the judiciary translates empathetic legislation into enforceable rights and obligations, thereby providing a safeguard even when public sentiment or political pressures might pull in other directions.[34]

PUTTING PEOPLE AT THE HEART OF POLICY

Connected to ideas of engaging people more in using their power and cultivating greater citizen engagement and investment in politics, empathy can be built into policy design and implementation processes at the heart of government. It can inform how politics is done. Such approaches can re-energise governance and offer valuable insights for policies that are more attuned and responsive to people's needs.[35]

Kit Collingwood-Richardson, a former policymaker in the British civil service, offers a useful toolkit for empathy in policy, having observed the shortfalls and problems of existing approaches.[36] When she was working on prison policy, she found there was no understanding of how women encountered unique challenges in prisons, especially relating to menstrual and reproductive health, and motherhood. No one had thought to consider how certain policies would have differential impacts on people, and this motivated her commitment to build empathy into the policy process. She offers a number of practical steps, which include doing more frontline user-research, where policymakers go to meet with people themselves rather than using commissioned research that provides a pre-digested summary. Policymakers should go where policy comes to life – where ideas become reality. They should go to schools, hospitals, job centres, and housing services, to see what happens when policy comes into contact with the people. She advocates that people go deeper and find out more about the local circumstances and context, and, as part of that, understand how people use and run the services being provided. Such an approach is dependent on a rich body of data that goes beyond statistics, to individual experiences, stories, discourses, and more eclectic insights.

This value of empathy in policy is not just a nice idea; it is being put into practice in the United Kingdom. His Majesty's Revenue and Customs have begun a process of incorporating empathy into both their workplace culture and their policy process.[37] Following a series of episodes that revealed a disconnect between the organisation and British taxpayers, there have been internal changes designed to put the citizen first. The initiative, led by Andrew Clark-Jones and his team, aims to build empathy among staff, so they understand citizens' needs better across the organisation, and to incorporate citizens' experiences into the design and implementation of policy.

The 'Customer Immersion Team' engages with small groups of citizens to understand how they interact with the department, and how policies might affect them. For example, with self-assessment tax deadlines coming up, the team will explore what challenges are arising for those submitting claims for repayments and try to understand why some people would call so many times, revealing issues with the interface between the citizen and the department. Once understood, these findings can feed back into how policy rollouts are designed and delivered. The initiative is less about solving an individual person's problems than gaining a richer appreciation for the customer experience so it can be improved.

The team is small, but it has impact. Although it doesn't collect data on a large scale, or carry out extensive opinion surveys, the method of talking to people, and seeking to understand their perspective, facilitates new ways of considering problems and thinking creatively about solutions. In the process, it has high-level buy-in, exposing very senior policymakers to how citizens are thinking and feeling about tax affairs, and about where they encounter problems.[38]

Policy could be transformed if such a function existed across government, providing a gateway and source of dialogue between policymakers and the people, and equipping policymakers with the language of empathy. This case of the 'Customer Immersion Team' and other related initiatives offer insights into what works, and lessons about what doesn't, which can inform a wider initiative.

Other countries are making similar shifts and recognising the value of empathy. Olli-Pekka Heinonen is a former Finnish politician who now leads the International Baccalaureate. He has been prominent in policy for a long time, holding several ministerial positions and working in education as Director General of the Finnish National Agency for Education. From 2012 to 2016, he was the State Secretary in the Prime Minister's Office of Finland and he has written a book on how to improve politics based on his experiences.

When we speak, he recounts how effective it was to engage with the public more on education policy during the pandemic, and how it became a core part of their work. Yet it was not just about working with the public, but how it was done – in a way that conveyed curiosity, interest, and humility.

The important thing, he notes, is 'to free the discussion from the idea that we need to end up with an outcome. Then actually, people naturally start to connect more with each other.' Paradoxically, 'when you let go of the outcome, it enables the outcome to emerge'.[39] He tells me of how one of the breakthrough moments came during a series of initiatives around education when 'someone was courageous enough to say that they actually didn't know how they would solve a problem, and that was when the professional shields went down'.[40] When someone said: 'my spotlight is not enough to solve this challenge, then people start to connect with each other and start to see each other as humans'.

This highlights the importance of humility in policymaking, something the Finnish system has championed.[41] It offers a recognition that policymakers cannot have, and do not have, all the information. Such awareness should encourage them to seek out those who know more, or have the vital experiences required to feedback into the decision-making process.

While humility is an asset, it can be difficult. Some organisational cultures reward those who can champion themselves or who are unabashed about highlighting their own achievements, rather than being a part of a team. This depends on the metrics of success and what is valued within organisations, and indicates where changes can be made.

To practise empathy in a policy setting impels initiatives that engage the most vulnerable and least empowered in society. More people must be in the process from early on, informing policy design. There should also be a wider array of backgrounds and experiences among the policymakers themselves, and across government, to ensure cognitive diversity and a richer representation of society more widely.[42]

How we frame problems, what we focus on, the end goals we seek, and how we talk about them are critical to the solutions we find. This is about stories, and assumptions, and the power of ideas about what works and what is needed. There is a danger that when we see a complex challenge we resort to the same comfortable answers, or ways of doing things, and we need more imagination and creativity to rethink what it is we are dealing with and explore new avenues.

This can be harder in practice. Politicians have to weigh up the best course of action and make complex decisions, prioritising what deserves most attention. Their choices and options are determined not only by what they wish to achieve, but also by a careful balancing act of their party and its priorities and popularity, the various needs of their many constituents, the available resources and public appetite for any initiatives, as well as the wider international context. As a result, there will consistently be multiple competing interests and demands involved in how decisions are made.

Empathy can help the process, offering politicians a deeper and more nuanced understanding of how political choices might have an impact on others. It can also help them communicate the different elements of their decision or course of action – and articulate the trade-offs and considerations that have shaped their thinking. However, putting empathy into practice and changing how policy is designed and delivered will be a longer-term initiative as people gradually adapt to new ways of approaching problems and finding more collaborative solutions.

*

The challenges of our societies, our politics, our security, well-being, and environment, are all dependent on collective efforts to change and a dramatic intentional rethink of our approach. Expanding and adjusting our conceptions of power is crucial to this effort. The obstacles to such change can be found, in part, in the asymmetries in power, its uneven distribution within society, and in too-narrow ideas of what change means and how it should look.

To alter this, leaders at all levels have to be willing to choose the path less travelled in redefining what power means and how it is distributed. This involves an openness and willingness to explore new means of politics and include new voices. Leaders have to work to accommodate different ideas and perspectives, and navigate compromises on the result. Along the way, they have to be able to communicate the trade-offs and challenges of reaching some kind of consensus.

An important place to rethink power is in the ideas and ideologies that guide our societies. They have power over how we construct and find meaning. What stories do we tell as individuals? As communities and societies? And as nations? These stories, containing within them logics of how things work, and assumptions about how things are, shape our interpretations of the world and the meaning we accord to events. There is power in reimagining them.

5

Telling Richer Stories

On 11 May 1994, a day after swearing the oath as President of South Africa, Nelson Mandela announced the start of a new dawn for the country: 'Out of the experience of an extraordinary human disaster that lasted too long, must be born a society of which all humanity will be proud. Our daily deeds as ordinary South Africans must produce an actual South African reality that will re-inforce humanity's belief in justice, strengthen its confidence in the nobility of the human soul and sustain all our hopes for glorious life for all.'[1] It marked the end of Apartheid, and an attempt to heal the deep rifts within society. Creating a unity government, he set out a commitment to work together to craft a new story of the country, which did not shy away from the pains of the past but looked towards the future.

Nelson Mandela is often held up as an exemplar of transforma-tional leadership. His character was forged through long experiences in politics, and over twenty-seven years as a political prisoner. He centred empathy and compassion as part of his vision for peace and unity in South Africa. And he offered a new way of looking at the country and its potential future: including through the

1995 Rugby World Cup, famously captured in the 2009 film *Invictus*; or by inviting political opponents for cups of tea, then disarming them with his charm and helping them understand the scale and potential of his vision.[2] He demonstrated the possibility for transformation. It was a long and hard process, but it gave the people of the country a new story and changed the narrative internationally as well. Albeit this did not last as long as he had anticipated.

To create political transformation, we need powerful and creative stories that offer the possibility for change. Politics is about storytelling. As American sociologist Charles Tilly explained, stories 'do essential work in social life, cementing people's commitments to common projects, helping people make sense of what is going on, channelling collective decisions and judgements, spurring people to action they would otherwise be reluctant to pursue'.[3] An effective, powerful leader can articulate an idea and a vision for who and what a country or community can be, and how their leadership will realise that goal. How we speak about the world, and create meaning through words and actions and symbols, has a bearing on the significance and power we give to things.

Yet these stories don't just come from our leaders; they are co-created by society, by collective aspirations and ideas. Part of the process of reimagining power involves challenging our prevailing stories and how and where we confer meaning. We should question the way things work and whether they are the most effective for the societies and politics we seek. Empathy helps us in this process, by encouraging a richer understanding of the different identities in a society, and the diverse hopes and dreams people hold for their future, helping us connect with each other. Such stories have to be sustainable and part of a collective effort of shifting mindsets, ideas, and assumptions. This process of crafting new stories can help to build more trust and investment in the process, fostering connections between citizens and politicians and institutions.

STORIES OF WHO WE ARE

In our current moment, our identities are a source of division. They are narrower than in the past, more tightly held.[4] They are connected to more two-dimensional stories about what matters, what is important, and what is wrong, as well as resentment about how things are and should not be.

This form of politics can foster tensions and create in-groups. We feel more at home with certain political identities than others. We might position ourselves on the political spectrum – right, left, somewhere either side of centre – or we might find more resonance with certain ideas and ideologies – Conservative, Liberal, Green, Socialist, Nationalist. There is belonging in these spaces. In these contexts, empathy and emotions are used to create a comforting sense of acceptance and community. It has a moral quality, where people share in a sense of virtue or righteousness about their ideals of a good society and what truly matters.[5]

Stereotypes help us delineate what distinguishes us from others. They create easily understood, albeit incomplete, pictures of political opponents and those with whom we disagree – 'woke' lefties, 'new elites', 'eco warriors', or the 'alt-right'. However, such reductionist groupings over-simplify and remove elements of another's personality, experience, or values to which you might relate and find common purpose.

Moreover, using such designations against others does little to convince them of the value of your ideas. It shuts down dialogue rather than facilitating pathways to connection and mutual understanding.

At the more extreme end, this dehumanisation and denigration of the 'other' in politics obscures our capacity to see the humanity in people. All sides are guilty of portraying political opponents as more callous, less deserving, or corrupted by ideologies or interests.

Another person's dignity and humanity can be gradually removed through the language, imagery, and symbolism used about them. Professor of Philosophy David Livingstone Smith writes of dehumanisation not only as a way of talking about others, but as 'a way of thinking . . . It acts as a psychological lubricant, dissolving our inhibitions and inflaming our destructive passions. As such, it empowers us to perform acts that would, under other circumstances, be unthinkable'.[6]

This is very visible in how those who oppose allowing refugees and migrants to enter their country will use language that refers to them as 'hordes', 'swarms', 'poison',[7] or 'illegals'. This denies them their humanity and their dignity. When such terms are repeated often enough, it becomes easier for people to legitimise demeaning, degrading, and inhumane policies against them. UN High Commissioner for Refugees Filippo Grandi has spoken of how 'it is this type of language that stigmatizes refugees, migrants and other people on the move, that gives legitimacy to a discourse of racism, hatred, and xenophobia'.[8] Such discourses threaten and demean others, and can legitimise the use of violence. It is well documented how, in the years before the horrific genocide in Rwanda, Hutu politicians would repeatedly refer to the Tutsi minority as 'cockroaches' and 'snakes'.[9] In messages broadcast via radios across the country, they would stoke fear and anger, legitimising the terrible violence that was unleashed in 1994, eventually killing over 800,000 people.[10]

Scientific studies suggest there can be a natural empathy gap. Even though we may be predisposed to respond to the emotional states of others, this capacity seems to decline for those considered part of an out-group, compared to those in our in-group.[11] And, in times of competition, there can be different valuations of life.[12]

Our identities and political opinions may feel viscerally important, giving us a sense of certainty. Yet we should hold them lightly. They should not obscure our capacity to see the rich human complexity of others. We are all more than a label, and instincts and habits can be overridden.[13] We have to find universality within diversity.[14] There are levels, and points of contact, where we can break these divides: points of social connection, civic spaces, hobbies, and other interests. Food can be a great way to engage with people from different perspectives and is often used as a means to help bridge divides between conflicting societies. Empathy becomes easier once we find points of commonality with others, and a shared sense of purpose.

One way to approach differences is to genuinely listen to what diverse sides say. Giving them time and space to air their concerns and their hopes and reciprocate in turn. Even if you vehemently disagree with an Olaf Scholz voter, a Jeremy Corbyn fan, or an Anthony Albanese aficionado and cannot understand their choices, if you can get below their voting preference to the issues at hand, it may be that more areas of commonality or shared concerns emerge – about prosperity, security, about what they want their community to feel like, so they feel safe and valued. We should empathise with the outcomes, with what it is people are seeking to achieve and why, even if we do not agree with their position. It can be easier than we realise.

In 2017 Heineken released a powerful advert called 'Worlds Apart', based on an experiment showing pairs of strangers coming together despite their difference. The scene opens in a large workshop with many big boxes and parts of colourful overturned furniture in various states of disarray.[15] Interspersed in these opening scenes were short insights into who each pair of strangers were, their core political beliefs or identity. One claimed they did not believe in climate change, another felt women should know that their place was in the home, one was a feminist, another did not believe in gender fluidity. Aptly matched to their opposite, and without awareness of the other's beliefs or backgrounds, they found themselves engaged in a series of activities. In the first, 'The Icebreaker', they had to build flatpack furniture – a common source of tension in many homes – and work together to share the instructions where they were incomplete and piece the item together.

Once this was done, in the second part, each person was asked to describe themselves in five adjectives. They shared what defined them, what made them proud of themselves, the struggles they had overcome, their values, and their experiences, such as having been homeless or in the military. They complimented each other on their courage, their resilience, their warmth, or relatability. They shared what they had in common, and what made them feel connected.

Part three – 'Bridge-Building' – involved putting together the bar and the stools from the array of furniture, seeing the product of their joint effort over a few hours. Finally, they had 'The Decision'. Handed a beer, they watched the videos of their counterpart's opinions and beliefs and were given the option: either they could stay, share a drink, and discuss their differences, or they could leave. All chose to stay: to sit, to chat and engage, and reflect on how maybe their biases were not fixed nor entirely well informed. A study by Stanford reinforced the impact of this process, finding it to be an effective means of changing people's perceptions and ideas.[16]

We can be resistant to empathising with those from different identities, backgrounds' or perspectives. It can make us feel that we look weak, or as if we are conceding ground and compromising. It can also reveal our own ignorance about others. Yet a good step towards overcoming this resistance is to lean into curiosity.

In the heart of trendy Nørrebro in Copenhagen, there is a human library ('Menneskebiblioteket'). Based at Union, a culture house on Nørre Allé made of weathered brown brick, and surrounded by coffee shops and apartments, the library opens on Sundays to the public. There, in the outdoor space, among a collection of plants, trees, and seating areas' you can 'take out' a 'book' for free and spend thirty minutes with them.

During that time, the human book – a person who has offered to share their stories and experiences – will answer any question and share their perspectives. You can select a book or have one allocated at random. The open book I borrowed was a woman who shared her experiences with neural diversity. She was patient and honest with our group as she reflected on her life and on how she had learned to adapt to the challenges she had faced.[17]

Started in 2000, the idea has now spread in various forms to over eighty countries.[18] With books on a vast array of topics – from sexuality, race, adoption, and ADHD (attention deficit/hyperactivity disorder) to life in prison, homelessness, drug abuse, incest, and physical disabilities – the library addresses topics and taboos to make it possible for people to broach issues they do not fully understand or feel able to speak about. The books are volunteers and, alongside the open library events, the organisation offers more targeted educational initiatives. It is designed to create deeper understanding of one another, to tackle prejudice, stigma, and discrimination in society to help people 'unjudge' one another and contribute to more cohesive, tolerant, and diverse communities. Through the experience I learned the value of seeking to understand another and confronting our own ignorance or uncertainty. People are often willing to be asked difficult questions if this is done kindly and respectfully, from a place of genuine interest.

HEALING DIVISIONS: HOW WE COME TOGETHER

Being curious about understanding your family member with weird views, debating politics or sport with the guy you just met in the pub, or learning about how different people have overcome stigma is one thing, yet discussions around empathy are much harder when dealing with people who have harmed you, or actively want to deny your identity or your right to exist. Even if empathy is an integral part of how we come together, and overcome our current divides, it is a demanding and difficult task.

Jo Berry is one of those inspiring figures who, despite just cause for enmity, chooses empathy over vengeance or shame.[19] On 12 October 1984, when she was 27, her father Sir Anthony Berry MP was killed in the Brighton bombing. As a Conservative politician he was attending the party's annual conference and was at the Grand Hotel, where Patrick Magee of the Irish Republican Army (IRA) had planted a bomb under a bathtub on a long-delay timer. British Prime

Minister Margaret Thatcher and senior cabinet members were the primary target, with the IRA hoping to cause such a shock it would let the government know they were in it for the long haul and would not go away. When the bomb detonated at 2.54 a.m. it killed five people, including Sir Anthony, and injured over thirty-one others. Had it reached its full potential it would have killed far more. In sentencing Patrick to eight life sentences, for both the Brighton attack and other offences, the judge declared him 'a man of exceptional cruelty and inhumanity'.[20]

Remarkably, just two days after the attack, Jo made a private decision to understand why it had happened: to truly grasp the events and circumstances that had led the IRA to commit such an act. When she reflects on that period, she admits her approach and relative equanimity was partly informed by her time in India in her early twenties studying Gandhi, meditation, and the value of humanity. It was a choice further reinforced by a serendipitous meeting in the back of a taxi with a man from Northern Ireland whose brother had been in the IRA and had been killed by the British military. On the short ride, they shared their mutual pain, and a vision for a time when violence would not be the norm and the communities could live alongside one another in peace.

It was a tense and violent time in the United Kingdom. Between 1988 and 1994, British television would not permit the voices of Sinn Féin to be heard, meaning that leaders such as Gerry Adams would be dubbed whenever they appeared on TV.[21] It served, Jo admitted, to further dehumanise the other side.

After her decision to understand the conflict and why people were using violence to achieve their aims, Jo spent extended periods in Northern Ireland, meeting people and speaking of her experiences in various forums. She met with other survivors of the Troubles who articulated their own unique history of trauma, and actively sought to understand the perspectives of civilians, combatants, and politicians on all sides.

In the two years after the Good Friday Agreement was signed, over 400 paramilitary prisoners were released early. Patrick was released in June 1999. Eventually, in November 2000, they met.

Jo's intention and aims for that first meeting were, she says, to see evidence of humanity. Patrick had been given a bad label by the judge at his sentencing and she wanted to see beneath that, whether there was more to the man. She did not need an apology and had no expectation of seeing him again. But they ended up talking for ninety minutes. Justifying his approach, he discussed the political motivations of his act, and the suffering his community had experienced, including Bloody Sunday. As she was about to leave, prepared never to see him again, he admitted to being 'disarmed by her empathy', and so she stayed, and they spoke for another ninety minutes. This time the conversation turned to her anger and experiences, how humanity was lost through violence, and when he apologised it had a deeper meaning. None of this was without pain, and difficulty, but she speaks of the power she found in modelling humanity, in listening and respecting the experiences of another, without attachment to being right.

It is rare to commit to such a process, and far from easy. Some may be inspired by the courage it takes to face the man who killed your father. Some may be shocked, feeling justice and retribution have not been delivered, and that people should pay a higher cost for their actions. All perspectives are valid. However, it raises the question: where do cycles of hate and animosity lead us? This is a prominent theme when Jo speaks with me about her experience. Her calm demeanour belies the time she has spent processing and confronting these emotions and it has not been easy. Her reasoning for this vulnerable and confronting process of reconciliation, she explains, was because she did not want anyone else to be responsible for her healing. To hate Patrick would not change the circumstances, but consume her, and her own relationships. She recalls that often misattributed quote: 'resentment is like drinking poison and then hoping it will kill your enemies'.[22] It gives more power to another. Yet to offer the grace of empathy, and to be open to another's perspective on such a traumatic event, is a way to process grief and transform it into a dialogue for change. Listening, and being heard in return, becomes an antidote to shame, anger, and their corrosive impact on human relations. Individuals alone cannot transform societies, but they can offer a model for change.

While an individual may determine their own capacity and inclination to make such a shift, and to consider the context and justification for it, when societies transform the stories they tell, and come together after crises, conflict, and deep divisions, it is far more complicated. It involves a collective process of empathising across the divides, of understanding the grievances, the pain and trauma of different people, and identifying the kind of country they wish theirs to be. This is not a linear or simple process. Not everyone will be on board with or amenable to the process. Changing how people view another, especially in conditions of extreme enmity, takes years – or even generations.

Look again at South Africa – Mandela's vision was accompanied by action and concerted efforts to process the changes and to heal past wounds. The Truth and Reconciliation Commission, established in 1996 by the president and chaired by Archbishop Desmond Tutu, was an intentional effort to air the experiences of those who had been victims of gross human rights violations and injustices between 1960 and 1994. It also gave space for perpetrators to share their experiences and accounts, offering insight into events and sometimes revealing the missing pieces of what happened to the period's victims for their families. Guided by the *Ubuntu* philosophy that emphasises empathy and shared humanity, it was informed by the idea of forgiveness as a political necessity to move forward, and dependent on truth and honesty about crimes and injustices committed.[23] Confrontation is inevitable, as people are faced with diverse accounts and experiences of events, but it is integral to the reconciliation.[24] Although it was not a perfect process, as many senior political and military officials refused to engage, it offered steps forward for a country that had been divided, and a way to accord dignity to the victims, and paths to rehabilitation for perpetrators.

Empathy is an essential part of healing divides and can help in bringing conflicts and tensions within a society to an end. All such efforts require high-level political investment and visionary leaders who can hold their nerve and provide clarity and reassurance to the country about the benefits of such a process. Nevertheless, it requires not only leaders, but citizens and civil society who can create the space for understanding and legitimise and normalise new stories about who they are.

For former president Juan Manuel Santos of Colombia, empathy was key to helping transform the country after five decades of civil war and violence. When he came to power, the civil conflict between the Colombian government and the Fuerzas Armadas Revolucionarias de Colombia (Revolutionary Armed Forces of Colombia) (FARC) had been long and bloody. It had resulted in the deaths of over 220,000 people, displaced about 5.7 million, and led to the disappearance of over 25,000.[25] As defence minister under the previous president, Álvaro Uribe, Santos had overseen an extensive crackdown on the FARC. And he had been effective.

In four years as defence minister, he had done a lot to improve intelligence, to enlist the support of the US, UK, Israel, and others to ensure the government had the best information to succeed against the FARC. His approach was rewarded with electoral success, achieving a landslide win to become president with 69% of the vote. Yet the experience also confronted him with the realities of war. Each week he would have to travel across the country to attend funerals of fallen soldiers and citizens, and to hear of the traumas and human costs of war and violence, often far away from the relative security of the capital.

Over his career, however, he evolved from a hawk to a dove. By his own admission, his ideas of what was needed for successful politics changed.[26] When he became president, he was questioned by friends and advisors about what he wanted his legacy to be: continued conflict, more deaths, or an effort at peace? He recounts how, knowing the president's inclination for peace, a former commander of the army offered his advice: 'Treat FARC not as enemies, but as adversaries – enemies you defeat, adversaries you beat, but you have to live with them for rest of life. Treat them as human beings.'[27] Such a move, it was argued, would facilitate dialogue with them, while helping to ensure the president held the moral high ground.

President Santos has spoken frequently of the vital power and significance of empathy in his leadership and as a prerequisite to peace. He had to learn to cross the divides within the country, and to listen and genuinely hear what different parts of the population were saying. Former ambassador to the UK Mauricio Rodríguez Múnera was closely involved in the process. Reflecting on President Santos's character as a leader, he emphasises how Santos 'had this very deep, profound intellectual, emotional, spiritual commitment to peace ... that's what kept the process alive'. Even when some of those around him were despairing, he persevered.[28] This kind of vision, tenacity, and conviction is essential for effective leadership, especially in such circumstances.

Although President Santos had made that shift in his thinking. Convincing the Colombian people was far harder. In Colombia, as in other countries, many of the elite were removed from the remote regions where the violence was most intense. Their children were rarely the ones fighting, and they did not have to live with the immediate consequences or disruption of war. There was a disconnect between events, realities on the ground, and wider societal understanding. When speaking with business leaders in the country, some of the biggest opponents of the peace process, Mauricio Rodríguez Múnera found that the majority did not fully comprehend the scale or toll of the conflict, nor the level of inequality within the country. They had no sense of how little the average person living in poverty had to spend each day, nor the disproportionate distribution of wealth in the country.[29]

It is hard to feel empathy if your perspective is rooted in a reality that is black and white. Especially as to fully understand the scale of the problem, on all sides, means confronting the restrictive nature of labels like 'guerrilla', 'communist', 'criminal', and 'oppressor' that flatten people into neat ideas of good or bad. These labels may give an illusion of moral certainty but do not capture the more complex reality or the humanity of the people involved. It is through seeing the other as more than their label and finding points of connection and understanding that space can be created to move forward.

The process in Colombia was far from easy. Violence continued during the period of talks, which were facilitated by Norway and Cuba and lasted over four years. During this time, most of the country remained polarised and unconvinced by the process – sentiments that were stoked by the political opposition. Colombia was prey to internal structural weaknesses that had contributed to cycles of violence. There was an absence of governance in the regions, with local people rarely seeing politicians or officials. This was compounded by a culture of impunity for those in power, meaning a lack of justice and accountability for those who abused their position. In the absence of this, armed groups and illegal economies grew. The peace process was a significant step to address this.[30]

On 26 September 2016, the Colombian government signed a historic deal with the FARC after extensive negotiations in Havana, Cuba. All dressed in white, with a pen made from a bullet, and accompanied by Beethoven's 'Ode to Joy', the signing was an occasion replete in symbolism. To cheers and applause, the FARC leader, Timoleón Jiménez, familiarly known as Timochenko, apologised to 'all the victims of the conflict' and asked for forgiveness for the pain caused. 'We are being reborn to launch a new era of reconciliation and of building peace . . . Let us all be prepared to disarm our hearts.'[31] It was the first time he had ever addressed the nation on television.

For those in charge of the FARC group, the agreement was considered largely beneficial. It both addressed some of their grievances and facilitated their political engagement.[32] Yet many were still disadvantaged by the process, and there was frustration and dissatisfaction from groups on all sides. It would be a tumultuous transition to new relations.

On 2 October 2016 a referendum on the peace agreement rejected it by a small margin – 50.2% against 49.8% in support. It involved around 13 million voters, and just over 53,000 votes separated them. Notably, a lot of people – about 62.8% of voters – abstained, approximately 22 million Colombians.

The political environment of this period and the campaign surrounding the referendum was hostile. Mauricio recounts how opponents spread lies, based on fostering a sense of indignation and misplaced fear that the agreement was too favourable to the FARC members and would implement gender ideology and threaten ideas of the family.[33]

Although this was a setback, President Santos was determined not to be defeated. He embarked on a National Dialogue, bringing together former president Andrés Pastrana and former president and opponent Álvaro Uribe, who had been strident in opposition to the process.[34] He also listened to people across society about their concerns, and what it really meant to forgive and rehabilitate those who had participated in the conflict. He was aided by the efforts of young people, and rising protests in public spaces calling for peace. When Santos was awarded the Nobel Peace Prize on 7 October 2016, it was, Mauricio recalls, 'like manna from heaven'.[35] On 24 November, after incorporating the views and concerns they had received from the National Dialogue into the process, the government and the FARC signed a revised peace agreement, which was agreed and ratified by both Houses at the end of November.

Shifting ideas and opinions was not only about making the case for peace but also about exposing the people of Colombia to diverse perspectives and provoking new ways of thinking. For a country rich in art, literature, and music, these cultural dimensions were a central ingredient in bringing together the different experiences of the Colombian identity. Leaders can marshal a different story, but it is also essential for the public to be invested in it, and the media plays a critical role in facilitating vital shifts in perspectives and new stories about what people's identity means and how their country can move forward.[36]

In Colombia, photojournalist Jesús Abad Colorado was one of the prominent cultural actors.[37] He has won awards for his contribution to documenting the conflict and the people involved. His powerful images revealed the realities on all sides that few wanted to confront and drew attention to the peripheries of the country – the spaces political and social elites did not want to see. Through imagery he gave dignity to the people affected and helped to humanise all those involved. In this way, photography served as a form of memory and record that contributed to a richer and more honest narrative.[38] It is a contribution to changing the story.

However, those divides have still not healed. It is a lot to rest on any person's shoulders. As Björn Krondorfer explores in *Unsettling Empathy*, who has a right to extend empathy on behalf of a group?[39] How do people know if such empathy is sincere or not, especially if it is not shared by those they claim to represent? Violence and insecurity continue.[40] As do the structural challenges of a culture of impunity, absence of officials in the region, and a perpetuation of illegal economies and illicit drug trafficking. It will take a much more intentional and sustained process to deliver on the hope of 2016. Many harmful beliefs about the other, and their intentions and interests, continue on all sides and make it hard to de-escalate conflict.[41] And many people remain disadvantaged by the process, and are left feeling that justice has not been done.

It takes time to move beyond the legacies of the conflict. Successive governments and leaders have had their own perspectives regarding the peace process and have undone some of the good work achieved. Empathy is far from a given – even when it has the strength to effect change, it remains fragile.

To transform society, you have to understand it, and to feel in a genuine way how different people experience it. This goes beyond mere cognitive reasoning. It means feeling people's pain, their anger, their perceptions of injustice and inequity, and then seeking to address them. To do so requires an extended process of listening and really understanding where people's perceptions and ideas come from. This takes time and needs to be supported by evidence that can alleviate people's fears.[42]

Today there are new initiatives to inculcate dialogue in society. They are a way of rewriting a country's story, exposing dividing lines and grievances, and working through common aspirations. These are also operating in countries that are not in conflict.

In Finland, a country that is doing a lot to innovate and connect citizens with politicians, national dialogues are a regular feature of politics. They offer opportunities for citizens, authorities, and communities to share their ideas and their concerns.[43] The aim is not to gain unanimity or reach policy decisions or conclusions, but more to raise all the issues that are most pressing and to examine how they are experienced from different perspectives. It is less a citizens' assembly, more a process to generate richer understanding and help create more cohesion and engagement across society.

In South Africa, after the African National Congress lost its majority in the May 2024 elections, it joined forces with the Democratic Alliance (DA) and the Inkatha Freedom Party (IFP) to create a new National Unity Government. As part of efforts to re-energise the country and heal some of the deep divisions, politicians and members of civil society have been seeking a renewed dialogue in the country. President Ramaphosa invited 'all parties, civil society, labour, business and other formations to a national dialogue on the critical challenges facing the nation'.[44] Scheduled to take place between May 2025 and 2026, it will follow a series of phases, and engagements ranging from the local to the national. It intends to cover topics including 'Poverty, inequality and hunger; Economic transformation and job creation; and Governance, accountability, and participatory democracy'. A key aim of the dialogue is to foster more social cohesion and forge a new social compact looking ahead to 2030 and South Africa's development plan.[45]

Klaus Kotzé works at the Inclusive Society, a think tank in Cape Town, and has worked on developing a framework for the dialogue. It is, he argues, a potent opportunity for change. However, it has to be truly inclusive and representative of the whole of society.[46] Such dialogues cannot just take place among the political classes. Investment in a shared vision for the future requires a true dialogue with the people. Yet there is a risk that such dialogue processes become talking shops for political agendas and turn into missed opportunities that do not genuinely seek to listen to the public.[47]

Moreover, society so often lacks the space for such collective processing. There are few leaders who can give voice to the complex and unquantifiable dynamics of collective emotions and navigate people through them. Yet ignoring a society's past and the facts of historical experiences does not make them any less real. And while dwelling in the past too long can be disruptive, you cannot move forward with a more inclusive politics if you cannot reconcile the past. There is real power in the process, offering politicians and the people the chance to tell a more accurate and nuanced account of the country's history, to attempt to make amends for past harms, and then to write a new national story and vision for the future.

When trying to address grievances and concerns, attempting to evoke shame in people who have done wrong can feel cathartic. It is a way to call such people out, to highlight injustices, and frustrations, and affirm proper modes of conduct. Yet it is often counterproductive. Shame does not follow a simple logic that compels people to change their behaviour or their ideas, in fact it often forces people to entrench themselves in the very things they are being shamed for doing or thinking.

This feels counterintuitive. And, unfortunately, it asks for a disproportionate level of magnanimity from those who have every right to want others to feel shame or guilt for their actions. This was the case with Jo Berry, and it was what President Santos was asking of the Colombian people who had been victims of FARC violence for years when he sought reconciliation. There is a balance to be struck between, on the one hand, justice and acknowledgement of guilt, and on the other, according space to those who have done harm to speak and to seek forgiveness and common ground going forward. It is not an easy ask, nor readily achieved. Yet, if invested in the process of rewriting a story that does justice to the past, while creating a different vision of the future, it is an integral part of the process.

Shame is not processed logically. It is unpalatable. None of us like feeling it, and it is an emotion few of us want to have. At an individual level, shame can prompt anxiety, self-loathing, and unhelpful introspection. It can cause us to act out or seek validation in different ways. At a collective level it is more complex and equally nonconstructive. Research suggests that it is less compatible with empathy than guilt.[48] What is more, people are less likely to seek to repair when feeling shame, whereas guilt is more pro-social, offering opportunities to apologise or make amends.[49] However, there still needs to be accountability, and people need to take responsibility for their actions. Providing space for forgiveness, and honesty, as was the case in the South Africa Truth and Reconciliation process, can facilitate this.

Another critical emotion is remorse – a key part of reconciliation and opening new pathways for change. This is significant not just in conflict situations. In the current political climate, evidence of remorse would go a long way to address some of the tensions and frustrations people have with governments and politicians over the state of the economy, the lack of housing, diminishing opportunities, and the inefficacies of government. It is powerful, but rare, to see politicians capable of recognising they are at fault, or admitting to errors and expressing remorse with a willingness to make amends or change their approach. Remorse must be followed by repair and constructive efforts at change. Otherwise it quickly looks empty.

CREATING MORE INCLUSIVE SOCIETIES

Change arises from a greater vision for a country, and a desire to transform the culture. Given the scale of marginalisation and polarisation in societies, there needs to be more than just kind words about diversity and inclusion: there needs to be action. Evidence suggests that we do become adaptable to difference.[50] It is not just through stories but also legislation that change can occur, by actively creating initiatives that compel shifts in behaviour and attitudes.

Canadian Prime Minister Pierre Elliott Trudeau had a significant influence on the country's politics and society with his vision for a tolerant, inclusive, and multicultural nation.[51] He had a strong political philosophy and envisioned an inclusive, pluralistic Canada. He considered nationalism sinister and wrong, whatever guise it took.

Over the course of more than fifteen years in office, he turned ideas into action. Among the legislation and initiatives he introduced, he institutionalised bilingualism, creating a country and a bureaucracy that could work in both English and French, and provided pathways from people of both languages to play a role in politics and policy. He decriminalised homosexuality and homosexual acts in 1968–69, famously exclaiming that there was 'no place for the state in the bedrooms of the nation'.[52] He saw vibrancy in diversity, centred on ideas of understanding and empathy:

A society which emphasizes uniformity is one which creates intolerance and hate. A society which eulogizes the average citizen is one which breeds mediocrity. What the world should be seeking, and what in Canada we must continue to cherish, are not concepts of uniformity but human values: compassion, love, and understanding.[53]

The logic is that 'vibrant ethnic groups can give Canadians of the second, third, and subsequent generations a feeling that they are connected with tradition and with human experience in various parts of the world and different periods of time'.[54]

He was himself a product of the country's multiculturalism, having been born and raised in Montréal, Quebec. At a time of nationalist tensions between Quebec and anglophone Canada, he could argue persuasively in English and French. His style was hip and urbane: he was a charismatic leader and media savvy. Capitalising on the growth of television and radio, his team ensured he had wide appeal and cultivated a distinctive public image: part intellectual, part renegade. He could be haughty, guided by reason, and with a tendency to do things his own way – pirouetting for the cameras in Buckingham Palace on a visit to London.[55] He combined a touch of the dramatic with a straightforward, no-nonsense approach and was, by various accounts, warm and charismatic, but also intolerant of fools and with a clear vision of the country he wanted to see.

When he entered the Liberal leadership race (which would subsequently make him prime minister) in 1968, the media spoke of 'Trudeaumania', comparing his popularity with the emotional appeal of The Beatles and capturing the widespread enthusiasm for him. He won easily. Although he was not someone who embodied empathic leadership in the way others might, being quite cerebral and aloof, empathy is evident in his vision for a culture of understanding, compassion, tolerance, diversity, and multiculturalism. It was a part of his intellectual priorities and aspirations for the kind of country he wanted to live in.

In 1988, after his second premiership had ended, the country passed the Multicultural Act, becoming the first in the world to enshrine such ideas into law.[56] The intention of the legislation was to enhance awareness and respect for diversity, promote intercultural under-standing, and ensure access to participation.

Until recently, Canada maintained this global image of a welcoming, vibrant country. In 2015, Pierre Trudeau's son, Justin Trudeau, ran on a similar multiculturalism platform, and won the election with an outright majority in October of that year. Just two months later, in December 2015, Trudeau welcomed the first flight of Syrian refugees off the plane at Toronto airport as part of his plan to resettle 25,000 by February 2016. Yet such initiatives, though well intended, also contributed to tensions. Canada has not been immune to the present-day rise in nationalism, and to concerns around the number of recent immigrants living in the country. In response, in 2024, there was a shift of tone, and steps to restrict who could live and work in the country. Some may argue this was because multicultur-alism and immigration have gone too far, but it could also be that, as elsewhere, successive governments have failed to address the under-pinning structural and systemic failures within society and see immi-gration quotas and curtailing diversity as a quick salve for deeper, more comprehensive issues around economic security, opportunities, and well-being.

As Justin Trudeau acknowledged, multiculturalism is a constant work in progress.[57] However, there are continued efforts to promote these values of diversity and multiculturalism in Canadian culture. Each September, Canada holds an annual Welcoming Week to cele-brate new arrivals and create a virtuous circle. The more welcome people feel as they arrive in the country, the more likely they are to contribute to their local community, easing integration and fostering community and familiarity.[58]

We need this kind of visionary leadership, which embraces multi-culturalism and champions diversity and humanity, to break through some of the limited ideas and regressive nationalism we have seen in recent years. This does not mean immigration should be unrestricted or all borders open, but the discourse has to give a better account of the richness within all our societies, and bring that understanding of different cultures into our national stories. Education and public awareness are integral to such shifts.[59] It has to be equally matched by efforts to address the underlying structural and systemic issues that are contributing to people's grievances.

*

Even though empathy as an idea can be a powerful lens to transform our politics, it must go beyond abstract aspirations. As an approach, a mindset, an ethos, and an aspiration, empathy has to be rooted in concrete and pragmatic steps. This means embracing the discomfort and hard work of seeking to understand.

Its ability to make a difference is shaped not only by the force of our commitment to the idea of empathy, but also by the political environment and its compatibility with a different approach, the media's capacity to tell more complex and nuanced stories, and our engagement as citizens with the process.

6

Creating a Healthy Ecosystem

If ideas and ideologies are the visions and assumptions we have for how politics should or could work, then culture is the environment in which they are shaped and brought to life. Our ideas of power, of what is possible in politics, and of the nature of political leadership are influenced by the prevailing political culture.

Yet the concept of political culture can seem amorphous. Political culture is 'the particular national character of a people, its historical development, and the whole complex of both its social and political relations'.[1] It shapes citizens' knowledge, feelings, and judgements of the system and their own role in it.[2] There is no one political culture, nor does it follow a linear or neat trajectory.[3] It is dependent on a country's historical and social evolution, and the constellation of politics and institutions within wider society. Who has access to politics? Who is heard? Who is at the table?

Systems shape the outcomes. For empathy to be able to transform politics, a vibrant, inclusive, and supportive ecosystem is required, that brings more people into politics and rewards understanding and connection. In part this requires a rethink of the underlying structural issues of many current democratic systems, which limit the capacity for elected individuals to be empathetic. This might involve reforming campaign financing and lobbying, which can limit politicians from speaking their own truth about what they think and feel. However, it also requires more incentives for politicians to work across parties and be more collaborative, in order to deliver more comprehensive and longer-term solutions for the people.

This involves addressing the workplace environment and the often toxic nature of politics to help get the best out of those who represent us. Standards for good professional conduct must be upheld. Our institutions may not be capable of empathy as organisations, but the people within them are, and attention should be focused on what is required to facilitate that. A significant priority is to rebuild people's trust in politics. This is also about cultivating more inclusion, valuing and celebrating diversity, and inculcating it into society. Politicians can actively create a space where people can feel seen, heard, and understood, and then contribute to dialogues that move the conversation forward, while acknowledging disparate views and experiences. Finally, greater political awareness among citizens is necessary – about their role and responsibilities within society, and how politics works – so they can hold politics to account, but also gain a deeper appreciation for the challenges and complexities inherent in democratic decision-making.

WORKING ACROSS PARTY LINES

Our politics has become too divisive, too partisan, and too heated, at least in public spaces. This means that empathy, understanding, and tolerance are not sufficiently modelled by those involved. Yet the biggest challenges we face today – such as economic inequality, socio-economic deprivation, climate change, and the provision of healthcare – require parties to come together and collaborate in the common interest.

Speak to most politicians and they will have friends from across the aisle, or recount stories of how, behind closed doors, many politicians work effectively across party lines. Jennifer Nadel, of the think tank Compassion in Politics, noted positively that behind closed doors politicians from diverse parties in the UK are working together on new ways of doing politics, and the organisation has launched a number of initiatives to clean up politics and create a code of conduct that have received cross-party backing and engagement.[4]

On committees, in realising legislation, and in championing change, politicians frequently collaborate irrespective of their political affiliations. For Sir Nick Harvey, a former British Liberal Democrat politician and defence minister, it is through these initiatives and through working on committees that you learn a lot about the opposition and their vulnerabilities, and by choosing to work as a team, can build trust and collaboration.[5] This is how lasting change is achieved.

Having become a member of the Federal Opposition following his swearing in to the Australian House of Representatives in 1995, Brendan Smyth, a former member of the Liberal Party, explained how it was that a senior minister in the government showed him a shortcut to the Chamber for a vote. Albeit the more senior member wryly noted it might be the last time he helped someone of the other side.[6]

Before he became president, Joe Biden was known for his bipartisanship. As a senator since 1972 he had built up relations with his counterparts in the Republicans and was known for being friendly, and a good negotiator. In his role as vice president for Barack Obama, Biden was able to work across the aisle to achieve policy objectives, and as president he achieved more bipartisan initiatives than any other president on either side in a generation, signing into law over 400 bipartisan bills.[7]

Research from the United States shows that politicians who gain a larger proportion of co-sponsors from opposing parties on their legislation are more likely to be successful.[8] It can therefore aid the longevity of an initiative if there is cross-party investment in its success.

However, while behind closed doors such collaboration is often standard, it is not always public.[9] In many countries, what the public sees is politicians locked in an adversarial and fraught relationship, with little scope for dialogue or cooperation.

One way to transform this is to break down the hold of two-party systems, which will permit a plurality of voices and interests. When only two or three parties dominate, it can constrain debate and limit choices. In systems where there are more options, it can help drive more engagement from the public: they are more likely to find a candidate whose views and ideas resonate with them. It compels a need for dialogue as parties have to learn to coexist.

In Australia, the rise of prominent Independents, such as former Rugby Union player and now Senator David Pocock, who has represented the Australian Capital Territory (ACT) in the Senate since 2022, reflects growing shifts to political attitudes and interests that are insufficiently captured by either of the main parties.[10] Many of these Independent candidates and elected officials build strong local bases and align with different parts of the political spectrum according to issues and interests, rather than a standard party line. It also helps ensure that those in the dominant parties don't take their seats for granted. The Teal Movement in particular has been a powerful force in unsettling traditionally Liberal seats.

The nature of the political system can influence this capacity for plurality and cooperation. Proportional representation (PR) systems – such as in Australia and Denmark – mean that when people vote, their choices are more likely to be reflected in some form in the outcome. It permits the growth of more parties and compels coalitions. Such systems force parties to work with others, meaning it is not always an easy or comfortable alignment. At elections, smaller parties can become kingmakers or can end up with more influence than their share of the vote suggests. For parties to achieve at least some of the platform that they stood for in the elections, they have to compromise, and in the process of political debate they often have to be more careful about the tone of discussions: you cannot afford to alienate too many parties, as there is a chance you may need them later. This system is not perfect – arguments abound about its limits – but it inculcates more reciprocal relations and efforts to understand what different people need and want, and where their red lines lie. Coming from a British first-past-the-post system to Australia, it was striking to watch the Australian federal election in May 2025 and see how much more representative the outcome was. Australians have much more agency in identifying their political preferences on the ballot paper. Instead of just putting a cross next to one name and party, they rank the options. This means they can select a smaller party first, to show their inclinations, and then give second or third choice to more dominant parties.

First-past-the-post systems, on the other hand, ensure only one party governs. This can yield greater stability, in some regards. The winning party takes all and sets about delivering their mandate, albeit constrained by the size of their majority and strength of the other parties. Yet the trouble can be that each time a new government arrives in power they overturn their predecessor's policies, leading to short-termism, and to a lack of common groundwork towards collective national interests.

In this respect, civil society can help, by creating the space to legitimise topics or raise the issues for change to be pushed forward. This has been the case with gay rights and equal marriage, where civil society-led movements have been vital voices for change and have shaped and influenced shifts in public perceptions and attitudes.

Nevertheless, in order to facilitate values of cooperation, dialogue, and healthy robust debate, significant changes are needed in how politics is done, including substantial electoral reforms.

REBUILDING TRUST

Seeing politicians working together for a common cause and the collective good would go some way to improving public trust. It would demonstrate the potential of compromise and conciliatory dialogue.

Trust is essential for well-functioning democracies. It is the belief and feeling that someone, or some entity, such as a government, is operating reliably in your best interest, even if they could exploit their position of relative power. It is 'the expectation of no harm in contexts where betrayal is always a possibility'.[11] It reinforces the promise of the social contract, a belief that the state is working for your best interests and does not seek to cause unnecessary harm. For citizens, trust is built on feeling seen, understood, and included in policy considerations. Levels of trust reveal how people view the quality, strength, and reliability of public institutions. However, over the years trust has steadily declined. In 2025, the Edelman Trust Barometer identified that 61% of people had a moderate-to-high sense of grievance, which they define as 'a belief that government and business make their lives harder and serve narrow interests, and wealthy people benefit unfairly from the system'. This has detrimental impacts for trust. Those with the highest sense of grievance expressed the lowest trust for institutions, the media, and businesses.[12]

Trust works in different ways. It is not only about how much the people trust politicians and political institutions, but also how much politicians trust citizens, and how much citizens trust each other. The latter, societal or social trust, is important for social cohesion and feelings of community and security; it will be discussed further in Chapter 9 on the value of society's engagement in politics.

For over twenty years the Edelman Trust Barometer has shown how the social fabric is weakened by the erosion of trust, culminating in greater polarisation and disconnect from official institutions.[13] Trust is eroded by factors including, but not limited to, levels of corruption, disconnection between politicians and the electorate, and perceptions of politicians pursuing self-interest that suggest politicians are not putting people first or acting in their best interests. It breaks the tacit promise between politics and the people.

The Organisation for Economic Co-operation and Development's (OECD) survey of trust in public governance reveals a similar decline, and yet offers a more nuanced picture of both the vibrancy of democracies and the challenges.[14] While governments could be better at responding to the concerns of their citizens, and there are genuine issues regarding public perceptions of integrity,[15] the very freedoms democracies accord to citizens mean that they can express their low trust. It is part of a larger dialogue.

In the majority of OECD countries, from the Asia-Pacific region to Europe and North and South America, there are common democratic freedoms of expression, association, and opinion, and regular free and fair elections. Yet there is a craving for more engagement. Citizens want a greater role in determining the direction of their country, and a greater say in the decisions taken at the highest level.

In order to restore trust, therefore, leaders will have to acknowledge how the current system has failed. How jobs have not been equally distributed, the promises of wealth and security and opportunity still not met. This means understanding and really getting to grips with how people see politics, the source of their distrust and frustration. Leaders have to be able to demonstrate that they truly understand how politics has translated into people's everyday lives. This is where more participatory and deliberative democratic settings can help, giving politicians access to more nuanced information and citizens' voices.

In the process, crucially, political leaders also have to get better at trusting citizens. In the age of soundbites and 'easy solutions', there is an underlying assumption that the public is neither smart enough nor interested enough to engage with the reality of contemporary issues. The ubiquitous quotation, misattributed to Winston Churchill, that 'the best argument against Democracy is a five-minute conversation with the average voter', captures the sense of disdain with which some people feel they are regarded by politicians.[16]

When politicians assume the electorate is not intelligent enough to understand, political messaging is reduced to snappy phrases that do not convey the depth or complexity of political choices and policies.

This does a disservice to the public as well as to the challenges of the job of those in politics. It reflects a lack of courage in communicating what it takes to devise policy solutions, and an unwillingness to convey the compromises and patience required. Many people can recognise insincerity, and dancing around complex problems does not make them any easier to solve. Trust could be enhanced by giving more respect to citizens, enabling them to appreciate the choices politicians are having to make, and giving them a role in the process.

Polling done in September 2023 by University College London and More in Common, a British research organisation, thought incubator, and consultancy founded following the tragic murder of British politician Jo Cox at a time of heightened divisions over Brexit, reinforced this. It showed that the public value respect from their leaders. Respect may be slightly different from trust, but it indicates a level of trust in the people to make the right choices, and a positive regard that is essential for a healthy social contract between state and people. The data shows four key attributes of respect in politics. First, recognition of the contribution people make to society beyond their qualifications or social standing. Second, the importance of empathy, and having politicians with the ability and desire to understand people from all backgrounds and the struggles they face to counter a pervasive sense that politicians are detached from the real world, and lack the lived experience needed to make informed choices. Third, leaders who are authentic and true to themselves rather than feigning a character for the public eye. Finally, honesty, and politicians who can communicate in a clear and no-nonsense way about the challenges faced and the difficulties that might be besetting the country. People do not want to be patronised or talked down to but want to feel trusted with the proper information about what is going on and what is being done to address issues.[17]

Increasing the political trust of the electorate can strengthen engagement and the two-way flow of information about the nature of problems, and the most appropriate solutions. It pushes back against the patrician mindset that assumes those in power know what is best for the people.

Further evidence supports this. Data from the OECD shows that trust is built when the electorate are engaged and represented, not only through the ballot box but through more participatory democratic processes.[18] Monica Brezzi is a leading trust expert from the OECD, based in Paris. When I spoke with her about her work she emphasised that what emerges strongly from the data is the feeling people have that they are not heard, and that they do not have a voice.[19] It connects again with perceptions of powerlessness among citizens. Those who feel more marginalised, including women and minority groups, tend to feel lower levels of trust. Building more inclusion into political systems can reinvigorate the iterative relationship between politics, people, and the vital political and civic institutions in our societies. Empathy and the imperative of listening and seeking to understand what different people think and feel are therefore critical antidotes to disconnection.

Some electoral systems are more conducive to this form of participation and representation than others. Switzerland, as a federal system, scores highly on trust and engagement, as well as on stability indicators.[20] According to the OECD, around 62% of Swiss people have high or moderately high trust in their federal government, far higher than the average of other countries at 39%, and 52% in their national parliament.[21] Multilingualism is built into the fabric of Swiss society, given the federal arrangement between Swiss German-, Italian-, and French-speaking regions.

Direct democracy, and the frequent voting on measures, creates more incentives for citizens to be informed, to understand what options are on the table and what they can vote for.[22] It serves other purposes too, as it can constrain politicians from pursuing personal interests as it makes them more regularly accountable to their citizens.[23] Switzerland is found to have lower polarisation and to be less divided than many other countries.[24] Albeit nowhere is immune.

Such measures to connect politics with people are important. It is not just our politicians who are determinants of trust and engagement in politics. Monica Brezzi emphasised that trust is also dependent on whether the civil service is considered credible and efficient, and is respected.[25] This helps 'generate a more positive view of the entire political system, although it doesn't necessarily mean that these countries are immune to democratic challenges and democratic crises'.[26] Countries like Australia and Finland fare well in this regard, being seen as relatively effective and with low levels of corruption. In Australia, a survey by the Australian Public Service about trust and the delivery of public services in the regions identified that trust means integrity, empathy, loyalty, and delivery.[27] Empathy here was about a duty of care, respect, and understanding, and perceptions of the kindness, friendliness, and patience of government employees and public servants.

TRANSFORMING THE ORGANISATIONAL CULTURE

As well as encouraging politicians to work across party lines, and to reinvest in creating institutions that the public can trust and have faith in, there needs to be a recalibration of the environment in which they work.

A key part of this is addressing campaign financing and lobbying. As the money that flows into politics can distort priorities, lobby groups can wield disproportionate power on political agendas, making it harder for politicians to pursue the causes that matter most to their constituencies. The hold of the gun lobby on American politics has made it near-impossible for concerted action on gun violence in the country, despite having a significantly higher rate of gun deaths per capita than other industrialised countries.[28] The same is true regarding the interests of big oil and gas, which constrain the potential for governments to enact truly innovative climate change policies or shift to more renewable forms of energy.

What is more, in many countries, politics has become toxic. It is not only that the public are losing trust in politicians, but that politicians are becoming less civil to each other – especially in the public eye. There are increased ad hominem attacks, targeting people's character rather than their ideas. During debates, especially in more adversarial legislative chambers, jeering and booing signal disrespect. It is derisive and diminishing. Politicians may enjoy the sport of it, and find themselves hardened to the manner of engaging, but for those on the outside it can look juvenile and unprofessional. In his memoir of his time in office, former politician and diplomat Rory Stewart shared his deep frustration and sense of shame at the parlous state of British politics and the quality and tone of debate.[29]

More recently, politicians have been able to make wild and unsubstantiated claims. That dishonesty has become so commonplace, and politicians have not been penalised for it, contributes to a low level of public faith in political standards. More in Common[30] and Compassion in Politics, in the United Kingdom, are working to address this.[31] Through their work they are calling for a change in the language of politics, to make it more respectful and avoid any signs of inciting violence. They want to see more debate that favours consensus-building – especially in a UK context where the very nature of the House is adversarial, and they want to ensure professionalism and respect between and across all members of parliament.[32] It is already having some impact.

In response to this work, in Wales, the Senedd has indicated it will progress such measures ahead of the elections in 2026, especially to counter the ability of politicians to make misleading or false claims, and mispresent themselves or their agenda. While there is a danger that any such efforts appear tokenistic, they spark essential conversations about what we tolerate and what is expected. It helps restore faith that politicians, too, are aware of the problems with politics.

Empathy is often valued as a counterbalance to the bad behaviour and the challenges in these spaces, albeit with varying effect. In

Australia, the political culture has traditionally been quite exclusive and misogynist, with denigrating and demeaning remarks made openly about women in parliament, and Indigenous and other under-represented groups. After an incident in 2021 where Queensland Liberal MP Dr Andrew Laming was found guilty of harassing two women online, Prime Minister Scott Morrison ordered him into empathy training.[33] Noting the value of such a move to rectify the culture, Deputy PM Michael McCormack, the leader of the Nationals and junior coalition partner, ordered similar training for his party, stating: 'If we can learn from an expert ... and actually learn a few tips on how to not only be better ourselves, but how to call out others for it, then I think that's a good thing.'[34] However, such moves were largely rhetorical and political.

Journalists from the *Sydney Morning Herald* observed a group of Australian politicians in a short version of such training that outlined nine core competencies, including emotional literacy, taking perspective, self-regulation, practising kindness, and moral courage.[35] Katherine Teh, a Melbourne-based entrepreneur, activist, and advisor who trained the politicians on the value of empathy, reflected that the opportunity to engage with the ideas and consider their application individually and institutionally failed to shift their awareness of how underlying political norms entrenched an exclusive and adversarial – often misogynistic – dynamic that was anti-empathetic. While she is convinced about empathy's importance, her experience has made her cynical about its prevalence.[36] Katherine was concerned that the cultural resistance and the lack of structural follow-through meant it was perceived more as a 'tick-box exercise' than a genuinely valuable leadership competency. 'When power is used to silence, not listen; to posture, not problem-solve – empathy is easily dismissed as weakness. Without internal change, such training risks becoming a performance, not a transformation,' she said. 'True empathy must be systemically embedded – in the way power is shared, decisions are made, and ideas are debated.'[37]

Yet at the same time as seeking better politics, we can expect too much from leaders – an infallibility of character that is unattainable for any human. As citizens, we need greater awareness of the competing challenges and demands that face politicians, and appreciation for the personal sacrifices they make – time away from families, living in two spaces at once, working long hours, and under constant scrutiny.

It is hard to expect empathy in a culture that can be toxic, exhausting, and relentless. Marcos Peña, a former politico from Argentina, admits that politics can lead to the loss of personhood, given the intensity and demands of the work.[38] If we want politicians who can take care of us, they have to be able to take care of themselves too. There is a precarity to being a politician that can make some more focused on retaining their position than bringing in radical new ideas.

Controversially, perhaps, for those who see politicians as on a constant gravy train of benefits, we cannot expect the best from people who are constantly burned out and stressed. This does not mean politicians should be living a life of luxury, with long holidays and easy hours, but there should be a balance. If we are overwhelmed and struggling to look after ourselves, we are likely to lack the mental space to countenance the complexity of the challenges that have to be addressed. Even though, from experience, a lot of politicians operate very effectively on adrenalin, are used to demanding schedules and long hours travelling, and being 'on' and accessible to the public, it can only be sustained for so long. 'If good people can't sustain themselves in public life because it is just too punishing and zero sum – if the opportunity cost of the life of public service is just too high, if a life in politics just doesn't feel worth the personal sacrifices that are made – then we have a serious problem.'[39]

For many there is no way to prepare a politician for the dramatic shifts in life that follow election. It brings an emotional, psychological, and physical toll, however passionate you are about your work. There are the constant emails and communications, the demands of your team for more time in your already overstretched diary, calls from the media (national and local) on the priorities of the day, and the need to squeeze time with family and friends around work commitments – both in the parliament and in the local area. This can deter precisely the kind of people we need in politics: the people who care about the issues, who know their local areas and want to make a different but feel they will be scorched or affected by the environment.

Love Politics is an organisation that aims to address both of these issues. It works across Germany, Austria, and Switzerland.[40] Through courses, training, and network creation, it brings more people into the political space and gives them an insight into life as a politician. It has multiple objectives: to encourage them to run, to equip them with the vital skills to make a difference, and also to prepare them for the uncertainty of the political afterlife. Sonja Jöchtl, one of its original founders, had a long career working with Austrian politicians. She wants to see more inclusive, diverse, and responsive politics that promises real change. 'People want something they can say yes to,'[41] and in the present moment many voters are feeling uninspired by the choices available to them.

In the countries Love Politics covers, Sonja notes, those in politics often come from very similar backgrounds, and are not truly representative of the people they serve. Yet 'politics should reflect the diversity of society to build trust'.[42] This is about making politics accessible to more people and providing a richer insight into what the country needs.

The task of getting the best people into politics, however, has become harder. Sonja explained that in the past in Germany and Austria, politicians could rest assured that on leaving politics they would find a suitable, comfortable job for post-political life. Nowadays, the political brand has become so toxic that this is no longer so easy.[43] So not only can a politician find they are working all hours, at great personal cost, but that the pain is not necessarily worth it once they leave. This is not unique to these countries. In the UK, talented politicians who suddenly lose their seat after an election can struggle to find rewarding jobs, and can face a period of economic and professional uncertainty, especially if their party is out of favour.[44] This has a greater impact on those without independent sources of wealth or additional positions outside of Parliament, and can deter those from lower incomes from entering politics.

Given the current political climate, organisations like Love Politics have to help politicians to be more resilient. And with the training courses they deliver, they teach potential politicians about the inner workings of politics, about coalitions, negotiations, and finding solutions, since 'to change a system, you have to know how it works'.[45]

Elsewhere in Germany, the Robert Bosch Foundation leads an initiative for relatively new politicians to learn more about the practicalities of policymaking.[46] I spoke with Susanne Zels, who was involved in this initiative between 2022 and 2024. She is the co-founder and manager of Values Unite, a non-partisan organisation that advocates for European values and political participation, and has long been active in politics, both as an advocate and as a candidate. In 2019, she stood for the Christian Democrats in the European elections. As a result, she has a long-standing commitment to fostering more engaged and representative politics, and is motivated by questions like 'How do we secure our democracy?' She explained the initiative and its importance. By bringing together a cohort from across most German parties, the initiative fosters cross-party relations and opportunities to address some of the tensions in the House in a more collaborative space.[47] Like Love Politics, the foundation has an extensive training programme, designed to expand people's perceptions of what is possible, exposing the cohort to external experts and different political systems, to cultivate more of the resilience required, so people can find ways to cooperate across party lines. Each cohort is together for four years, helping to develop longer-term relationships. And alumni remain involved, so it builds a broader community and deepens connections. The training includes practical skills, like how to run an office, as well as how to present yourself to the media. And she notes how where people live – either in rural or urban areas – can shape politicians' capacity to consider policy issues from a more regional or global perspective.[48]

To complement these efforts to improve politics, we also need greater public awareness of the complexity and challenges incurred.

CULTIVATING A CIVIC CULTURE OF EMPATHY AND POLITICAL AWARENESS

As citizens, our tolerance for change in how politics is done is dependent on our understanding of what really goes on behind the curtain. Very few people, even some of those who spend their lives working around politics, fully understand the complex procedures and processes involved in turning a bill – an initial piece of legislation or a proposal for consideration – into a law.[49] In a Westminster system, such as the United Kingdom or Australia, this typically involves several 'Readings' in the House of Commons/Lower House where the proposals and principles of new legislation are scrutinised, subject to committees and debates, and then amended through a series of debates and drafts to address specific concerns of opposition MPs as well as those on the party's own backbenches. It then proceeds through a similar process of readings, committees, debates, and amendments in the House of Lords – or the Upper House – before returning to the Commons for approval. Once both Houses are happy, it proceeds to Royal Assent and enters into law. Given the sheer number of bills being debated it can take weeks or months to reach the final stages. Other democratic systems have similar steps and procedures.

Such a deliberative and considered democratic process is designed to avoid any one person or party pushing through legislation without scrutiny. It gives all members a chance to have their say and to engage with their constituents. Yet, from the outside, it can appear that it takes too long for real change to be introduced and, when the debates seem dry, few of us care to follow the minutiae of where to insert a key detail in Section 6, Subsection (4), line 32, even though that small addition may have a direct impact on the quality of our daily lives.

All of this is made harder by the huge array of sources of information, often offering different accounts of events – newspapers, websites, news channels – and then thousands of social media accounts seeking to provide snappy bite-sized accounts of complex political procedures. It is little wonder that, overwhelmed by details and information, we can resort to what instinctively feels right, or good, without sufficient context of what is achievable.

If we are more cognisant of the inner workings of political institutions, and what happens when we raise a concern with our local politicians, there is a chance we may be slightly more patient with the speed of their efforts, the compromises they have to negotiate, and gain a more human account of their work. This might help us get better at upholding standards for politics, and become less tolerant of lying and the manipulation of information.

The enduring perception is that the public do not sufficiently understand politics,[50] and demands for greater civic awareness typically increase after electoral shocks. Unfortunately, such calls might be perceived as the product of elitist assumptions about those who voted differently from the way they were expected to. Yet, with rising polarisation and divisions, calls for more civics in schools are typically rooted in the assumption that this will strengthen a sense of national identity[51] and contribute to greater societal resilience and readiness,[52] helping people identify efforts to undermine or weaken democracy, make more informed decisions, and develop critical skills.[53] In the process it enhances their role and capabilities as active agents and citizens in society.

In the words of American President F.D. Roosevelt:

Democracy cannot succeed unless those who express their choice are prepared to choose wisely. The real safeguard of democracy, therefore, is education. It has been well said that no system of government gives so much to the individual or exacts so much as a democracy. Upon our educational system must largely depend the perpetuity of those institutions upon which our freedom and our security rest. To prepare each citizen to choose wisely and to enable him to choose freely are paramount functions of the schools in a democracy.[54]

A great place to look for this is Finland. Although it is a relatively homogeneous society, since the 2010s Finland has been championing the importance of civics education, alongside its belief in multiculturalism and pluralism, as part of its national education system. This is embedded across schools at all levels. Courses at schools explore misinformation and disinformation, and encourage students to critically evaluate different perspectives and the veracity of news. Such an approach has contributed to the country being at the top of the media literacy index,[55] alongside the other Nordic nations.

Eenariina Hämäläinen is a schoolteacher in Tampere, teaching upper secondary students. She also has a PhD on the role of ethics education in the country's schools and has been an author of some of the country's textbooks on civics and politics education for over fifteen years. She generously gave me time and valuable resources (which she very kindly translated for me) on the essentials of the country's approach to education. She explains how Finland has a tradition of civics education since the 1960s, and demand has grown. Often it is connected with history, and she points out how empathy is a feature there – helping students imagine how it must have been to have lived at that time. The aim of civics education in Finland is to engender a strong sense of citizenship and belonging. Across most age groups, there are substantial and consistent classes that examine different facets of a citizen's role, their place in community, and their political responsibilities. These courses deepen each year, getting more complex as students grow and become more conscious of politics and their role as active citizens.

Courses have to do more than just deliver facts or dry details; they have to make the idea of civic responsibilities and rights real and relevant, and connect with a sense of people's identity. Politics, and how citizens engage with society, is not the only feature of civics; it also includes philosophy, religion, and what is translated as 'world-view, culture, and ethics' (*Elämänkatsomustieto*) or 'life-standing' courses for those who do not do religious studies.

A compulsory course, for example, on 'Society and Me' (*Minä ja yhteiskunta*) in upper secondary school encourages students to reflect on their own identities, and their position within society. It emphasises the importance of community for humanity. The core content is centred around seven themes: critical thinking, understanding the media, evaluating ideas and values in society, being an active citizen, economic and political power, human dignity and rights, and global justice and sustainability. It is a comprehensive mix, intended to equip students with critical reasoning skills and the ability to reflect on ethical questions and make informed decisions.

Such an approach is not without its challenges. Eenariina notes that sometimes politicians take issue with the contents of civics courses, if they feel their party is not represented as they'd like. And students are still distracted by social media, which can present a challenge for conveying the broader themes of connection and community.[56]

And, while empathy may not always be explicit, the emphasis on tolerance, plurality, diversity, and respectful debate are part of the necessary practice and essential attributes for a more understanding and inclusive political culture. Indeed, it is vital. Eenariina also expresses caution about the potential for empathy to favour one group or story over others, and so teaching the concept alongside other ideas of freedoms, moral motivation, and ethics gives these ideas more weight, and stronger foundations, embedding them early as part of an intrinsic civic attribute.

People can be trained in the practice of empathy and this can inform greater awareness.[57] There are explicitly empathy-led initiatives. Ed Kirwan is a former science teacher from north London in the UK, and a talented photographer and filmmaker who is passionate about the value of empathy, emotional resilience and well-being in education. In 2020 he founded Empathy Week, now Empathy Studios, which builds the skill of empathy in 5- to 18-year-olds. I met Ed in 2020 and have supported Empathy Studios ever since. It is one of the most practical, inspiring, and creative ways to build the practice of empathy from a young age.[58]

The Empathy Programme uses short films, no longer than ten minutes, to expose children to the unique stories of people from around the world. In its first year, the films took children to India, and the work of Slum Soccer,[59] embracing the universal power of football to spark connection. Since then, the videos have featured people from countries including Nepal, the UK, and Mexico, each time bringing different cultures and experiences into the classroom. By exposing young people to diverse experiences, they learn to practise understanding. The films explore wide-ranging themes such as grief, family, gender equality, mental health, culture and identity, and disabilities, and help students to discuss and unpack what they have learned.

There are teacher resources, lesson plans and student activities designed to accompany all these videos. These reflect a core framework to their approach, centred around three fundamental pillars – 'Empathy for Myself', 'Empathy for Others', 'Empathy in Action'.

If students can see part of themselves reflected in these films, it can help them feel less alone in their struggles, or provide a sense of perspective and context regarding the challenges they encounter. As Ed explains, 'the world is nuanced, and context is important'. So often, when we want to make sense of the world, we try to put things in neat categories, but these films explode those neat lines. Empathy Studios have expanded their work to provide vital training and support to schoolteachers, helping them to guide conversations and providing practical steps to embed emotional literacy and awareness of our shared humanity across cultures throughout the year. Already schools from Darlington in the UK to Dhahran in Saudi Arabia have incorporated empathy skills development into their whole-year curriculum.

Alongside the student skills programmes, Ed also leads a non-profit global festival: Empathy Week is an annual festival of film, storytelling, and events. It is a successful and rapidly growing initiative. By 2024, it had reached nearly 1.5 million students in over fifty countries. And Empathy Studios have partnered with organisations like Amnesty International to do live workshops and bring students together, growing a community and sparking vital conversations. This work continues to expand.

Crucially, the work has substance. As a former science teacher who is obsessed with evidence-based approaches to education, Ed's work has been reinforced by research from Cambridge University. Participating teachers reported that the programme yields marked improvements in students' empathy skills, curiosity in other cultures,[60] and student behaviour.[61] It 'gives students a chance to speak' and helps them become more compassionate with themselves when they encounter struggles or make mistakes.[62] Such findings further reinforce the increasing amount of research that shows that empathy is something that can be taught and developed at all ages.[63]

Yet such educational initiatives go beyond empathy. They are also about learning to be comfortable with difficult conversations, being able to regulate ourselves emotionally when we encounter confronting experiences and perspectives, and finding ways to retain our humanity. Such efforts to train empathy encourage people – children and adults alike – to lean in with curiosity, not only to understand other people or groups better, but also to gain greater insights into ourselves. Instead of responding immediately on instinct, they encourage us to interrogate our feelings: Why are things the way they are? Why does something make us feel uncomfortable? How can we dig deeper to understand what is going on, and its source? Are there points of connection or areas where we can develop common interests? Classrooms are vital spaces for these kinds of discussions.

This kind of education has an important long-term vision. If you introduce the Empathy Programme to every school year and take a child from 5 to 18 on this journey, they will have experienced multiple countries and dozens of real-life stories by the time they leave school.[64] Along the way, they will have discovered diverse themes and communities, while learning more about themselves and points of commonality with others around the world. There is a natural implication for our politics, as Ed asserts: 'These are the students that will go on to be our politicians and determine the future of our world.'[65] Even if they do not enter politics, they will all be future voters, who may seek such a world reflected in their choices. It is planting a seed for a more sustainable transformation.

*

There has to be the capacity within societies and within our political cultures to tolerate, accommodate, and even celebrate differences. And, as citizens, we must also be more informed about what politics truly entails, so we are more understanding not only of its complexities and challenges, but also of its significance in our everyday lives, and the responsibilities we have, as citizens, to play a part in democratic processes.

It takes conscious, deliberate effort, and a lot of time and patience. It is a process, often slow and necessarily intentional. Such change is dependent on several additional factors, including – as we see through subsequent chapters – drastic efforts to improve gender equity and realise political parity so we see far more representation of the whole of society within our politics, and especially in leadership positions. A fairer, more accountable, and pluralistic press is required, that can not only accommodate and celebrate the diversity within our society but also tell richer, deeper, and more complex stories about life, our common humanity, the challenges we face, and the efforts already under way to address them. Finally, and critically, the engagement and efforts of all of us are necessary – to step up and be active participants in our politics and society to exemplify the change we wish to see.

7

Embracing More Inclusive Politics

In the early days of the pandemic, Norwegian Prime Minister Erna Solberg held a long press conference for children, no adults allowed. Joined by the Minister for Children and Family Kjell Ingolf Ropstad and the Minister of Knowledge Guri Melby, she took time to listen to her young audience and answer their questions about what the crisis meant. Children's television programmes, such as *NRK Super*, and the paper *Aftenposten Junior*[1] helped reach a wider audience and relay questions from those who could not be present. It was a display of kindness and empathy, acknowledging the uncertainty and fear that the crisis had provoked across the whole of society, and recognising the impact that it had had especially on the younger members of society. A few weeks later, ahead of the Easter holidays, New Zealand Prime Minister Jacinda Ardern took similar steps, addressing children in her country directly, and declaring the tooth fairy and the Easter bunny essential workers.[2] Due to the situation, she explained, both the bunny and the tooth fairy might be very busy with their own families, so children should not be disappointed if they did not make it to their homes this time. Instead, she suggested, maybe children could use it as an opportunity to connect with other children in their neighbourhood in an Easter egg hunt and help those who were not as fortunate. Both these women conveyed maternal qualities, comforting children who might be struggling to comprehend the crisis and how it was preventing them from seeing friends and going to school. It conforms to a gendered image about women in leadership positions that became more pronounced during the pandemic.

At the height of the crisis, it was observed that countries that were managing better, including Germany, Taiwan, Denmark, New Zealand, Norway, Iceland, and Finland, were all led by women.[3] These countries seemed to weather the uncertainty and insecurity of the early stages of the crisis with fewer deaths, more proactive policies, and better social compliance. Certain gendered values were associated with their success. Women were seen to be more empathic and compassionate, to have communicated honestly and clearly in spite of the difficult messages they had to convey, and to have taken decisive action across a range of portfolios – health, economy, borders – that had immediate impact on the numbers affected by the crisis.

Women are often associated with this kind of leadership that prioritises care, understanding, and other maternal qualities. And research suggests they can be rewarded for these traits.[4] While this is generally positive, such gendered assumptions about the nature of women and the qualities they bring to leadership can also be constraints and overly reductive. These very traits can be, and have been, used as explanations for why women may not be strong enough to deal with the harsh realities of power and leadership. Conversely, when women demonstrate strength, or assertiveness, or step out of preordained perceptions of how they should act, as former Indian Prime Minister Indira Gandhi (1980–84) or former British Prime Minister Margaret Thatcher (1979–90) did, they are often seen as anomalies – proving the complexities of being a woman in politics. Some women have even been charged with 'behaving too much like a man' or performing masculinity to get ahead,[5] a criticism former US presidential candidate and Secretary of State Hillary Clinton frequently encountered. A strong man in leadership is considered the default, but such a stereotype oversimplifies, doing an injustice to all genders. None of these examples provides a complete picture of women's role, potential, and contribution in political life. On the flip side, the stereotype points to limiting views and expectations of men, and masculinity in politics, that can be equally constraining and detrimental – not only to politics but to society at large. Men are equally capable of empathy and compassion, and prominent men such as South Africa's former president Nelson Mandela have shown these qualities can be matched with strength, courage, and vision.

The conversation around empathy and gender is an important one for several reasons: First, it reveals how our stereotypes and assumptions about genders influence our perceptions and expectations of people in politics and leadership roles. Second, it emphasises the necessity for equal representation and inclusion in politics, as at all levels in our society. Third, it shapes the issues and priorities of our national politics, evident in the disparity in care for women's health and well-being. Fourth, it exposes some of the challenges involved in an essentialist view of gender, empathy, and politics, and the limits to more inclusion – particularly as many women themselves have traditional views of their role. Finally, when extended to all genders, empathy can help mitigate feelings of marginalisation and reveal the complexities of gendered experiences of the world. The topic asks: Are women really more empathic than men? And how can empathy provide a means for more inclusive and representative politics?

GENDERED ASSUMPTIONS OF LEADERSHIP

Politics has often championed the myth of the 'Great Man' – the prevailing idea that a strong, powerful man could steer his country in a new, successful direction and rewrite its history. People like Charles de Gaulle or Napoleon Bonaparte of France, or President Abraham

Lincoln in the United States. The assumption is that great leaders are born not made, and they are predominantly male. Certainly, powerful men have managed to achieve notable feats of leadership at critical times, but there is a lack of imagination in assuming that women are incapable of similar success.

The problem is there are too few women in leadership positions. And if there are women in such positions, they are too often given 'family' or 'women'-oriented portfolios, such as health, education, welfare, or development, rather than those associated with more 'masculine' characteristics such as defence, the economy, or trade. This can reinforce the idea that, while women politicians are valuable, they are not quite 'tough enough' for top office.

One of the challenges is that the language used to define leadership qualities is often gendered. Traditionally masculine ideals of strength, courage, determination, and power are held to be superior to traditionally feminine ideas of care, kindness, and support. Men are stereotypically, and incorrectly, assumed to be inherently more rational beings, while women are seen as emotional. Such arguments assume emotionality and rationality are part of women's biological wiring, and unavoidable. They reinforce outdated notions around traditional gendered roles – women should be at home and in positions caring for others, whereas men should do the hard work of leading a country. They can also be used as an excuse for women to be excluded from office because of prejudices that they are too emotional, hysterical even, and by inference therefore, irrational. In the current evangelical Christian movement against empathy, part of its critique is that women are more susceptible to empathy because they are weaker and overly emotional, and this can distort their priorities – with the implication that they should not be in office.[6]

Emotional expressions are connected with perceptions of competence, authority, and the ability to make difficult decisions. This is particularly noticeable in how society responds to the image of an 'angry woman'. Whereas anger and aggression are typically seen as commanding and decisive, a sign of strength and virility, in men, when women express anger, they can be dismissed as hysterical, irrational, or shrill, lacking the warmth and geniality people associate with them. These double standards reflect our discomfort with women who do not conform to societal expectations or narrow gendered roles. It also binds them between the perceived weakness of care and the irrationality of anger.

This is the kind of double standard that former Australian Prime Minister Julia Gillard pushed back against so powerfully when she delivered her 'Misogyny Speech' on 9 October 2012. During a heated debate, the prime minister responded passionately and eloquently to accusations of sexism and hypocrisy from the Opposition leader Tony Abbott. Speaking unscripted, but fuelled by what Gillard herself attributes to 'a big dose of cool anger',[7] she declared that she 'will not be lectured about sexism and misogyny by this man. I will not. And the Government will not be lectured about sexism and misogyny by this man. Not now, not ever.'[8] She listed many of the Opposition leader's double standards and sexist comments, and encouraged him to look in a mirror. It followed months of sexism in the media, with denigrating language, insults, and excessive comments about her wardrobe, her marital status, and her personal life. Her decision not to have children was held against her, and seen as a failing – 'How could a woman not conform to society's expectations of her purpose'? It was a speech that resonated not just in Australia but around the world. And is, unfortunately, a common experience for so many women in leadership.

These unwritten codes of behaviour can force women to temper their emotions and exert more control over their expression, leading to them appearing insincere or inauthentic. As former US Secretary of State Madeline Albright remarked: 'Many of my colleagues made me feel that I was overly emotional, and I worked hard to get over that. In time, I learned to keep my voice flat and unemotional when I talked about issues I considered important ... In the end, I successfully changed opinions.'[9] Modifying her emotional expressions may have worked for her and contributed to her influence in American politics. And it makes sense to adapt to survive in an environment that punishes natural human expressions. But we should also want authentic human expressions, and leaders who can connect emotionally with their audiences without moderating their experiences.

Anger, rage, and fury can be critical sources of political change. Especially now. They provide the fuel and impetus to address injustices, to call out oppression, and to mobilise people. In particular, as Rebecca Traister argues, confronting anger, and seeking to understand it as one emotion among others, provides insights into how people may feel powerless, or marginalised, or hurt,[10] and offers ways to rectify problems. It is a crucial element in reparative and radical politics that seeks deep changes to systemic injustices.

Men are not immune to judgements about their emotionality. This can be in beneficial ways or further perpetuate limited ideas of masculinity. Winston Churchill was famed for his capacity to cry.[11] During the Blitz in London in September 1940 he visited an air raid shelter where the people gave him such a welcome that he 'broke down completely'.[12] They saw it as proof he truly cared. He cried after powerful speeches in the House of Commons, at funerals of soldiers and the former prime minister Neville Chamberlain. In contrast, more recently, Canadian Prime Minister Justin Trudeau was criticised by some for being 'soft'. One Tory senator, Jean-Guy Dagenais, sent him a box of Kleenex for Christmas because of his tendency to shed a tear at tragic or emotionally intense events. Trudeau notably cried during a funeral for people killed at a mosque in Quebec in 2017, after reuniting with a Syrian refugee whom he had welcomed to Canada, and also on the passing of Guy Lefleur, a professional Canadian ice hockey player,[13] and Gord Downie, the vocalist and frontman of Canadian rock group Tragically Hip.[14]

Part of this is undoubtedly connected to the character and personal image of the leader themselves. When US President Barack Obama spontaneously sang 'Amazing Grace' following his eulogy to Reverend Clementa Pinckney, who had been shot in the Charleston church shootings in June 2015,[15] it was a powerful and raw moment of emotional expression from the president. Even though he was known for championing empathy, Obama was often seen as being cool and cerebral. The moment boosted his popularity. A week after the events, a CNN/ORC poll found his approval rating had risen above 50% for the first time since May 2013 – a sizeable jump from his 45% rating the previous month.[16] There are few leaders who would get away with such expression.

These emotional conventions and norms, connected with our ideas of how men and women should behave, are not insignificant. They influence how expressions of empathy might be interpreted in our politics. If expressing care or understanding or trying to listen to the perspectives of others is seen as at odds with how leaders should behave – strong, decisive, and assertive – this hinders its expression or leads to it being seen as evidence of a weakness. While New Zealand Prime Minister Jacinda Ardern put empathy at the heart of her government's approach and ethos, she came under growing criticism from her opponents on the right for not being ruthless enough to tackle the big questions.[17] This stifling of genuine emotion prevents a richer and more nuanced appreciation of people as human beings on their own terms, with all their virtues, flaws, feelings, and complexities. We need people in power who can show strength and courage, while also being able to connect, demonstrate authenticity, and communicate what they feel.

When photos leaked of Finnish Prime Minister Sanna Marin dancing and drinking with friends at a private event in August 2022, a number of her political opponents criticised her for not taking her work seriously enough. It was seen as an error of judgement, at odds with the formality of office, especially with the pandemic and rising tensions with Russia on the country's border. In response, she gave a powerful address: 'I am human',[18] she remarked. And as much as she worked hard, and her government had handled the pandemic well, she also wanted joy in these dark times.[19] She received an outpouring of support from women and men around the world who called out the gendered double standards and posted videos of themselves online dancing, sharing the hashtag #SolidaritywithSanna. It may be just one example, but the prospects for gender equality in leadership is partly dependent on societies' willingness to view women as whole, red-blooded, flawed individuals, as much as men can be. The demands of formality and seriousness are at odds with the desire for authenticity and presence from leaders. For women it can feel like a lose-lose situation.

Fortunately, as will be examined shortly, people are pushing back against these narrow assumptions, calling them out, and showing the power and strength of diverse forms of women's leadership.

Yet at the same time as women's rights and gender equality are rising on national agendas, there is a trend towards so-called 'traditional values' and exaggerated ideals of masculinity and femininity being championed by political leaders and winning significant support. Around the world, politicians and political movements are galvanising votes by invoking traditional ideals. Their political visions recall a simpler time, when people knew their role in society and when gender was a less fluid or flexible concept. Here empathy encounters friction. Such leaders advocate a return to a former status quo that rejects more inclusive and diverse politics and sees the move to greater understanding of others – such as those who identify as trans or as non-binary – as weakening politics. Sometimes they even co-opt the language of empathy in the process, reflecting back concerns they feel they share with their audience about what inclusion does to 'traditional values'.

In the public space, figures like Vladimir Putin in Russia, Donald Trump in the US, and Jair Bolsonaro in Brazil, are keen to convey their strong 'masculine' qualities. They ride horses bareback, refuse to take health precautions against contagious viruses, and emphasise their own virility and unique qualifications. In Brazil, right-wing President Jair Bolsonaro prided himself on his masculinity, his strength, and his power. During the pandemic he invoked gendered language to encourage citizens to face the crisis 'like a man', refusing to implement the extensive measures of countries such as New Zealand or Denmark, led by women. There have been reports of misogynistic language and behaviour, including telling a left-wing congresswoman, Maria do Rosário, from the Workers Party, 'I wouldn't rape you because you don't deserve it.'[20]

Such politicians are not only focused on performing masculinity and demonstrating the strength of being a 'real man', they also reinforce and impose gendered ideals on society. Among populist leaders especially there is a fear of women gaining too much power, or men and boys becoming 'feminised', or too soft. In the People's Republic of China, Chairman Xi Jinping and the leadership have been introducing a number of initiatives to limit women's voices and restrict feminist activists. At the twentieth Communist Party Congress in October 2022, Xi Jinping introduced an all-male Politburo,[21] and throughout the party women are vastly under-represented, constituting less than a third of members, and absent from the upper echelons of power. Women make up only 26.54% of China's Congress.[22] This has been coupled with initiatives within the country to weaken and suppress feminist movements such as the 'Feminist Five',[23] and to reaffirm traditional female roles.[24] Even so, in an interconnected world, China's feminists remain inspired by, and part of, global movements, to continue the push for women's rights and representation.

These political leaders and gender ideologies are reinforced at a societal level by popular and powerful influencers on TikTok, Instagram, and Snapchat, who offer bite-size advice on how to be a 'high value' or dominant man or a 'trad wife', offering relationship advice and guides to life that replicate traditional gender binaries.

The power and popularity of such figures reveals some of the challenges to the vision that empathy offers; there is widespread resistance to diverse gender identities and understanding of how gender shapes different people's experiences. In some ways society is going backwards. In many countries there is a growing gap between men and women in their vision of society and their voting preferences.

This is especially visible in South Korea, where gender was a prominent feature of the 2022 and 2025 elections. In 2022, leaders of both main political parties – Yoon Suk Yeol of the People Power Party, and Lee Jae-myung of the Democratic Party – made it central to their campaigns in efforts to win over young men. They promised to look after those who felt sidelined by feminism and pushed back on initiatives designed to increase gender equity, including the Ministry of Gender Equality and Family, denying the experiences of systemic and structural inequality faced by many women across the country. While women were hard pressed to find a candidate who reflected their interests, Yoon won the election with support from 58.7% of men in their twenties (36.8% of the same demographic voted for Lee).[25] Although Yoon was later impeached, in April 2025, after having declared martial law in December 2024, in the election to replace him in May 2025, gender remained a prominent feature. Many women still felt let down by the offerings of the main parties.

Such gaps are occurring in a social context where women are increasingly educated, independent, and enjoying the freedoms of equality, which is making marriage less appealing. Feminist movements are growing, with the more radical 4B movement, started by Korean feminists amid frustrations at a culture that has traditionally prioritised men, rejecting marriage, children, and relationships. In contrast, South Korean men are struggling to find partners and get married, which is making many, especially those still unmarried, less supportive of equality.[26] Some even see themselves as victims of reverse sexism and women's power, and anti-feminism is growing online and across society.[27] It presents a challenge to a dynamic country with a decreasing birth rate.

Such a trend suggests a critical disconnect between the experiences of many men and women, and a lack of dialogue and communication in the political space.

ARE WOMEN REALLY MORE EMPATHIC?

Nevertheless, the assumption that more women will transform politics in an empathic and progressive way is not a given. Even while it is essential that there should be equity in politics, and equal representation, women do not have a monopoly on empathy, nor is it guaranteed that such empathy will lead to more left-leaning politics. Debates around gender and empathy require more nuance and more latitude. Women, like men, are not a unified homogeneous entity.

Across the world, women are the public face of populist movements actively championing more traditional ideals of women and their rights. In Italy, Giorgia Meloni, a member of the right-wing Brothers of Italy, was elected the country's first woman prime minister in September 2022, creating a governing right-wing coalition. Her engagement in politics began in 1992, aged 15, when she joined the student movement Youth Front.[28] Many of her political allies are from these early days in politics, when as a woman, she was not only in the minority but also underestimated as a political force.[29] While gender is a strong feature of her platform for change, it is through the lens of traditional ideals of the family, pushing back against gender ideology, the LGBTQ+ community, and access to abortion and a woman's right to choose.

Before her, in France, Marine Le Pen, daughter of the National Front leader Jean-Marie Le Pen, has successfully managed to soften the party's image and move it away from the stereotype of skinheads and neo-Nazis that it was associated with in the 1970s, 1980s, and 1990s under her father. She claims to represent 'the forgotten' and sustains an anti-elite rhetoric despite her own position as a member of a wealthy political family.

Language and emotional signals are a powerful force in this rebranding. Both Meloni and Le Pen, as well as other women on the right, mobilise the gendered ideas of care and femininity, and claim the language of 'humanity', 'empathy', and 'understanding' for those who are left behind, misunderstood, or marginalised in contemporary politics. Friends and colleagues of Meloni speak of her trustworthiness, and how you can rely on her to show up[30] and keep her word: a popular trait seen as a rarity in politics.

A further challenge to the view that more women in politics would transform politics is visible in the large numbers of women who vote for populist politics and subscribe to similar traditional views of gender. Women are not a unified block, nor do they hold a universal view of women's rights or what women need. We need to get better at understanding that. Despite his politics, and after four years in office, in 2020 President Donald Trump won over 74 million votes,[31] 46.8% of the total. As a total of the popular vote, it is more than any other presidential candidate in history, with the exception of his rival President Joe Biden. Strikingly, between 2016 and 2020, his popularity grew among women to 44% in 2020 compared to 39% in 2016.[32] Although many women did oppose him, and many people around the world of all genders took to the streets to protest his election on 21 January 2017, the day after he was inaugurated, his politics are shared, or at least tolerated, by large proportions of the population. In 2024, even though more women voted Democrat overall, the figure was lower than 2020, with a growing number of white women voting Republican, and higher rates of younger women (with 40% of young women voting for him in 2024 compared to 33% in 2020), and Latino women turning to Trump.[33]

Being a woman does not equate to being a feminist or believing that all women are equal or should occupy the higher levels of office. While Margaret Thatcher played on a public image of a savvy and thrifty housewife,[34] she eschewed the stereotypes of female emotionality. Given the moniker the 'Iron Lady', she made use of her reputation as strong, steadfast, no-nonsense, and unsentimental. It may have been a survival mechanism for an unforgiving and male-dominated political culture. However, during her eleven years in office, she promoted only one woman to her cabinet and pronounced that she owed nothing to the women's movement.

Equally, among women's movements, empathy can be inconsistent and selective. During the feminist movement in the United States, as elsewhere, in the 1960s and 1970s, Black women and other women of colour were often marginalised, under-represented, or undervalued. Shirley Chisholm, the first Black woman to enter Congress in 1968, and the first to run for nomination for president in 1972, spoke of the challenges she encountered when white feminists did not rally to support her and many women chose George McGovern as nominee. Not only were women of colour not represented or included on panels at conferences and events championing women's rights, but many feared their white counterparts did not really understand, or care, about some of the unique hurdles they faced.[35] There was a lack of awareness among white women of their own privilege even while fighting a common cause. Yet such gaps are not restricted to history. Former Democratic presidential candidate and Vice President Kamala Harris faced awful racist and sexist slurs during her election campaign in 2024. Research by Pew in the same year suggested that 71% of Black women, and especially women under 50 years old, believe the political system in America is designed to hold them back. And across both genders, two-thirds believe that Black public officials are more readily discredited than their white counterparts. This contributes to a high degree of mistrust in politics, and probably presents a barrier to entrance and greater representation.[36]

The #MeToo movement was initially founded in 2006 by Tarana Burke to create a community of advocates against sexual violence.[37] When it went viral in 2017 following high-profile cases of sexual assault by figures including film producer Harvey Weinstein, there were criticisms of those who sought to universalise the experience of women, given that many women of colour are under-represented, marginalised, and subject to additional prejudices. There is no simple or easy solution. Gender should not be essentialised, nor should we assume universal experiences as women, men, trans or non-binary people. Our experiences are diverse, shaped by culture, by socio-economic conditions, the situation and context of our lives, and the opportunities afforded or denied us. Here empathy can reveal the nuances and variety, helping find points of connection and difference between all of us that can strengthen democratic politics. Yet power remains a dominant influence in shaping how people engage, who has more agency, and how privilege is replicated within groups.

In her science-fiction book *The Power*, Naomi Alderman offers a fascinating exploration of the pervasive and universal nature of power once the tables are turned. When women gain the ability to project electric shocks they become the dominant sex, able to turn the tables on traditional patriarchal power structures. Among their ranks there are the healers, the community builders, the vengeful, and the coercive. The book reveals the intricacies of power and its use in exerting control, and abusing and harming others, as well as in caring for others and helping to transform society.[38] It captures well the limits of gender essentialism. As explored in Chapter 4, power has a character of its own, and changing politics requires change in how we think about it, its utility, and its potential.

Beyond these limited ideas of gender that constrain men and women alike, there is space for a more diverse and authentic form of politics.

REPRESENTATION IN POLITICS

Greater representation is crucial to cultivate empathy because it brings in more diversity in thought, experience, and backgrounds. When it is visible at the highest levels of politics, it also helps model more inclusive societies and encourages people to pursue opportunities and dreams irrespective of their background or identity. At the same time, we should be encouraging people to exercise empathy with others regardless of their background.

There is a long way to go, however, to achieve gender equality in politics. It is estimated that 'in 81 percent of the world's legislatures, women hold less than a third of seats'.[39] Shockingly, according to the 2022 *Gender Gap Report*, it will take 132 years to close the gender parity gap at the current speed and trajectory.[40] In most countries, women were not accorded the right to vote until the 1900s, and even then it did not apply to all women equally. In different countries, women were excluded based on factors such as race, economic and marital status, ownership of property, and literacy. New Zealand was the first country to grant women the vote in 1893, but in some European nations equal voting rights were introduced only recently, including: Switzerland (1971), Portugal (1976), and Liechtenstein (1984).[41] This means women's voices and experiences have largely been excluded from or marginalised in political leadership and representative systems, reflecting their subordinate and unequal position in many other areas of society. Empathy in politics is difficult if the experiences and voices of half the population are excluded or considered marginal. It becomes even harder when they are not represented in the highest offices.

It was not until 1960 that a woman first became head of state, when Sirima Ratwatte Dias Bandaranaike of Sri Lanka became prime minister. Newly widowed, she took over the party leadership of her former husband Solomon 'Solla' Bandaranaike and, despite low expectations and scorn about her aptitude for office, proved to be one of the country's defining leaders, furthering social reforms, nationalising foreign companies, making the country a republic, and engaging in the Non-Aligned Movement. It was not a perfect tenure, and the minority Tamil population were often overlooked, but she made her mark and would later see her daughter assume the leadership. In the succeeding years, more women took leadership around the world, albeit still outnumbered by their male counterparts.

Twenty years later, Vigdís Finnbogadóttir became the prime minister of Iceland in 1980, at a time of heightened national discourse around the central role women in society and how they were under-valued. Five years earlier, on 24 October 1975, the women of Iceland had taken a collective day off – though the organisers of the move-ment were keen to stress it was not a strike. On this day, known as *Kvennafrídagurinn*, women left their homes and their workplaces – leaving men to see the extent of women's unpaid and additional labour and how essential they were. It was an exercise in compelling greater empathy, forcing the country's men to see how much silent and hidden labour Icelandic women did. Around 90% of Icelandic women participated, and it was effective: it led to the Gender Equality Act in 1976, the Gender Equality Council, and shifts in cultural and societal norms. It partly explains why today the country has one of the narrowest gender gaps.

Another country that frequently tops lists for gender parity is Rwanda. In 2022, women held over 60% of seats in its parliament. This is partly a result of proactive measures introduced as part of the country's recovery from the genocide in 1994 and speaks to the potential of concerted action to address inequalities. In the new constitution, ratified in 2003, lawmakers set quotas for female partici-pation, stating women had to hold at least 30% of seats.[42] Yet parity in representation does not necessarily translate to parity across society. Despite huge progress in representation in Rwanda and Iceland, and other countries, there are still massive inequalities between men and women in politics across societies.

Equality in politics is not only about metrics, numbers, and parity. There are multiple compelling reasons to increase the profile and representation of different genders in politics, not least that democratic politics should reflect the societies it serves. It is hard to have a nuanced and detailed insight into how the world is experienced by people if half of them are excluded or vastly under-represented in positions of power. More women in politics expands the range of experiences and perspectives that shape and influence political agendas, and opens debate to a wider array of voices. In leadership roles, women bring gender-related issues into the main-stream, championing issues such as healthcare and reproductive rights, and they are often more connected with the needs of their communities.[43]

Despite these benefits, there remain key barriers to women in political leadership.[44] These include having the right to stand and be elected; a willingness and desire to stand; a political culture that facil-itates and embraces female participation; selection by their parties; and being elected by the voters. Some of these barriers are structural. For example, women's chances of being elected to office are partly dependent on the voting system.[45] Proportional voting systems, where the number of seats allocated to a party equate relatively fairly with the number of votes they receive from the public, are seen to correlate more strongly with higher rates of women's participation. This is because parties can rank candidates in their lists to help enhance representation, putting more women at the top to ensure access. First-past-the-post systems and mixed systems, tend to have a lower share of women in parliament. Director of the Global Institute for Women's Leadership at the Australian National University Michelle Ryan and her research partner Alex Haslan found that not only were there limits to women in leadership, but when they do attain senior positions – whether in politics or the boardroom – it is often in a precarious situation, where they have to manage crises that can mean they are set for failure.[46] They are also dependent on funding available for their campaigns, and the support they receive, or expect to receive, if they are simultaneously politicians, mothers, and carers. Changes and incentives to increase proportionality are therefore culturally and country specific.

CULTIVATING INCLUSION

Gender cannot just be a concern of women or the LGBTQ+ community who are most affected by many of these issues. It has to be something in which everyone is invested. The oppression or denial of rights of anyone has an impact on the freedoms and rights of everyone. It was French socialist philosopher Charles Fourier who first coined the word 'feminism' in 1837, when he wrote that: 'the extension of the privileges of women is the general principle of all social progress'.[47] Among his works on political theory, English philosopher and politician John Stuart Mill similarly wrote on women's suffrage and equal rights, supported and influenced by his wife Harriet Taylor Mill, a prominent philosopher and feminist. Albeit these are all ideas women such as French author and feminist Olympe de Gouges and British philosopher Mary Wollstonecraft had expressed in their own works years earlier. Allyship is growing, but even more is needed.

Around the world, women and men are campaigning for equal rights. In Afghanistan, even as their rights are further curtailed, women have consistently risked severe punishment to protest the restriction of women's rights and freedoms since the Taliban returned to power in August 2021. In Iran, when Mahsa Amini was arrested, tortured, and tragically killed by the morality police in September 2022 for not wearing her hijab in accordance with the country's strict gender rules, protests and vociferous calls for change and women's rights erupted. And although women were the driving heart of protests, standing defiantly in front of police and security services, and walking with their hair free asserting their rights, they were not alone in fighting for equality and pushing back against prejudice and oppression. Across the country, many men were their allies, equally risking their lives. So too in the United States, women and men joined the #MeToo movement which became a powerful force for change from 2017 onwards. This is how it should be: women and men working together as allies for change. Gender in politics is not about men versus women, nor should it be. Instead, it is about societal change and challenges to outdated systems and structures of power to make them more representative and inclusive.

There are prominent initiatives promoting greater cooperation and solidarity. Actress Emma Watson was the public face of the movement 'He for She' in the UN in 2014, calling for men and boys to get involved in feminism.[48] The movement is still growing, offering courses, practical toolkits, and campaign guides to promote more engagement and allyship from men in gender issues.[49] However, while they are all positive steps towards emphasising the huge gap in gender parity across society and in the highest offices of state around the world, there is a danger that such initiatives are given lip service but little concrete action follows. There is also a risk that they are seen as 'gendered' and are predominantly attended only by women. In 20 September 2022, when the United Nations initiated the General Assembly Platform of Women Leaders to raise issues of gender equality in the multilateral forum, it was mainly attended by women.[50] It is important for women to speak and share their concerns and ambitions in such spaces, but if men are not included in such dialogues, if they are not at the table, then such forums risk being considered women's spaces, and remain separate from mainstream thinking and leadership. How can men gain understanding if they are not part of the intricacies of the conversation and are not present to take part?

In addition, although a focus on gender and political leadership typically focuses on men and women, empathy has to extend to all genders and sexualities. While women face multiple obstacles and barriers, transgender people and members of the LGBTQ+ community encounter unique stigma, prejudice, and challenges in politics. Many have experienced attacks or threats of violence, or fear expressing their true selves. Often, they are under-represented in the highest offices. Icelandic Prime Minister Jóhanna Sigurðardóttir became the first openly gay political leader only recently, in 2009. Although, unsurprisingly, most want to be known for their abilities and vision rather than their sexuality – heterosexual politicians rarely have to declare their romantic preferences – their rise to prominence and ability to be more open signals positive shifts in attitudes within society. The openness with which politicians can share their sexuality and their partners suggests signs of progress and wider acceptance. In Ireland, historically known for its more conservative values, Leo Varadkar was elected the first openly gay Taoiseach in 2017. There are also growing numbers of openly transgender politicians, facilitating changes in debate and challenging stereotypes and misperceptions.

In Taiwan, Audrey Tang (Tang Feng) has been a prominent and dynamic figure of change. Originally a programmer and civic activist, they served as the country's first digital minister, leading innovative approaches to digitalisation and citizen-driven engagement. They are also the first openly non-binary, transgender person to be in the executive cabinet. They describe themselves as a 'post-gender', conservative anarchist (and accept the use of any personal pronouns to describe them). It is this rejection of neat binaries, in work and in life, that they credit with being able to see things from different sides, helping them to empathise with others and work across traditional hierarchies.[51]

By making politics more inclusive and safer for people, irrespective of their gender, sexual orientation, or identity, a diversity of experiences and worldviews can enrich our politics and give greater insights into where change is needed. Yet this is dependent on a deeper curiosity, with people encouraged to understand how different people experience the world through a gendered lens.

We need to encourage men to not shy away from vital conversations about sexual assault, women's reproductive health and well-being, and the inequality they experience on a regular basis; as well as to appreciate how society has been designed with men in mind, as

Caroline Criado Perez's book *Invisible Women* eloquently demonstrates, and how that creates unanticipated obstacles.[52]

Male politicians should campaign for reproductive rights, or access to treatments for the menopause, or better childcare, with the same frequency as women. Not because they are husbands or fathers, but because half of the people they represent will experience these challenges at some point in their lives and not addressing them has implications for everyone. Such behaviour models care and concern for wider society.

Critically, the importance of the gendered lens works all ways, offering insights into the double-edged constraints and gendered norms of society for men. Having more open conversations about gendered experiences of the world can similarly shine a light on how men are facing challenges in society.

There is growing recognition that men, and especially young men and boys, are feeling marginalised and disconnected. They are experiencing lower educational outcomes, and higher rates of mental ill-health and suicide than their female counterparts. Often they lack a supportive environment in which to share their struggles, because of social pressures to conform to outdated ideas of masculinity and the stigma around men talking about emotions. There is also a lack of sufficient visibility for positive male roles that normalise different ideas of what it means to be a man, though so many exist.

The rise of 'bro' culture, and cult figures like Andrew Tate, who advocate for regressive and traditional views of masculinity and ways of treating women, championing ideals of wealth, fitness, and material success at the expense of emotional connection, play on this sense of disconnection and frustration. It raises growing concerns about how men are being let down by the system and society.[53] Attuned politicians can tap into such disconnect and further stoke divisions, as is evident in Korea.

Society has empowered women, but not yet equipped enough men to handle these changes. Yet, in the process of seeking to understand what is going on, we have to avoid demonising men or implying they are toxic, stymying opportunities for genuine dialogue, compassion, and deeper awareness that might lead to better solutions. More vulnerable conversations about their experiences should not be dismissed because of predominant perceptions that, even though they face challenges, they still have privileges on account of being male. Recognising and understanding how men feel left behind or out of place, and validating that, is not incompatible with continuing to address systemic and structural inequalities.[54]

Expanding the field of vision shines a light on how gender shapes all our experiences of society. It plays a central role in how we have been conditioned and socialised, and how we experience the world. Understanding this and discussing its implications can contribute to changing systems and structures of power and inequality that do not work for anyone.

Such shifts are essential not only for our politics, but also for our societies and our closest relationships.

*

Across many societies, we are still not ready to see women in positions of power, and consistently judge them by harsher metrics. Yet equality, inclusion, and representation are crucial to effective political change. Gender offers a vital lens through which to understand and critique systems and structures of power, and associated asymmetries and inequalities. Rectifying the present imbalances will contribute to increasing representation of women, but it is also not just about women. Politics should reflect the plurality of our societies and give voice to its diversity. A huge amount of work is still needed to facilitate this parity and create the conditions and political culture where everyone can feel seen and where equality is the norm. However, achieving greater equity in our politics demands wider shifts not only at the highest levels of office, but also within society and the media.

8

Transforming the Media Landscape

Australia's Indigenous Voice Referendum on 14 October 2023 was a prominent attempt to redress some of the country's historic injustices. Put forward by Prime Minister Anthony Albanese, it proposed that Indigenous peoples should have a greater consultative role in politics and policy and a formal body to give advice on laws. Building on decades of work by many Aboriginal and Torres Strait Island Peoples, and on the Uluru Statement from the Heart in 2017, it sought reforms to the political system, greater rights, and more say over the laws and decisions that affected them.[1] It was an effort to grapple with the country's colonial past, and the legacies of violence and discrimination against Indigenous Australians.

It was a passionately contested and significant campaign, bringing some of the most difficult parts of the country's history to the fore. However, the initiative was introduced relatively hastily and not given sufficient time to mature. Although both the Yes and No sides were umbrellas for a diverse range of arguments and opinions,[2] for the Yes camp it was predominantly a chance to create a more inclusive politics, address historical injustices, and rectify the marginalisation of Indigenous people across the country. For the No camp, in contrast, there were concerns that it was risky, would cause more divisions, and add unnecessary bureaucratic layers into the political process. People on the No side felt it would create more tensions and give too much scope to a new body. When arguing against the Indigenous Voice in parliament, leader of the Opposition Peter Dutton echoed the language of Martin Luther King's vision of a country where they would 'judge each other on the content of our character, not the colour of our skin' (a reference one wonders whether Dr King would have endorsed). This vote, he contended, would re-racialise the country and stoke new divisions.[3] The No campaign was highly effective, aided by a catchy, efficient slogan that played on voters' uncertainty about the implications of the vote: 'if you don't know, vote No'.

In April 2023, polling put the Yes vote in front by 51% to 34%, yet by October the picture had changed dramatically. Across all states, with the exception of the Australian Capital Territory, home to the nation's capital Canberra, citizens voted No. It was a shock result. Certainly, the referendum was not a perfect offering, and questions were raised about why it needed to take place when other mechanisms may have been more effective in changing the political system (referenda have a tendency to not go as planned).

Despite the deep disappointment over the outcome of the vote, when I met him in Sydney, Thomas Mayo was frustrated at the turn of events, but remained hopeful. A Torres Strait Islander, author, prominent advocate for justice, assistant National Secretary of the Maritime Union of Australia, and signatory of the Uluru Statement from the Heart, Mayo has been at the forefront of efforts to close the gap between Indigenous and non-Indigenous people in Australia for years. For him, 'Australians are not lacking empathy, but there is this collective amnesia and forgetting of recent history.' Bad actors, and the media, he notes, amplified people's fears and lack of familiarity with Indigenous peoples and their history. Bipartisan politics broke down.[4] Irrespective of the outcome, around 87% of Australians support the idea that First Nations people should have a say over matters that affect them.[5] The media was an influential force in telling a different story about who Australia was, and who it could be.

Across the campaign, the media was critical in generating support and opposition. Just as in Colombia during the referendum over the peace negotiations, the media put forward their own agenda. Sky News, owned by Rupert Murdoch, created specialised channels for the Indigenous Voice vote, whose predominant message was that the vote was a bad thing and a Yes vote would weaken the country.[6] More broadly, misinformation and falsehoods were spread, not only on social media, but on mainstream platforms where they were insufficiently challenged[7] and critics questioned the impartiality of the debate.[8]

In the midst of heightened national discussions, Indigenous experiences of colonialism, and King Charles III's coronation, Stan Grant was another prominent voice. An Indigenous Wiradjuri man with a long career in journalism, he came under fire for comments about some of the negative implications of the British monarchy for Indigenous peoples. His words were distorted and used as proof of hatred for his country. As a result, he announced a break from the media, to recalibrate his relationship with it:[9] 'We in the media must ask if we are truly honouring a world worth living in. Too often, we are the poison in the bloodstream of our society. I fear the media does not have the love or the language to speak to the gentle spirits of our land.'[10] 'The media sees battlelines, not bridges.'[11]

The media is a powerful feature of our democracies, and a critical element in how we understand empathy in politics. It can be a vehicle for sowing divisions, or a means to bring people together. It can share stories that humanise people or stoke rage and fear of others. The media shapes our engagement with leaders, with ideas and ideologies, and perceptions of risks and challenges. Traditionally, television, print media, and radio have contributed to shaping the stories we tell of society, helping to create collective meaning, guiding national and local priorities, and focusing our attention. Since 2004, the emergence of Facebook, Twitter (now X) and other social media platforms has offered new ways of sharing and disseminating news. The space is being transformed by the reach and resonance of these new technologies, and the plurality of voices with different agendas who can share news content. Some of these changes are positive, democratising the space, allowing new voices to come to the fore, holding power to account, and revealing the reality of situations through real-time videos and near-instantaneous news reporting. However, it too has its own political lines and agendas. And, as we have seen from disinformation campaigns across numerous elections, it can heighten insecurity and mistrust in our political systems and erode the core fabric of democracy. There is a need for change, for more accurate reporting, and for more complex, nuanced stories, and local voices.

THE ROLE OF THE MEDIA

We operate in a dynamic and complex media environment. News is instantaneous and easily accessible. On television, rolling news channels detail every new development on events as they unfold, coupled with rolling insights. The print media, once released in daily or twice-daily instalments, is constantly updated, with fresh comments and opinions on the latest issue of the day. Check your phone and, for many people, you will be overwhelmed by notifications and possibilities. Any one of the major platforms can inundate you with their stream of news, opinions, and stories. Not only can it be exhausting, it also presents challenges for our attention and our care. As Jamil Zaki explains, it can overwhelm our capacity for empathy.[12]

Since the early nineteenth century, with the extension of suffrage to more members of society, the media has been a key asset in the expansion of politics to a wider audience and electorate. It keeps us informed and offers us a medium through which to understand not only news and current affairs, but the state of our politics. It reveals some of the complexities of politics; the inevitable trade-offs between what we want, what we can afford, and what is possible given the constraints and parameters of resources and political will.

As it has evolved, disparities in how different generations get their news have meant political leaders have to diversify how they engage and communicate. For older generations it is more often through traditional television or print media, whereas a larger proportion of younger people get their news online.[13] Nevertheless, in such a pluralistic media environment, there is a space for critique and debate – enabling diverse voices to engage and give insights and perspectives on the dominant stories of the day through a wide array of platforms.

The media mediates trust through the narratives it tells about leaders and institutions, the credibility or frailties of those in power. The proliferation of media sources, often critiquing the trustworthiness or agendas of mainstream outlets, makes it harder for people to trust in either the media or politicians. Our trust – or mistrust – of politicians is partly dependent on which news sources we watch and read, and who they promote as a credible and capable figure looking out for the needs of the people.

News is always more than just facts and information. It involves stories, ideas, opinions, and accounts of how different people view the world made accessible and relevant for us – depending on what we seek and where we look. As professor of journalism at Columbia University, Michael Schudson argues that journalism has a function in supporting social empathy: 'journalism can tell people about others in their society and their world so that they can come to appreciate the viewpoints and lives of other people, especially those less advantaged than themselves'.[14] Certainly there is no guarantee. A story or an image does not guarantee empathy. It can also provoke feelings of revenge, outrage, disgust, or calls for action.[15] Yet it is a crucial means with which, and through which, we learn about the world.

The connection between the personal, the political, and the public helps stories to resonate more, and to sell. Human interest stories are a vital tool for the media to illustrate and make real the implications of social issues such as poverty, homelessness, or inequality. It is a part of creating what C. Wright Mills terms the 'sociological imagination',[16] which emphasises how, as individuals, we are situated in the context of broader systems and structures. This interrelationship of the personal and the societal helps us to link our own experiences and personal challenges with broader social issues. Yet the logics of a story – and the underlying assumptions about how things are and should be – can constrain our capacity for creative ideas or solutions, especially if they challenge or inconvenience those with the power to shape the agenda.

For, in telling these stories, the media is rarely impartial. It can set the agenda. It chooses and curates the narratives, the personalities, and the events we see. This is partly due to time and space constraints, at a time of constantly competing stories and unfolding world events, and the demands of an insatiable audience. Yet this matters, as it can distort our empathy. Privileging certain stories over others and therefore directing our concern and our attention in certain ways comes at the expense, sometimes, of giving a bigger and more nuanced picture. We have seen this in reporting of the conflict in Gaza, and how little we see of conflict in the Yemen or Sudan. Certain voices and perspectives matter more than others through the media's lens. This is also evident in how conflicts are covered and whose deaths are seen to matter. It was notable that during the early days of the conflict in Gaza, the passive voice was used far more to explain the deaths of Palestinians who 'starved' as 'no food entered Gaza',[17] 'were buried' under the rubble of their bombed homes, or 'died' by drone strikes. Such language avoids accountability or responsibility. And it contrasts with the language of Palestinian violence against Israelis, which is expressed in a more direct, active voice.[18]

Even if we can resist being told exactly what to think and are not as predictable or as narrowly focused as some would assume,[19] still, as Bernard Cecil Cohen wrote in 1963, the media guides people in 'what to think about'.[20] 'The world looks different to different people, depending not only on their personal interests, but also on the map that is drawn for them by the writers, editors, and publishers of the papers they read'; even more than a map, which might be too confining, the media is 'an atlas of places, personages, situations, and events'.[21]

What is more, this tendency we have to want neat or compelling storytelling, heroes and villains, catchy soundbites and charismatic or endearing figures, narrows the aperture of political life and removes some of its vital complexity. Politics is not easy. It requires compromises and dialogues, and the intrinsically complicated process of accommodating diverse ideas and experiences into a national or communal narrative of meaning and identity. Too often, the media can flatten both content and character. And it can be unforgiving in its depictions.

It is not just what the media says that matters, but how it says it – and how we engage. When the media was predominantly print, radio, or television, there was a hierarchy of news, or sections – current affairs, international, finance, sport – that bracketed issues.[22] Our media literacy itself has been transformed. The current news environment has a far weaker sense of prioritisation. It is led not only by editorial choices but by likes and clicks, which may or may not lead to accurate reflections of what actually matters for us to know. It is therefore vital that we ask ourselves: What does the media not show us? What do we not see? Whose lives and identities are shown to matter, and why? Whose stories are silenced?

Certainly, there is a lot of cultural variety in this environment. In France, for example, regular political panel shows give voice to experts and politicians from across the political spectrum. They debate at length, engaging with audiences and offering different sides of a story, reflecting a society where debate is embedded in culture in a particular way. In some countries, such as India, Facebook (or Meta) is increasingly a source of news rather than newspapers, which can mean the news is more accessible to millions online, but also has dangerous implications now that Meta has stepped away from fact-checking, given the scale of disinformation that can proliferate on its platforms. And in authoritarian countries, the government's close hold on the media stifles dissent and critique. There is little to no space for opposition or accountability.

Attacks on the media from politicians and officials who feel threatened by independent journalism and the analysis of critical journalists constrain the space for empathy. Efforts to suppress the press, and to limit whose voices are heard, further narrow our ability to access different perspectives. Worse, they penalise those who seek to offer alternative points of view. In Hungary, for example, a country that has moved towards authoritarianism under the leadership of Viktor Orbán, critical parts of the media have been penalised or closed, helping Orbán consolidate his hold on power. Such moves concentrate the narrative of what is happening in politics and in our societies in the hands of officials who have an interest in telling only their story through their own filtered light. This has serious implications for the freedom and fairness of elections, and the quality of public debates, further degrading democracy.

Problems with accountability, opposition, and freedom are also partly due to the current media model. With declining advertising revenues, and fewer people paying for the news, given its free availability online, the economic model of our media is too often determined by clicks and likes. To generate vital revenue, clickbait is designed to keep people on the page for longer, with snappier structures and enticing headings. What is popular is privileged, rather than what might actually be important for public awareness and social change. 'If it bleeds it leads' was a common refrain for determining which stories appeared on newspaper front pages and at the top of news bulletins, yet there has been a bigger shift towards infotainment. News packages resemble entertainment, with short segments to keep people's attention, which lack the nuance needed for a genuine depth of understanding.

Furthermore, while concern about the influence and power of a few 'press barons' is not new,[23] today the majority of media outlets in countries from the UK to the US and Australia are concentrated in the hands of a small number of wealthy billionaires. As such, the success of national leaders can be dependent on their relationships with the owners of media outlets. Media mogul Rupert Murdoch was an important figure in the election of Tony Blair in 1997, and also considered instrumental in the failure of Australian politician Malcolm Turnbull. How we perceive leaders, and the nature of the press coverage they receive, can therefore be dependent on their popularity with key figures in the industry.

AMPLIFYING VOICES AND REPRODUCING ECHO CHAMBERS

Social media has further transformed how we consume news and engage with politics. It democratises the media environment, allowing the public to offer a diversity of opinions and perspectives or to report on news as it unfolds where they are. It can humanise topics. In some countries in Africa, for example, social media is being used as an effective means of storytelling to reduce stigma around HIV,[24] and as a way of building community around ideas of belonging. It has also contributed to a growth in storytelling and meaning-making within societies. Who we are, what we value, and the change we seek in society are now in the public space, open to discussion and debate and interpretation. We connect over humorous videos, make sense of topics, and find solace in the comments section.

Social media simultaneously expands our perspectives, bringing the world to our palms, while reinforcing our echo chambers.

When, in 1759, philosopher Adam Smith, best known for his economic treatise, wrote about the limits of people's sympathy for others far away, he could not have imagined how communications would change. Even with a horrific disaster, he argued, one might lament it, but it will not change the everyday actions of most people or occupy their mind too greatly. It was beyond the immediate circle of their concern and there are far more pressing issues closer to home.[25] There is truth in that still, and yet the evolution of the media, new technologies, and especially social media, have transformed the situation. Suddenly we can care about those who live in distant parts of the world, because we gain intimate access into their lives, their fears, their hopes. The connective power of stories is amplified in these spaces, coupled often with a dose of humour or a catchy angle that resonates with people and enables the story and the storyteller to go viral and contribute to collective efforts to interpret or articulate events or ideas.

The Arab Spring in 2011 was an early indicator of the power of social media to unite and mobilise people in opposition to leaders and corrupt governments from outside the immediate area of action. Although it may not have been so powerful a tool as some Western media outlets claimed, as there were multiple factors at play, social media made the uprisings visible and accessible to citizens around the world in a new and dramatic way.

More recently, with the conflict in Ukraine following Russia's invasion of the country in 2022, social media has been at the forefront of Ukraine's fight back and efforts to gain international support. Using Instagram, TikTok, Telegram, and other channels, civilians are sharing their stories and realities from the frontline. These accounts of the conflict and innovations in storytelling by citizens and digital warriors are humanising the conflict for a global audience. Rather than being driven by the central political leadership, they are more often organic: the product of digitally literate citizens – citizen journalists – who want to create, share, engage, and amplify their experiences to galvanise support for their country. Such initiatives highlight how the political centre does not own the prevailing narrative, cannot maintain control of it, and must be prepared to adapt rapidly.

The danger is also that social media, and the formats that make it so popular, reduce complex stories into bite-sized snippets, offering compelling and familiar stories with heroes and villains, good and bad, erasing the grey space where the really interesting stuff actually happens, and where most genuine explanations can be found. Reality is rarely black and white.

In addition, social media can prevent us from seeing the bigger picture. Non-news – or worse, 'fake' news – can occupy not only our newsfeeds but also our time. We get absorbed in doom-scrolling or following the rabbit holes that social media algorithms present as the next compulsive watch. Further, it is hard to maintain care or outrage over a sustained period. People can experience compassion and empathy fatigue, or a sense of overwhelm. From behind our screens, we can feel helpless to affect events around the world – such as in the wars in Gaza, Ukraine, Sudan, Yemen – and yet we cannot stop consuming news. It is like fast food that targets an immediate appetite but leaves you less healthy and more unsatisfied.

It is part of the nature of social media and YouTube to give the impression that those sharing the news are really talking to you, specifically. There is not the formal veneer of the BBC or FranceInfo, and hosts will talk about what these stories mean for 'us', a collective group bound by shared concerns and insights. For those who already feel unheard or marginalised by the mainstream media, social media with its algorithms aligning you with others who think similarly, and specific forums for discussion, can cultivate a sense of belonging. What we read, watch, and are exposed to shapes and influences our sense of political identity.

Social media has implications in the physical world. Technology and platforms like X/Twitter, Facebook, Instagram, and TikTok have opened up alternative means of connection, while simultaneously removing us from personal contact and reducing our bandwidth for difference. They enable us to be a part of global communities and gain an insight into the lives and experiences of people on the other side of the world. However, though they offer a world of content, the limitations of their algorithms and the tendency to create echo chambers has been well documented. In such spaces, outrage and heightened emotions go viral, while more considered, well-researched, and nuanced reporting has to fight through the noise. Even more problematic is the rise of misinformation and disinformation that such platforms facilitate. Bot farms actively proliferate rumours and fake news, or stoke anger, to crowd out other voices and distort debates.

One of the biggest challenges is that we all seem to exist in our own media ecosystem. Algorithms on news sites and social media feed us more of what we have already consumed and then seem to push towards the extremes. If your only diet is Fox News or the *Daily Mail*, it is not surprising that your perception of the world is more fearful, and that there is frustration and outrage at the many ways in which politicians and political institutions have failed you. Outlets like Rumble, a Canada-based platform founded in 2013 that prides itself on giving a voice to smaller content creators, offer a space for video content and live-streamers to share their views. They are popular with conspiracy theorists and can exacerbate this narrative of fear, outrage, and mistrust.[26] Such platforms provide counterpoints to mainstream news, and accessible, catchy explanations for why you are sad and mad with the establishment. How can we bridge that gap between the conspiracy theories and platforms that promote them, and reality?

Social media platforms pose further problems for our attention span and capacity for deeper, richer consideration. The nature of the news agenda is to prioritise certain stories and voices over others, creating a hierarchy of care, and distorting priorities and the capacity to respond.[27] When we increasingly consume our news in neat soundbites rather than lengthy reads or more in-depth analysis, we miss the nuances of a situation and the deeper causes. Such media snacking may give us a more eclectic sense of what is happening around the world, but it cannot give us the substance and details needed to appreciate why, nor help us grasp the broader context and implications. The format often means experts can be overlooked for commentators with a profile who know the language and demands of that media environment: the people with the quickest, catchiest 'hot take'. Instead, we need nuance and depth, and more context. This will likely involve more critique, uncomfortable truths, and fewer neat answers.

We have already seen the influence of social media on elections and political campaigns. The rise of disinformation and misinformation, fake news, and manipulated videos erode the fabric of democracy, and contribute to growing rates of mistrust in politics. This requires technologically literate politicians, who can work with technology entrepreneurs and the leaders of the tech giants such as Alphabet and Meta to find a balance between ensuring access to the potential these technologies present, while regulating their more deleterious implications.

As our news sources have become more pluralistic and diverse, people have increasingly questioned the veracity of facts. In the United States, Donald Trump made the term 'fake news' part of the everyday lexicon and regularly lashed out at the media, challenging its account of his leadership. Alternative news outlets offer stories that connect with elements of truth but distort them to offer alternative worldviews that galvanise those who mistrust political elites, and sow discord. It becomes so much harder to find common ground if we cannot even agree on the type of ground we are standing on or we dispute the veracity of facts.

This development has also revealed the depth of divisions within society and helped to amplify them. There is a comfort in our echo chambers. They reflect back to us what we feel is right and provide more evidence to support our views. The anonymity of online platforms has also permitted more toxic and harmful cultures, where shame can be weaponised[28] and people in prominent positions threatened. It is not surprising that people may not want to socialise as much, that we find security behind our screens. When debates are heated and visceral, people can disengage. This spills over into the real world, where we seek solace in our phones. As Rebecca Solnit writes: 'The desire to withdraw, to seek smoothness and avoid the potential friction of contact, arises from the view that nonparticipation is self-protection, in contrast to the older idea that being urban is a participatory sport.'[29] Creating a more empathic form of politics involves changing the culture of these spaces, engaging more with real people and gathering a wider array of viewpoints.

Yet we must also avoid empathy becoming performative. On these sites there is a compulsion, and expectation, that you must share how much you care in order to signal virtue. Performative outrage – railing against events with righteous indignation – may indeed be well meaning, but it also tends to drive likes. How much of it is matched by genuinely caring action? Does it dissipate the moment a new, more popular and current issue arises? Some studies suggest that social media use decreases empathy, instead increasing narcissism,[30] creating a further obstacle to the humility and tolerance required for meaningful connections.

Our outrage online makes it harder for us to build bridges with others, to be confronted with the emotional states and personal experiences of those around us. We engage with each other as if behind the comfort of walls, forgetting the impact of our words and behaviours have real-world implications. Philosophy professor Byung-Chul Han argues that social media has resulted in a 'digital swarm' that hinders the creation of meaningful community and connection. This is so pervasive it erodes political discourse and the potential for action.[31] A current feature of such technology, as MIT Professor Sherry Turkle has argued, is that we lose the ability to engage in conversation in person,[32] and to have sincere, robust, and difficult debates. Online we can hide behind anonymity, removed from the consequences of our actions. In person we are more conscious of how others receive our words, especially if we are critiquing ideas intrinsic to their being. This has implications for how we overcome polarisation and find more paths to connection, a feature of the next chapter. One example of how people are putting this in action can be found at an initiative that began in the Netherlands. At the Offline Club people are responding to an appetite among people to disconnect from their online worlds and be more present. At the club's events, people are invited to unplug, lock their phones away, and spend time with people away from their screens. People turn up to coffee shops, churches, or community spaces to knit, read books, play board games, and talk to friends and strangers in their community. What is more, they are willing to pay for the experience. It is already spreading with chapters now in London, Barcelona, Paris, and Dubai.[33] Similar ideas are gaining ground around the world, and starting to shape how people experience music gigs and raves.[34]

Finally, the growth of artificial intelligence in this space only compounds an approach to news that is motivated by metrics that may not necessarily correspond to what truly matters. What do we lose when we start to let artificial intelligence tell our stories? Data-driven storytelling will be easier to produce and more accessible, but what happens to the richness of the human experience and the originality of our stories?[35]

MEDIATED IMAGES

At a personal level politicians (and their communications teams) use platforms to convey a sense of who they are. More than heavily managed party-political broadcasts, X, Facebook, Instagram, and TikTok afford a closer (albeit curated) insight into their lives. Disseminated in bite-size chunks, these videos and posts can create an impression of intimacy and proximity, as politicians comment on their day and their recent engagement in the community. Newer generations of politicians are more adept at this format. Congresswoman Alexandria Ocasio-Cortez had an online community even before entering office. There is a critical balance. Politicians have a right to a private life, to a life out of the spotlight where they can be themselves. As a leader there is always an element of performance, of playing a role, but it is important that that is not led by social media and is not overly curated.

Nevertheless, such methods are important. For most of us, our understanding and opinions of our political leaders and representatives are formed through the media rather than in person. We get a sense of who they are and what they stand for through how they present themselves in the public eye, through the speeches they give, reports of their politics, their behaviour, and their efforts to deliver on their promises. We rarely get access to their private selves so have to discern what type of person they might be, and whether we trust them, or find them likeable, or credible, by the image they convey. Yet research suggests we can feel that someone cares without liking their politics.[36]

Some politicians have been very effective at using the media to connect with citizens. On 12 March 1933, American President Franklin Roosevelt began a series of 'Fireside Chats' that lasted until 1944.[37] In his warm tone, and with clear language, he welcomed 'his friends' to the radio and proceeded to explain a series of changes to the banking system, why they were made, and what it meant for the American people. It was shortly after the Great Depression in 1929, when the Wall Street stock market crashed, prompting a severe economic downturn with disastrous implications. In America, and around the world, there was mass unemployment, social and economic dislocation and deprivation, and widespread poverty, with the effects lasting over a decade and contributing to the rise in fascism. At the time of his first broadcast, Roosevelt was speaking in this broader context, and to a more recent loss of confidence in the banks and panic in the system, which had led to a rush for people to get their money and hoard their savings. The banks had been unable to function properly, and many had been forced to close temporarily. As he detailed the efforts of his government to address this situation, he acknowledged the hardships and inconveniences the people were facing:

I recognize that the many proclamations from State Capitols and from Washington, the legislation, the Treasury regulations, etc., couched for the most part in banking and legal terms should be explained for the benefit of the average citizen. I owe this in particular because of the fortitude and good temper with which everybody has accepted the inconvenience and hardships of the banking holiday. I know that when you understand what we in Washington have been about I shall continue to have your cooperation as fully as I have had your sympathy and help during the past week.[38]

This was the first of many such chats, which were well received, building the perception that he cared and was accessible.[39] This kind of empathy in communication connects leaders to the people, makes politics relatable, and offers an opportunity to demonstrate care and concern for changes people may encounter. It also helps to shape behaviour, in this instance providing reassurances to counter the panic in the market and offer directions for how to proceed in a constructive way.

The advent of television added new dynamics. After the US election in 1960 a politician's image and public presentation became even more important. During the presidential campaign, Republican nominee Richard Nixon was the more seasoned and experienced politician, at the time serving as vice president under President Dwight Eisenhower. John F. Kennedy, in contrast, was a relatively new senator. In the first presidential debate, those who listened to the radio felt that Nixon had won, whereas those with a television believed Kennedy was the stronger candidate.[40] Their appearance and the physical impression they made had a bearing on their ability to connect with the audience through visual media. One aspect of this was Nixon's five-o'clock shadow. He had to shave regularly and admitted at one point to journalist Walter Cronkite that: 'I can shave within 30 seconds before I go on television and still have a beard.'[41] In contrast, Kennedy had a fresh-looking tan (possibly a symptom of a chronic illness) that gave him a healthy glow, and a Hollywood charm and confidence. The tide may have been turning on the Republicans' election fortunes regardless, but the message many politicians and their teams took from the event was that appearances matter. Such an assessment has been supported elsewhere.

In the UK, political leaders have often unintentionally undermined their electoral chances through an unfortunate or mistimed image. In 2014, while campaigning for local elections, and a year before the 2015 general election, the media made hay out of then Labour leader, Ed Miliband MP, eating a bacon sandwich. The image quickly became a widely shared meme on social media with people further contributing, unfairly, to this idea that he was laughable. While it was not the image alone that had such an impact, it played into a broader account of him among opponents and in the media, as being someone awkward and geeky, lacking the credibility for the top job.[42]

More recently, the 2024 general election in the UK began with Prime Minister Rishi Sunak announcing the election at the exact moment a rainstorm broke. Standing there alone, soaking wet, against a lectern, with no umbrella, this became a defining early image of the campaign. It conveyed a sense of a leader who does not have the foresight to run a country – how had he not checked the weather? – and who lacked the support of his own colleagues.

The media can make or break characters. And there is a real problem that the media sets people up to fail. They want the 'gotcha' moment, the awkward photo that makes people feel vicarious embarrassment but diminishes the standing or credibility of the person targeted. The problem can be particularly acute for women. Across all platforms, women in politics receive greater scrutiny, especially for what they wear, how they behave, and for their marital status.

In the UK, newspapers created elaborate interpretations of what then Prime Minister Theresa May's leopard-print shoes revealed about her.[43] Or Australian Prime Minister Julia Gillard's empty fruit bowl, which the media unkindly connected with commentary on her decision not to have children.[44] In the United States, figures like Hillary Clinton and Alexandria Ocasio-Cortez have had their speeches and activism reduced to their outfit choices.[45] It is an effective way to diminish a woman: reducing her to her fashion tastes or body type, with implications about what such things say about her character, rather than focusing on the substance and quality of her ideas and political vision.

Certainly, men are not immune from such commentary. In autumn 2022, French President Emmanuel Macron sparked discussion when he used his fashion choices to aid his policy agenda, sporting a black turtleneck under a suit to encourage new ways to cope with the rising energy prices in winter.[46] Former Canadian Prime Minister Justin Trudeau has frequently been the feature of 'thirst trap' photos,[47] and US President Barack Obama caused a media storm when he wore a tan suit for a press briefing in 2019, prompting claims he lacked seriousness.[48] However, despite such coverage, men do not encounter the same kind of sexism as women, coverage that belittles their ability, or seeks to shame them to undermine their authority.

A problem with the media's need for stories, and for 'characters', sensationalism, tension, and intrigue, can mean that certain figures are given disproportionate airtime and attention. They 'sell'. They drive clicks to news outlets – even if this is only down to rage clicking – and they ensure airtime. Nigel Farage, a former Member of the European Parliament, a founder and later leader of the UK Independence Party (UKIP), and more recently the leader of Reform (UK), is a pro-Brexit champion with a charismatic media style. He is portrayed as a man you would share a pint with at your local pub, a politician who tells inconvenient truths and isn't afraid of the 'establishment'. In contrast to politicians who look and feel scripted and rehearsed, he can appear to his supporters as authentic and unalloyed. Former British Prime Minister Boris Johnson has similarly benefited from his well-crafted but seemingly natural public persona.

These caricature figures give catchy soundbites, and easy-to-sell stories – it's immigrants, it's 'the elite', it is political correctness gone mad – and often have far more latitude in what they can say and how they behave because of their perceived 'novelty value'. Because of this, the media can give priority to certain voices. It may be framed under the idea of balance, but it amplifies those who are far more savvy and able to connect, sometimes irrespective of how representative they are of society at large.

Certainly, a core function of the media is to hold people to account, to shine a light on abuses, misuses, and failings of power and the powerful. But this has to be done in good faith, not by humiliating people unnecessarily and undermining public trust.

Politicians too do not help. Because they cannot trust the media to portray them faithfully, they become more heavily stylised and conforming, reducing the personal attributes and quirks that might get called out, but that also make them distinct.

An excessive focus on how one appears, and the 'ideal' of a good public image, can erase a leader's true personality. We do not see their ability to manage mistakes, their sense of humour. They can appear devoid of character and depth, which are key to fostering connection and encouraging the electorate to relate to them. Can we truly connect with, or trust, someone who feels like the product of a PR wizard or speech coach? Especially if many of them follow a similar model of never really saying much, and using the same ways of speaking, or well-considered gestures. Certainly, you want professional and articulate communicators, and speech coaching and communication classes should be a core part of political training, but the electorate also want to see a human, like them, able to answer questions, to speak to the pressing needs of the day, and show relatability. This is what cultivates empathy and connection.

This heavily stage-managed, image-conscious form of leadership contrasts with leaders like Donald Trump, Boris Johnson, and Jair Bolsonaro, who speak their mind, even when what they say is brusque or rude or lazy. Their appeal is partly that they appear more honest and 'authentic', not conforming to the neat, polished model of a leader.

Indeed, too scripted an approach to the media and one's public image risks politicians trying too hard to anticipate what people want to hear rather than focusing on what they may *need* to hear. Politicians often need to convey to people the importance of certain courses of action, or change how we see a situation. If a leader alters course with every wind and appears to have no firm anchor in their convictions or their vision, they can appear insincere, open to being influenced by whoever is the loudest or the most pressing voice. It suggests a lack of courage and an insecurity in their position; reiterating suspicions among some of the electorate that a politician's core concern is self-preservation.

There is also a detrimental side-effect to seeing politicians online all the time: it arouses suspicions about how much work is actually being done to effect change. How much is for Instagram, and the desire to appear to be working? Moreover, if everything is in real time, there is nowhere to hide, and little time to reflect. It risks contributing to this bite-size, easily consumed politics at the expense of the nuance required to build deeper literacy about current events.

Better politics requires less reactivity, and instead a more coherent and measured account of what is happening, why, and how it is a part of a larger picture. There are few places and spaces for such narratives, and social media reinforces our demand and appetite for constant updates, new information, and 'hot takes'. There are ways around this, to get a richer picture, and expand our field of vision.

HARNESSING THE POWER OF THE
MEDIA FOR POSITIVE CHANGE

Beyond its role in publishing news, the media also has responsibilities. This does not mean constraining the freedom of the press or reducing the capacity of the media to operate independently from governments. Yet given the ubiquity of the media and its influence on politics and society, it also has certain duties to contribute to a healthier media environment, political culture, and social change.

These include educating and informing, stimulating debate, holding power to account and being responsible with stories and sources. The media can challenge distrust in politics, increase political literacy, help foster community and connection, and publish stories that reveal more of the complexity of life and politics. But only if it so chooses. Certainly, we must know about the bad news, the atrocities, violence, abuses of power, and the challenges we face as societies. However, we should also cultivate a richer media diet that prioritises community, trust, belonging, awareness, and literacy, and inspires hope.

Some of these changes are about bolstering initiatives that focus on accountability and fact-checking. Such changes involve valuing those functions of democracies that fight disinformation and misinformation, and call out errors and wilful untruths. Organisations such as Hacked Off in the UK have been active in pressing for a different press culture, calling out malpractice and invasions of privacy in the pursuit of gossip.[49]

There is also a need for national and international conversations about the regulation of social media and working towards agreement on its limits and the balance between its benefits and its harms. This is especially important with regard to children's access to social media, and their mental health.[50] There are already initiatives to address radicalisation and extremism online, but more can be done. Plus, research suggests it works.[51] This requires communication and dialogue between politicians and the social media companies, generating mutual investment in change, but it also involves citizens. It is an area where citizens' assemblies might serve a valuable role in informing political debate about the appetites and aspirations of the wider public for their online lives, and especially their well-being.

A growing body of research has shown how social media is designed to occupy our attention span, to entertain and distract us. It hits our neurological wiring in ways akin to addiction. In the US in 2023, a lawsuit was brought against Meta about the impact of Instagram and Facebook on young people.[52] Addiction to social media is an alarming trend with significant implications for mental health and societal well-being.

It is not just news that shapes us, but stories. In this environment, the access we have to more voices and richer, more complex stories gives us opportunities to think and engage differently. Guided by curiosity, we should ensure we have a diversified media diet: reading and watching (and scrolling) critically across multiple platforms and outlets. We should think about how we create healthy change in the same way as we approach nutrition and health. We need to balance what we consume to ensure a combination of vital information and trustworthy data about political developments and the state of the world, coupled with lighter news on positive changes and inspiring human interest stories.

We need the time and space to process the multitude of data we have coming at us, to avoid the empathic overwhelm. And we need to be better equipped with the tools to critically assess the validity and biases of news stories. We must be more media literate and aware. Where is this information coming from? Who or what purpose does it serve? How does it restrict or silence other stories? What other accounts of this story are available? Who is reading them? Who is a trusted source?

Our priority should be human stories mediated by fact-based reporting and a fair representation of the messy complexity of life. We need more context, complexity, and nuance. One way to create such understanding is to cultivate local journalism. Yet across many countries, local journalism has been suffocated by financial constraints as we move to online readership and free news on social media, as well as by corporate buy-outs. Larger media empires have subsumed these smaller outlets, centralising them, aligning them with the larger corporate agenda, or resulting in them being closed down. For those local papers that do remain, too many become a barrage of dodgy ads and weird clickbait (possibly out of financial necessity), lacking nuance and in-depth reporting, deterring people from engaging more intentionally with them. In the UK, a report in 2022 showed that local papers are no longer seen as the 'community glue' that foster a local identity and 'collective emotions'.[53]

For more connected, inclusive, and humanised politics, we need this local perspective. Local journalists typically have a more nuanced appreciation of their region and of the changes in local circumstances. They are able to translate national policies for the more local level, keeping the public informed, and also holding officials to account, especially at a regional and local level. Undoubtedly, local journalists may have their own political agendas and are not immune to telling one story at the expense of another. However, local journalism offers an opportunity to share some more of the good news and to restore faith in politics and each other. It can champion local heroes and offer spaces to gather and cultivate a greater sense of belonging. These are the stories we need to tell: the stories of our communities, of local initiatives, and of what we have in common and how we can get involved in our area.

One of the UK's most successful local papers is the *Bristol Cable*.[54] At a time when corporate takeovers by organisations like Newsquest and National World have subsumed many local news outlets in the country, the *Cable* has been resilient. Now over ten years old, this pioneering news cooperative has successfully raised sufficient funds, from a number of sources, to keep going for over ten years. People pay to be members, of which there are about 2,600 people, and they help make it free for others to access. Hard-copy papers are distributed for free in the city, supported by advertising in its pages. Eliz Mizon has worked for the paper for several years and has been a member since its inception. For her the value of local news, and the *Cable* in particular, is that it shares human stories from the local area, depicting the vibrancy of the social fabric. It is a lot less reactive than national news, with no breaking stories, meaning that it has time for longer-term investigations into local scandals, the mismanagement of services, or gaps in policing. In this way, it enables scrutiny of local politics, councillors, and services, which would not be given space in a national paper. There is, she argues, 'quality not just in the stories, but in how you build infrastructure', in how local news conveys the social dynamics of a city and its people.[55] These local news sources also build local trust and connection, giving information on community events and developments. While it cannot do everything, by telling the story of normal people it adds to the wealth and vibrancy of the city. However, even these local news sources are under threat, as funding dries up and important organisations, like Luminate, that typically support local news direct their attention elsewhere.

This is not just a matter of how we build community and belonging in our own countries. In a world where the global is also local, and we are more connected than ever to countries overseas, the media has a duty to convey what is going on more widely. A similar challenge in the international sphere is that in the mainstream media the stories of other countries and people are often told through lenses of pre-existing beliefs and narratives. It is important to address these to give people a deeper appreciation of foreign policy, and also because such beliefs and narratives also inform the stereotypes and awareness we have of other people and cultures in our own multicultural societies.

Given our decreasing attention spans, and the sheer amount of news available, we often only get the top lines and headlines – stories from foreign capitals and tales of the worst excesses of violence or crisis, without a more nuanced reflection of the events and dynamics in the country as a whole. At its worst, this can perpetuate perceptions of an 'oriental' other, accustomed to chaos and conflict in contrast to their more 'civilised' Western counterparts.[56] Our knowledge of Egypt is largely limited to events in Cairo. Yet if our lenses were to shift to Alexandria, Luxor, or outside of the major cities, we might get a deeper appreciation for the complexity of the country and its people. Few capital cities, with their wealth, political elite, and cosmopolitan centres, are typical of their country. To challenge this tendency, a number of international and regional initiatives are leading the way.

Dina Aboughazala is the founder and CEO of Egab, based in Egypt.[57] She grew up familiar with the workings of the media; her dad was a journalist for whom accessibility and readability was important – 'if the man who ran the printer didn't understand what he'd written, he would change it'. After working for several years as a journalist, including for the BBC, she grew frustrated by the erasure of local stories, and the projection of stereotypes and inaccurate depictions of events in the mainstream. Her organisation works to change that, empowering local people to share their stories, revealing more of the granularity, complexity, and human face of the Middle East and Africa, and giving mainstream outlets regionally and internationally access to more diverse and original news stories.

Dina and her team give voice to people who cannot publish their stories in the media without help, either because they are from communities with no access to editorial networks, or because they are unsure how to begin getting published. They do not have to be journalists, but they do have to have a good idea for a compelling story. Her team helps them craft the story and the pitch before it is sent to a news outlet. These stories, by people in local communities can counter Western tropes and generalisations, offering nuance and richness and human insights into the region. She shares a great story by Reyya Mozhami about women in Yemen who become mobile phone technicians to counter sextortion, which featured in the Spanish newspaper *El País*. It told of how when Yemeni women's phones broke down, the male technicians who were fixing them were using confidential content that might reflect badly on the women's honour, for blackmail and extortion. Such local reporting captured a dimension of the story that would have been missed by the mainstream, and gave a more nuanced insight into the country and its people.[58] Dina's vision is to amplify such stories, and 'create a world where the news is a trusted source for accurate and holistic representation of events and communities in the Global South'.[59]

The imperative for local media is becoming greater, she emphasises, as artificial intelligence (AI) is forcing the media to change and adapt. AI, she notes, cannot identify the local stories, or give voice to local people. The real cutting-edge news comes through people on the ground sharing their experiences in ways the mainstream cannot.[60]

In Barcelona, Preethi Nallu is the Executive Director of Report for the World, an initiative of the Ground Truth Project.[61] She is a journalist, a filmmaker, and a creative advocate for change and representation whose career has taken her to countries as diverse as India, the UK, Egypt, Palestine, Myanmar, Denmark, Lebanon, and Spain. Noting the dramatic decline of local news outlets and reporting, the mission of Report for the World is to counter the detrimental implications this decline can have on political accountability, government investment, corruption, and public awareness of issues like health, welfare, and the environment. By harnessing local journalists around the world, it aims to empower local voices, strengthen communities, and inform and engage citizens.

When we speak, she offers an alternative vision for local news: what if reporters covered not only war and violence but also turned their lens on compassion and the stories of those who help?[62] We don't see enough of that, but what kinds of stories would they tell?

For Preethi, empathy in the media is designed to compel a response from the audience, either to do more to support an initiative, or to counter or put a stop to certain behaviours or actions. Her motivation to be a journalist came through researching the world, with a desire to distil what she found and its complexities into more 'human-centric' language. Refugees and migration, conflict and displacement, are all central themes in her documentary work and reporting.

She conveys the meaning and implications of events through the eyes of people's experiences, sharing diverse voices with new audiences and expanding people's awareness of the world. Her aim is to make events into a story 'so someone walking down the street could understand why it matters and do something about it'.[63]

*

The media can, and should, tell more complex stories. The constant barrage of negative headlines and news stories on every platform and outlet can contribute to apathy or empathy fatigue. We need to know this bad news, and the details of the crises and the tragedies that are occurring. It would be naïve to try to be immune to, or disconnected from these realities. But if the media can share a wider picture of life and humanity, it might help counter the apathy, or sense of overwhelm we can experience. It is impossible to maintain a consistent level of care for a world the reflects back to us all that is wrong with humanity. Climate grief and emotional burnout is real.[64] When everything is disastrous, and all solutions feel futile, it can leave people wondering why they should care.

If the media were to contribute to a culture that valued empathy, it would tell more complex and richer stories about a wider diversity of people and seek out the humanity in the subjects. It would be able to show different sides of a story, to hold space for difference and disagreement, while also holding people to account. It would prioritise facts and nuance over sensationalism and soundbites.

However, more empathy in politics is dependent on our own capacity to broaden our horizons, to be receptive to more variety and complexity in the stories we are exposed to, and to increase our tolerance for uncomfortable news. Empathy requires attention and intention. It demands a curiosity about what lies beyond our immediate vantage point, and a willingness to embrace diverse stories and expand our understanding. This is also what makes it hard and costly. There is a comfort with easy news. Widening our own apertures and reading around our traditional sources can be confronting. We also have only finite time and energy, and in the current climate news can feel over-whelming and depressing. We need balance, and a commitment to a healthier media diet. There are ways to realise this. One is to start small, at a local level. By engaging as active citizens with our communities, we can often find seeds of hope, and stories of change and optimism, about the way our politics and our leadership could be.

9

Engaging Society

Before he ran for the presidency, in 2006, the young senator Barack Obama spoke to graduates of Northwestern University about one of the biggest challenges facing America: its empathy deficit. The financial crisis and federal deficit were not the only problems for the country, he argued; the challenge was that 'we live in a culture that discourages empathy. A culture that too often tells us our principal goal in life is to be rich, thin, young, famous, safe, and entertained. A culture where those in power too often encourage these selfish impulses.'[1] Empathy has been a golden thread through his writings and reflections on life and politics.[2] And in that moment he shared his hope that the graduates, and all those who would hear his speech, would expand their 'ambit of concern', 'because our individual salvation depends on collective salvation'.[3] It was, and remains, an important and hopeful vision: a call for people to look beyond their immediate world to see connection with the wider community and society.

This might involve, as Obama suggested, actively seeking to understand the experiences of those who have different backgrounds to you – the man who has fled a warzone and has moved to a new country seeking a better life, the woman who has recently lost steady employment and is working multiple jobs to make ends meet for her family, the child at school who is shy, awkward, unsure, and on their own in the playground. It extends to our homes and daily lives. No doubt, it can be incredibly hard and uncomfortable. Dinner parties, family gatherings, and social meet-ups can reveal the challenges of listening to, and engaging with, those with very disparate views. However, empathy is not just about understanding how different people live, and seeing a shared humanity with them, but also involves moving away from a centring of self, to prioritising community and connection. As growing data is showing, this is vital to our wider well-being.

While empathy is critical to effective politics and leadership, it is also integral to creating engaged, empowered, and vibrant societies. Changes in our politics and the character and quality of our leaders and representatives is partly dependent on our capacity to create change among ourselves. It involves our active investment and commitment. Are *we* ready for a different kind of politics? Are *we* prepared to engage with different perspectives and experiences within our own communities and societies? A desire for more empathy, tolerance, and understanding at the highest levels of politics equally requires a willingness to practise and embody it ourselves.

Despite the frustrations with the failures of politics and the challenges of the moment, there is a huge amount of hope and potential in citizen-led initiatives, and in movements and activism that are pushing back against regressive, materialistic, or self-interested ideas of what politics is and what it is for. There is magic in these gatherings.[4]

CHALLENGING POLARISATION

The sense of despondency with current politics, and the desire for different approaches and solutions, has motivated many new organisations to emerge that are led by citizens wanting to empower more people and give them a voice. People may feel angry and frustrated or apathetic regarding the current state of affairs, yet such organisations offer hope, as well as proof that empathy can contribute to valuable change across society.

In September 2019, one such organisation, America in One Room,[5] brought 526 voters together over one weekend near Dallas, Texas, for a process of deliberative democracy.[6] These voters represented the diversity of American society, from across the political spectrum. Over several days they debated some of the big issues of the moment: immigration, climate change, and the economy. For the most part the conversations were respectful, and people emerged largely hopeful about the state of democracy in the country, and the ability to find common ground.

One year on, after the elections and the 6 January riots, the mood was more despondent. Yet when the *New York Times* interviewed many of those who attended they found that even in the more cynical environment, the participants were more engaged in following presidential politics, and, while mainly still aligned with their traditional party, they were more open to reasoned debate about the challenges facing the country, and how other people saw them.[7]

Another citizen-led organisation, Braver Angels, reflects on 'patriotic empathy', where the process of understanding and engaging with people from across the political spectrum is essential to the prosperity and strength of the country.[8] It has over 15,000 members across the country and regularly hosts debates, events, and workshops. As a large cross-partisan and volunteer-led organisation, its intention is to foster spaces where people can talk across the divides in society with respect, dignity, and curiosity, and it leans into the value of community and connection. It does this through multiple channels. At a political level, it uses workshops, town halls, and resources to encourage representatives to work across party lines and engage in deliberative and collaborative approaches. It works with schools, providing educational materials to help students cultivate critical thinking and have dialogues across divides.[9] It brings together faith leaders around ideas of dignity and respect, not agreement, and prompts conversations between Christians and Jews about how people of faith can overcome polarisation.[10] Through such initiatives, Braver Angels normalises hard conversations, and the importance of dialogue, and creates a practice of empathy in the service of improving politics.

BridgeUSA, an organisation led by and for students, helps people talk across the divide on campuses and in other educational settings. I spoke with Manu Meel, one of its founders and leaders, as well as host of podcast *The Hopeful Majority*, and he explained how the organisation emerged organically in response to growing cancel culture and polarisation on campuses.[11] Members of the leadership team have very different politics, but leaders and participants alike are committed to the idea of dialogue and the search for unity, based on the principles of empathy, introspection, and effective action. Their mission is not to turn everyone into a centrist or to change people's minds, but to engage students across campuses in overcoming divisions by becoming more tolerant and understanding of different beliefs and ways of thinking.[12] It also contributes to building robustness in engaging with others, normalising again the discomfort of dialogue. They run regular workshops and other initiatives on campus, and their discussions are centred on four core norms, intended to produce more constructive discussion: '1. Listen to listen, not to respond; 2. Don't interrupt or have side conversations; 3. Address the statement, not the person; 4. Participants represent only themselves and not the groups they belong to.'[13] In 2025, BridgeUSA has ninety-four college chapters and continues to grow, showing an appetite for such spaces among young people. It is also just one of many similar initiatives seeking change at the civic and community level.

Outside of the US, More in Common takes a more global perspective. It is an organisation that uses data and research to understand the underlying sources of polarisation, discontent, and frustration in our current moment.[14] Focusing on seven priority countries (the US,

UK, Germany, France, Poland, Spain, and Brazil), their research seeks to understand the stories people tell and the hopes, fears, experiences, and values they share, and to identify how people form groups and connections, and where there are gaps. Using a growing body of evidence, they tailor their initiatives to the local context of each country. For example, to connect strangers in France in 2019, they worked with La Fête des Voisins (the Neighbours' Party) to bring together around 9 million people across the country. Through their research they discovered that the game of bingo was an effective tool and so provided community facilitators with bingo kits to cultivate community. And, in Germany, they are doing survey and listening research to identify how people feel about the climate and identify where the current movement leaves some people feeling left out, to create a more inclusive debate.

What these organisations do is increase exposure to diversity and difference and encourage people to lean into their community and to see the intrinsic worth and dignity of everyone, even if they come from diverse backgrounds or hold different views. In the process, this helps rebuild the trust in each other that enables societies to thrive.

TRUSTING EACH OTHER

Research by Pew shows that social trust correlates with higher civic engagement and feelings of belonging to a community, increased confidence in democratic institutions, and reduced likelihood of depression and anxiety.[15] And even while social trust is relatively high among the advanced economies, it is low among young people and those with lower levels of educational attainment. This is an indicator of which groups of people are being left behind and where efforts to foster trust should be directed.

Denmark leads in such metrics of the highest level of social trust, closely followed by many of the other Scandinavian countries. In part this is because of the political and social culture, and how community is centred in Danish society. There is even a word in Danish and other Nordic languages – 'tryghed' (pronounced troeg-hel)[16] – that captures this notion of trust and a positive sense of the mood and feeling of security in society. In English-speaking countries, we lack a word that sufficiently conveys a positive feeling or atmosphere of communal relations. In the same way that English has adopted the Danish word 'hygge'[17] to imply cosiness, missing its richer and more nuanced meaning about enjoying the simpler things in life, fostering contentment and conviviality with others, and restoring the spirit,[18] tryghed is also not easily translated. In the English language, it is commonly translated as 'security', but this has connotations of a freedom from danger threat, or anxiety. It tends to be connected to ideas of protection. Instead, tryghed is more about secureness, a sense of security that comes not only through protection, but through the feeling of safety that accompanies peace of mind and the knowledge that you are supported by your community.[19]

Tryghed has deep roots in Danish society, and there are similar words in other Nordic languages. Originally it meant 'safety', akin to English and German ideas of the term security or 'sicherheit'. In the 1700s, during the Enlightenment, it evolved to take on more expansive meaning, with more romantic ideas of a feeling or sensation of security.[20] That it is connected to ideas of trust is no surprise given that Denmark enjoys one of the highest levels of public trust in the world.[21] Yet this is not just trust in leadership and political institutions, but also in each other, in their communities, and in strangers. A strong welfare state, robust political institutions, and low levels of corruption are partly responsible. Yet so too is a broader societal ethos and investment in the value of tryghed. It encapsulates a community-mindedness, a sense of responsibility towards others, and the value of trust, connection, and belonging.

What could this mean for better politics elsewhere? Primarily, it involves thinking more concertedly about what we want our societies to *feel* like. How can we foster a deeper sense of belonging and connection for all in our communities? What do ideas of prosperity, opportunity, and security mean? Beyond *tryghed* or security, what does it mean to feel part of a vibrant, empowered, and cohesive society? And what will it take for our leaders and ourselves to create that?

Empathy is a key part of helping to rebuild communities in this way.[22] Yet it requires contact, familiarity, and exposure to a wider range of people. In psychology, the idea of contact theory, put forward by Gordon Allport in 1954,[23] suggests that prejudice and intolerance can be reduced the more groups have contact with others. The theory has evolved since then, with a more refined ideas of contact, but the principle stands: exposure to difference, especially early on in one's life, has longer-term benefits for social harmony.[24]

However, finding areas of commonality with others and under-standing different points of view at a deeper and more nuanced level is made harder by the decline of civic space and changes in society and how we connect. Across many countries, a long-term trend of budget cuts and funding shortages has meant there are fewer public areas where people can meet and interact in person within their communities.[25] Libraries, playgrounds, youth centres, community groups, sports clubs are invaluable to communal relations and to fostering a civic spirit, and a sense of engagement and ownership in local communities. Where such spaces are shrinking, budgets may make savings, but there is a cost to us in connection and community. There may be a correlation between the vibrancy of civic life and the cultural norms of clubs and community engagement, and the high levels of public trust that make countries like Denmark and Finland some of the happiest countries in the world. Such spaces contribute to the quality of a country's political culture, to the civic spirit, and the environment within which our politics operate. They facilitate relations with others and the contact necessary to know people in better and kinder everyday ways. They allow people to join groups and take part in activities like dance, sailing, tennis, or crafting, where they can meet people, and learn new skills. Yet these spaces require more investment and intentional design. If properly valued, they can play a vital role in re-energising communities, exposing people to shared passions, and areas of commonality.

Simple community-led initiatives can have a genuine impact. In Canberra, Running for Resilience (R4R) is a local and unstructured, informal, running event, which happens several times a week, first thing in the morning and in the early evening.[26] It is free, beginning at a pub on the lake at Kingston Foreshore and involving hundreds of people who show up to run with others before enjoying a drink. It has branched out into yoga and has inspired some of its members to take on longer running challenges and raise money for charity. Designed to promote awareness around mental health, and especially suicide, it aims to eliminate suicide in the capital by 2033, and figures released in 2024 suggest that due to mental health initiatives, targeted support, and organisations like R4R, suicide is already down by 44%.[27] It may be a small part of the city's life, but it is a well-known institution and an opportunity for people to connect outside of work and feel a sense of belonging in their local area while getting fit. Such points of connection may feel small, but their effects ripple out more widely.

CITIZENS CREATING CHANGE

Around the world citizens are turning these sorts of engagement into deeper political engagement and change at the local and national level. In the southwest of the city of Aarhus, north Denmark, in a collection of offices and meeting rooms connected to a large brown brick building that used to be a school, is Sager der Samler (which translates as Citizen Change).[28] Founded in 2012 by Paul Natorp, Karen Ingerslev, Brett Patching, Kristin Birkeland, and Morten Petersen Daus, it was designed with the intention of creating an initiative and training programme to contribute to society and solve problems in the local community. Over time it has become an engine-room and hub for a 'community of action'.[29] The organisation supports and empowers people to take the initiative to work with others to transform their community. It is one of many initiatives that exist around the world that are trying to create change from the grassroots, and it offers valuable ideas for citizen-led action.

On the wall of the communal hall, written on the back of an old and weathered white wooden door, with red titles and painted script, are the guiding principles:

Egen Virkelighed – tag udgagspunkt i din egen livssituation
Øjenhøjde – Gør noget med (ikke for) andre
Frihed – start der hvor du ikke skal spørge om lov eller bede om penge

That is:

Start in Your Own Reality – take your starting point from your own life situation and what needs to change. Help create change that benefits you and others.

Engage at Eye Level – do something with (not for) others, change is something done together.

Use Your Freedom – start from a place where you do not have to ask for permission or ask for money [which means building on your own responsibilities and authority as an agent within society].

The idea is to start where you are, build on your own strengths, and use your own experience and understanding of the world to foster connections and create change. When I met Paul Natorp he emphasised the importance of empathy to such an ethos, using awareness of your own position and circumstances to gain understanding about how different people experience the world.[30] Dialogue, exchange, and insights into how different people live offer opportunities to find points of commonality across the community.

There is a wide and varied assortment of initiatives or causes. One initiative to help vulnerable people access healthcare and be supported during medical appointments has been so successful it has expanded to other cities in Denmark. One woman takes politicians and city leaders out in wheelchairs to experience how the city feels to someone with limited mobility and gives them a first-hand insight into the practical challenges she faces when accessing shops and public services. Another woman organised a project that encourages people to imagine and empathise with how animals might experience the city, to encourage more discussion around protecting indigenous urban wildlife. There are around eighty members in the association itself, with several hundred involved in the different causes. The wider network includes hundreds of people from across the local community, incorporating businesses, citizens, and associations in Aarhus and the wider region.

The organisation also connects people with local political processes, with regular meetings before council meetings and with local politicians to inform the decision-making process, facilitate more two-way dialogue between people and politicians, and create opportunities to listen to and share concerns. Another hand-written sign on the wall, this time on a large sheet of paper, sets out the core principles:

Morgenpolitik:

- Vi sørger alle for en god tone og atmosfære
- Vi er her for at bliveklogere (ikke for at få ret eller blive enige)
- Vi værdsætter forskellige perspektiver

Which translates as:

Morning Policy:

- We all provide a good tone and atmosphere
- We're here to get smarter (not to get it right or agree)
- We value different perspectives

As a community, the organisation constantly strives to learn and grow, thinking about what makes for more sustainable and cohesive communities, which can empower all its members. Although it may not be city-wide, let alone nation-wide, it is growing, and offers proof of how a great communal ethos can be cultivated. Similar initiatives, rooted in the power of empathy, exist around the world. They could equally be started in town halls and local communities by those who are willing to work with others to develop political literacy, facilitate difficult conversations, and find common cause at a neighbourhood or parish level.

In Italy, in the northern city of Bologna, a place well known for its history of activism and progressiveness, and vibrant civil society, another initiative puts citizens in the driving seat of designing their local communities. The Citizen Imagination Office was invented in 2018 and managed until 2023 by Michele Alena, a dynamic figure with a mission, whose commitment to reimagining communities and politics means he works as a policy consultant, digital innovator, and community manager.[31]

The Citizen Imagination Office began at the ground level, organising meetings, assemblies, and focus groups. Michele explains to me how at a time of growing distrust, the office is designed to restore relations between communities and the municipality using methods and languages that are adapted to different contexts. It is directed at citizens, at engaging them in political processes. By going outside the traditional institutions to meet with people it revealed the power of proximity. Proximity agents work on the ground in the same area for extended periods of time to connect with people and get to understand the needs and requirements; it is empathy in action, with local representatives working closely with citizens to understand their concerns and what matters to them.

For Michele, the Citizen Imagination Office is centred on four key principles: Power, Place, Time, and Empathy. First, understanding power and how it is distributed; second, valuing that each place and area has its own characteristics and requirements, so they have to adapt and be responsive; third, it requires a lot of time (and patience) to build trust, and to overcome the disconnection between people and politics – investment in coffees, and meetings, and face-to-face interactions are required to create community bonds and networks; finally, empathy is essential to overcome departmental and institutional approaches and connect with people. On the frontlines, people talk about their needs not politics, so understanding these is key to shaping the approaches. Empathy is not just something for the leadership but is key for empowering civil society and citizens. As Michele notes, 'to strengthen democracy we have to recognise that our community knows the city better than us'.[32] Empathy also shapes the language used: it has to be accessible, relatable, and engaging.

Certainly, such initiatives are never without their problems. Local politics can be difficult and sometimes petty. As in national politics, there are diverse agendas and strong egos. Nevertheless, what so many of these organisations have in common is that they demonstrate new, dynamic forms of leadership centred on the idea that citizens are better equipped to know what they need, and so should be empowered to be a part of change. They share visions of sustainability for the future and a willingness to adapt to change. Those who work in them reorient the priorities of politics away from power and authority imposed from above, to more distributive and collective forms of engagement. There is acceptance of the compromises involved in democratic societies, and the costs incurred in working to create something better. Yet these are coupled with a more positive and empowering vision of what is possible when we rethink our assumptions about politics and participate in redefining it.

A key part of this is seeing ourselves as active agents and participants in politics and society. This focus on the power of people to come together and find new meaning is a theme Jon Alexander is passionate about. As a former marketing and PR professional, he is keenly aware of the power of stories to move people. Yet, despite it

212

being his dream job, over time he became disillusioned with what he was selling and its contribution to society. In 2014 he co-founded the New Citizen Project, and since then he has written about his vision for a change of story, and renewed hope in our capacity to change the status quo.

We have evolved, he argues, from subjects in a paternalistic and hierarchical society, where people are ruled over and kept safe by a (hopefully) beneficent ruler, to consumers, where the imperative is self-interest, looking after oneself, and meeting individual needs through material means. Although such a story offers the myth that through our individual empowerment we can create a better collective society, in truth, the consumer system keeps people disconnected, entitled and self-reliant.[33] In his book, co-authored with Ariane Conrad, they propose a new story: the citizen story. Instead of self-interest, this story places the emphasis on us all taking responsibility and working collaboratively to create and participate in the kind of communities we desire.[34] In the words of American author and activist Baratunde Thurston: 'citizen is a verb'.[35]

Citizens around the world are expressing their frustrations and their desire for change through protest movements and collective action. As we explored in Chapter 4, growing protests on climate change, human rights, and equality in recent years speak to a desire from citizens to do things differently and to be a part of the solution. For the most part, these protests are not threatening, but more another way that people seek to be heard and taken seriously. They also offer opportunities for politicians to engage and learn more. It can cause greater harm to repress such expression, thereby reinforcing a narrative that politicians do not care about, or are not interested in, the concerns of the people.

Nevertheless, as Jon observes, there is a balance. When social movements become about protest at the expense of progress, this can equally limit the capacity of politicians to engage. There has to be the capacity to let those in power evolve, albeit while holding them to account and setting clear standards and milestones. As Jon notes, there is a danger that some groups 'focus on defeating the institution but not creating space for the institution to evolve'.[36] The ideal of defeating an institution can skip over the next step, which often involves the recreation of new institutions, with their own problems and flaws. And these can end up replicating iniquities, injustices, and imbalances, as they are operating without the benefit of institutional memory and experience. Vision and transformation need to meet practicalities and process.

CONNECTING THE DOTS

This appetite for engagement and social investment in change at a citizen level presents opportunities for politicians and citizens to engage more intentionally and constructively with one another. A critical step is for politicians to listen more and connect with those outside the narrow confines of their own electoral base. If leaders only speak to, and act for, those who elect them, and not the wider country or community, then politics can become a merry-go-round of one set of vested interests replacing another set of vested interests, marginalising many. For citizens, it can appear that personal and political survival trumps working for national prosperity and well-being, and this contributes to disillusionment and frustration with those in power and democracy itself. Approaches to such situations can veer between anger at the injustices and failures of the system, to apathy rooted in the belief there is little that can be done to change it. Although there are some efforts to rectify this, they have variable success. Instead, Sir Nick Harvey speaks of the need to 'meet people where they are, not where we would like them to be'.[37] There will be no quick fixes.

In France, on 17 November 2018, the 'gilets jaunes' (yellow vests) began a series of citizen-led grassroots protests against plans to introduce more taxes on petrol and diesel. The taxes were designed as part of President Emmanuel Macron's efforts to move to more green energy sources, and change consumer behaviour, but they imposed a high cost for many among the lowest earners and most vulnerable French people. Rather than being led by any trade union or group, the protests gained ground online, through social media and online petitions. And, as with many protest movements, those involved had a wide array of concerns, grievances, and objectives. The movement became a broader symbol of dissatisfaction with the government, and frustration over the disproportionate impact of these policies on the lowest-earning French people. Especially in rural and small-town areas of France, people felt marginalised and unheard in the metropole. Such perspectives were reinforced by policies introduced to stimulate businesses which cut taxes for companies and for the wealthiest in society. The message was that those at the top, already enjoying innumerable benefits in a difficult financial climate, would be shielded from the crisis that was wreaking havoc across the country.

At its peak, on the first day, it was estimated that around 285,000 people joined the protests.[38] They took place each day, involving road-blocks and disruption, with some fringe elements engaging in violence or clashes with police. French President Emmanuel Macron's popularity took a hit. Between June and November he dropped fifteen points according to some polls, and a poll by Ifop (an international French market research group) in December 2018 showed approval for his leadership was at 23%, with 45% very dissatisfied.[39] Realising that ignoring or suppressing the protests would not work, Macron wrote a letter to the French people.[40] In it he set out his vision for the country, the pride for France he shared with other French citizens, and his recognition of the challenges many were facing and their impact. He also posed a series of questions relating to diverse aspects of politics – including taxation and public spending, the organisation of state and public authorities, the environment and the ecological transition needed for the future, and democracy and public citizenship.[41] These questions sought not only to gain different perspectives but also reveal the tensions inherent in political decision-making. For example, he asked: If you want to lower taxation, then what are you prepared to cut of public services? How can a country make the transition to a greener economy without further impoverishing, or making unnecessary demands on the most vulnerable of citizens? As part of his outreach, Emmanuel Macron embarked on Le Grand Débat National – the Great National Debate – involving a series of dialogues and town halls across the country.[42]

The idea, in theory, was a good one: the commitment and effort to listen is itself important. However, one of the problems with such initiatives is they can seem like cynical moves designed to perform care rather than a genuine desire to listen and learn so as to inform constructive change. Especially where trust is already low, it will take more concerted and visible effort, as well as time, to alter perceptions. Although his approval ratings did rise slightly after a series of town halls,[43] the continued resistance to President Macron's policies suggests the listening did not go far enough. This was partly because pension reforms in France – which sought to raise the retirement age from 62 to 64 to account for people living longer – prompted further widespread riots and disruption across the country. The surge of the far right, and how close they came to victory in the snap 2024 election, suggest the problems have not been solved.

Listening is a vital attribute for politicians, but often under-rated. We can sometimes see this when politicians speak in public: they seem to resort to their 'go-to' soundbite, the comfortable information they have to refute critique, without truly hearing what people are saying, or what lies beneath their words. Emily Kasriel, an expert in deep listening, emphasises the importance of intentions and attention, and showing up with humility to engage. It matters to people that they feel heard, and it's a vital skill for building connection with others.[44] However, with such an overload of information, listening can feel like hard work.

Cormac Russell is someone who motivates and encourages people to lean into shifts in power and works for greater collaboration between politics and people. Based in Ireland, he is a world expert on citizen engagement and the power of community. He travels internationally to advise governments, organisations, and local groups on the power of connection and community. And he wants to help people see that they are key actors and agents of change, not passive recipients.

Through his work he seeks to bring people into civic life and empower them to articulate and create the solutions to the problems they face. He looks at where the 'on-ramps' are for people to get involved, to partake of power. This can involve reframing the problems or offering creative outlets through which people can help. For example, maybe the local issues are less about crime and more about an absence of community or belonging. Citizens have far more agency to construct community and to keep an eye on each other than they do to fight crime, especially as 'the neighbourhood is often an effective unit for change'.[45] Changing the frame of reference, and seeing the problem from a different angle can open up more creative solutions or opportunities to direct funding or resources in ways that have longer-term benefits.

In such an environment, politicians can help translate what is going on and explain the possible levers and opportunities local people might be able to use. They can amplify concerns beyond the local level – representing them in parliaments or other bodies – while also bringing their political capital to support local actors.

When Cormac mentors and advises senior figures in politics and business, he asks a key question: 'What did you not do to enable people to step into their power?'[46] By not acting, by not needing to solve the problem, what creativity from others have you facilitated? For him 'empathy is the ability to foreground the capacity of others'.[47] It is about stepping back and letting local innovations flourish in response to local problems.

He points to Spain, where fascists were rioting and local citizens said 'not in our name'.[48] In the UK too, when the far right were violently targeting mosques and hotels where refugees were being held, it was local citizens who came out in large numbers to prevent the refugees getting harmed, and to stand against the right-wing politics of the rioters.

He finds that a challenge with grassroots change is that 'people retreat when there are too many bureaucrats, rules, or regulations'.[49] The feared 'red tape' hinders innovation and undermines trust. Removing these barriers is essential to co-create change, and share power more equitably. He recalls a commonly cited phrase, 'everything changes at the pace of trust', reiterating the importance of people in public life acting in a trustworthy way.[50]

He identified a critical way to increase the power and potential of citizen engagement, the idea of 'citizen orality'. Instead of political literacy, we also need citizens to be better able to articulate or speak about their problems, and then to identify the actions needed and take them.[51] An effective and powerful way to bring citizens into politics, and to foster deeper understanding not only of each other but also the intricacies of politics, is citizens' assemblies and other spaces of participatory and deliberative democracy.

RE-ENERGISING PARTICIPATORY
AND DELIBERATIVE DEMOCRACY

Held over several days, citizens' assemblies help foster interpersonal relationships, community ties and friendships between people who may not otherwise have met, and who represent an array of demographics and ideologies. Participants go through a process of random selection – called 'sortition' – commonly used in ancient Greece, that uses ballots or lots to ensure the composition of the assemblies is representative of the demographics of the community. Those involved spend several days in deliberations, exposed to diverse perspectives from experts and fellow citizens. The discussions are based on ideas of openness, equality of voice, fairness, respect, and empathy.

In Ireland in 2016, citizens' assemblies helped to shift debates on abortion and gay marriage. The Citizens' Assembly was established by the Irish government after a manifesto pledge from Fine Gael in 2016. A group of ninety-nine members and a selected chairperson was tasked with debating five distinct and emotive issues over a nineteen-month period. Among them was a discussion of the Eighth Amendment of the Constitution (on abortion). For a majority Catholic country, where abortion had long been illegal, it would be a contentious topic. Taking place over five sessions, a total of nine and a half days, between November 2016 and April 2017, the discussions on the matter included twenty-five expert talks, and participants reviewed 300 submissions (out of a total of 12,200).[52] At the end, the group presented their recommendations to the Houses of the Oireachtas (the Irish Houses of Parliament). Following their recommendations, the proposal was put to a referendum, and with 64% turnout, all but one constituency – Donegal – voted to repeal the Eighth Amendment. It is a striking example of the power of citizen participation to effect change.

There have long been calls for such assemblies and hundreds have already taken place. The OECD's Deliberative Database 2023 has captured over 730 recorded examples of deliberative democratic processes around the world.[53]

Assemblies offer a model to inculcate empathy into politics both as a leadership quality and an integral part of processes and practices of effective and deliberative democratic governance. However, they are not flawless. Academic Mary Scudder highlights how empathy can be limited in assemblies, the potential for projection rather than true understanding, and a tendency towards selectivity. Precisely because we are empathising with those who are different, she argues, it can lead to the exclusion of certain groups. There is also an ethical dimension; the concept's ethical connotations can constrain discussions, with ideas of what is 'good' or 'right' overlaying debates.[54] These are all valid critiques: empathy can be limited and variable. And it is right to be cognisant of its limits in these spaces.

Janet Rice, a former Green senator in Australia, is also supportive of participatory democracy as a core part of Green Party politics, but similarly notes that citizens' assemblies can be open to manipulation, and dependent on who is in the room. Although many people are good at engaging, from her experience, governments have few incentives to do so, and have to be willing to share power and take part in the process. People in government and in society both have to see their value for them to be worth it.[55]

Nonetheless, citizens' assemblies are growing in popularity as people seek to create a more participatory and empowering democratic process. They also remove some of the red tape and bureaucratic constraints from political participation that can be off-putting to people. Organisations like DemocracyNext[56] advocate for citizens' assemblies as a way for people to engage more meaningfully with politics, and create a 'more just, joyful, and collaborative future'.[57] Founder and CEO of the organisation, Claudia Chwalisz, has been working on democratic innovation for over ten years, motivated by addressing the disconnect between politics and the people. She is an inspiring advocate for such participatory processes and has seen a dramatic rise in their popularity.[58] The work of DemocracyNext is centred on five core pillars: creating the infrastructure to scale citizens' assemblies; establishing them as valid institutions that can contribute to, and reshape, power; harnessing innovation – including AI – to stay ahead of the latest developments; telling stories about an alternative democratic future, and inspiring people to engage; and finally, promoting systemic change that is rooted in communities and citizens. Through its mission DemocracyNext is training people in how to run citizens' assemblies, and cultivating a powerful and international community of citizens, policymakers, and activists.

Empathy is an intrinsic part of the process, even if not always intentionally. To make the case for their position, people who participate are confronted with what it might cost others and be willing and able to justify the trade-offs they anticipate. Grand ideas discussed with friends over a coffee or a pint suddenly touch reality when people realise their real-world impact; the ideas are then refined and adapted to accommodate a broader range of implications. This helps people to experience how strongly others feel about a subject, and why certain ideas or policy options are invested with such emotions and support. Those involved unpack what ideas of security, welfare, democracy, politics feel like to others, as well as what they mean and their practical implications. The process thus compels people to debate and discuss and to find points of commonality. It is a healthy function of vibrant democracies convened in a safe space that is conducive to dialogue.

Organisers of such forums remark on how people will so often find commonality across their divides. Laurie Drake led citizen democracy initiatives in Canada and speaks about how the process 'helps people grapple with how issues affect others . . . so they learn it is not just about "me" but "us"'. It is also, she notes, a process of 'collective reasoning', and she likes observing how people's attitudes and perceptions shift over the course of the process.[59] You may disagree on how to manage local education policy, but you discover, through the contact and dialogue the process creates, that you respect their candour and their experience, you find their jokes funny, or you share the same hobbies. This is true for wider society as well, but is too readily forgotten in contemporary media discussions that like to depict a near-constant state of division.

These assemblies go beyond the community and national level. The Global Climate Assembly ran alongside the COP26 in Glasgow in 2021. It used global sortition to convene participants around the question: 'How can humanity address the climate and ecological crisis in a fair and effective way?'[60] The assembly involved extended dialogue, and participants had access to experts and academic research, as well as experiencing the complexities of debates and policy ideas. A guiding value of the core assembly was empathy, enhancing connections between people and creating collective meaning.[61] It is considered an attribute to aid humility and therefore can facilitate collaborative decision-making. In addition to the core group, the Global Climate Assembly offered opportunities for anyone to run an event, and fostered cultural efforts to reach people through creativity and popular culture.[62]

Such processes not only fostered greater empathy among participants, but they aided political literacy, helping people understand how action plans, policies and implementation strategies translate into practice. The organisers observed how it seemed to contribute to decreased apathy, as people felt proactive in addressing what can feel like an abstract and enormous challenge.[63] The movement aims to have a global assembly by 2030 with over 10 million people involved around the world. An ambitious vision, but one that will also encounter some frictions. In the 2022 Global Assembly Report, despite overall positive feedback, there was a perception from some members that politicians did not take the assembly seriously enough, and uncertainty about whether the assembly could really make a difference.[64] These are challenges that are not insurmountable but point to the need for growing investment from politicians in the process.

Nicole Curato, a leading figure in the field of deliberative democracy based at the University of Birmingham, told me about how empathy informs these processes, based on the research she leads on the Global Citizens' Assembly:

When citizens learn to see the world through the eyes of those unlike themselves, they are more likely to generate inclusive, other-regarding collective decisions rather than decisions driven by self-interest, partisanship, or identity politics. Evidence suggests that when participatory spaces are intentionally designed to foster empathy, people are, in fact, capable of practising it. Participants in these processes often say, 'I may not agree with the recommendations, but I understand why others support them.'[65]

Assemblies offer distinct and more meaningful forms of communication, which are too rare in our current political environment. The design of the format gives time to slow down, and, as Nicole explains, offers 'the space to think carefully, weigh different perspectives, and reflect on our own values before forming a judgement. This stands in stark contrast to the norms of cancel culture, dogpiling, and clickbait headlines. Deliberation can transform politics by equipping us to listen across difference and to develop practical strategies for living together while embracing those differences.'[66]

There are big ambitions for such assemblies, as well as awareness of their limitations if they do not widen their parameters and consider the ethical implications of who is included, and excluded, from the dialogues. Nicole is now looking at how climate assemblies might contribute to a global ethos on addressing the critical challenges we face. As she explains it:

> The strength of a global climate assembly lies in its ability to disrupt the siloed thinking that national or local assemblies often reinforce. While many assemblies produce recommendations in support of net-zero targets – such as investing in green transport – these policies frequently depend on extractive practices in the Global South, like cobalt mining in the Congo or lithium extraction in Chile, which deplete local resources and harm communities. A truly democratic climate assembly must also be an empathetic one: capable of taking the perspective of people not in the room, and sensitive to the ecological impacts of its decisions beyond its immediate context. Without this broader ethical horizon, such deliberative processes risk reinforcing the very injustices they aim to address.[67]

Indeed, while citizens' assemblies and similar forums are vital spaces for democracy, they are not cost free. Nicole explains how they can be demanding of the 'time, attention, emotional energy, and cognitive capacity' of those involved. It is hard for people with limited time or resources to participate, even though, she notes, 'they arguably have the most to gain from them'.[68] To make them more effective, organisers have to manage the barriers to entry and be cognisant of the inequalities that can be perpetuated by the format, especially when people risk incurring costs for travel, accommodation, or childcare.

The challenge is incorporating such consultation and participatory structures into international and national institutions and policymaking. Their success is partly dependent on the legitimacy they are accorded by politicians and by the wider public. At present, politicians can engage with them or ignore them, according to their themes and findings. A climate change citizens' assembly in Paris in 2019–20 led to a series of policy recommendations and ideas, many of which were soon discarded by President Macron, who argued that while it had been a valuable source of perspectives and ideas, the assembly of just 150 people was not equipped to determine France's political priorities.[69] Finding ways for political leaders to work more effectively with assemblies, setting expectations, and maintaining and developing the dialogue are critical for the future. It is a constant work in progress. In 2023 there were some positive signs. Another French citizens' assembly came together, with 184 participants from diverse backgrounds who debated for twenty-seven days over four months. With a 92% consensus[70] they agreed on eighty-one proposals on assisted dying and end-of-life care that were presented to President Macron.[71] In response, Macron proposed that government and parliament should draft a bill for debate by the end of summer 2023, with further commitments to address the issue in the next ten years.

Elsewhere, city- and government-led initiatives are trying to engage citizens through participatory budgeting, giving people the power to help determine how budgets are spent within their communities. Such initiatives help to generate greater public awareness and understanding of the trade-offs and compromises involved in official planning, especially given ever-shrinking public budgets. It gives people shared responsibility, and a stake in the direction of society, aiding political literacy in the process. Confronted with the practicalities of limited budgets and infinite priorities, citizens are required to identify the most pressing needs and gain an insight into the complex decision-making involved in politics.

Tampere, Finland, is one city where participatory budgeting was introduced to engage people in deciding how money is spent within their communities. Those in charge often organise the process around core themes, focusing on specific problems or local requirements relating to education, public space, and everyday safety. This cultivates shared responsibility in the region, and encourages people to engage with political processes.

Certainly, there are cultural dynamics at play. Finland is a country of only 5 million people, and a high-trust society with a strong civic culture. The legal right of civic participation developed in the 1970s and has evolved since then, with a range of initiatives including innovations to create digital citizens,[72] and the principle of civic participation included as a core element of the constitution since 2012.[73]

Nonetheless, it is too easy to dismiss the success and feasibility of participatory initiatives as a result of a country's small size or civic culture. As demonstrated by the examples from France, despite mistakes and hard-learned lessons, there are signs of success and potential for larger and more populous countries. It is the limits of our imagination and willpower that restrict the capacity for genuine change.

Nevertheless, as much as communities' and citizens' engagement have to be critical components of democratic renewal and a better politics, there is a balance to be struck. When we work or engage only at the local level, we can sometimes miss the bigger picture, the constraints and responsibilities that governments have to manage. A closer relationship and exchange between citizens and the state is therefore critical, as the state, in theory, should have the data, the information, and a richer more complex picture in order to make informed choices. Enhancing the process of dialogue and communication across the political environment can help the government take people with them from the outset, while also helping citizens be part of shaping policies that are more attuned and responsive to their experiences and needs.

*

The challenges of politics do not reside solely at the top but are a reflection of broader societal divisions and insecurities. Building a healthier, fairer, more equitable society, where people feel more seen, heard, and engaged, means cultivating every part of the political ecosystem. We have a vital part to play.

If we want to see change, we must create it: in our communities, in the conversations and interactions we have around dinner tables, with our neighbours, in town halls, school classrooms, and office meetings. There are constant opportunities to do things differently, small shifts that can have big impacts. Democracy is only evident in the practice of it. Once we become more accustomed to using it, and see the benefits it provides, it will become stronger, more familiar, and more powerful.

The core pillars of vibrant, thriving societies – trust, cohesion, community, compassion – cannot be imposed from above. While they can be modelled by political leaders, and supported through initiatives and shifts in policy, they must also emerge through society itself, in the way we relate to each other and our communities. The growth of new initiatives, championing engagement, participatory democracy, collective action, and cooperation show there is a powerful, genuine, and growing appetite for change and greater engagement among citizens. Yet far more needs to be done, at scale, so that the calls for change and the investment in it gain momentum and become impossible to ignore.

10

The Case for Empathy

At the end of 2024, the American electorate returned President Donald Trump to the White House. It was a decisive win. The electoral map turned red far earlier than had been anticipated, as he quickly gained the crucial swing states. The result shocked Democrats, election pundits, and people around the world, and emboldened and boosted his supporters. His win meant he could no longer be written off as an anomaly on the grounds that the first term was just a sign of protest at the system that ended after his four years in office.

During the election, the Democrats had emphasised Donald Trump's lack of empathy. They pointed to his lack of care for women, minorities, and immigrants, in contrast to their nominee Vice President Kamala Harris, whom they championed for her own natural empathy. Yet as the surprising scale of Trump's historic return materialised, with the Republicans taking both the House and the Senate, the lens was turned the other way: maybe the Democrats did not fully understand the real economic conditions of millions of Americans, and maybe they had failed to address the genuine problems in the country outside of Washington DC. While offering a promise of progress, they had failed to offer concrete steps that could take the people with them. By focusing on what they were not and all they rejected in the Republican candidate, they did not offer a plan that spoke sufficiently to the fears and insecurities of those who had been hit by inflation, were experiencing difficulty accessing housing, were facing uncertain job futures, and did not want continued, costly engagement overseas. In his post-election analysis, Senator Bernie Sanders exclaimed that the Democratic Party had failed the working class, and misunderstood the mood and needs of the country.[1] To reinforce his message, he then began a tour of America, trying to understand and empathise with the concerns, the fears, the pains, and the hopes of those who had voted for Trump. And although it is a critique other Democrats rejected, there is something to it.

For too many, the Democrats' vision for the future was detached from the reality of the present. It misunderstood the needs and desires of the American people. Maybe, despite the criminal charges against Trump, his brash and vulgar language, his denigration of women and minorities, and apparent flirtations with fascism, the new president actually spoke to what many people feared and, critically, to what they wanted. He recognised the precarity of their situation, their frustration with the direction of political discourse and culture, their mistrust in politicians and political institutions, and he promised them solutions. He made these people feel seen, and heard, and important. It was not that Trump was empathic: beyond performative claims of care, it was that there were empathy gaps in the Democratic Party's vision. They could not take enough of the people with them.

This perception was exacerbated by the way senior Democrat figures talked to people who disagreed. Responding to hateful comments made about Puerto Ricans by a comedian at a Trump rally, President Biden remarked that 'the only garbage I see floating out there is his supporters'.[2] His jibe was reminiscent of Hillary Clinton's 'basket of deplorables' remark in 2016.[3] These phrases re-iterated a sense of disconnect and appeared to confirm the percep-tions of disdain many of Trump's voters felt they were held in by the Washington establishment.

For those on the left or in the centre, who cannot understand either the success or appeal of figures like Donald Trump, his win does not sit easily. Donald Trump does not embody empathy, even if he understands its rhetorical power. Nor is he likely to genuinely transform American society for the better. The language of his campaign was more aggressive this time, more openly hostile to those who had underestimated him, derided him, or humiliated him since his last tenure. After his first 100 days in office, the president championed his successes: prices were down, the borders were more secure, tariffs were re-energising industry and supporting car manufacturers in the country, and illegal criminals were being deported.[4] From elsewhere, the impact looks slightly different. The administration has released January 6 rioters from prison, berated Ukrainian President Volodymyr Zelenskyy (in part for not wearing a suit), imposed tariffs on allies, offered to rebuild Gaza into the next Riviera, stationed troops at the border with Mexico, and threatened universities with legal action or cuts to their funding. People with the legal right to remain in the country have been deported or questioned, and hundreds of migrants have been flown to a notorious Salvadorian jail. Internationally, America has seen its allies lose trust and confidence in the country, and domestically it is in a more precarious position economically and politically.

Donald Trump's last period in office coincided with the rise of empathy as a civic, political, and social necessity. People protested, wore T-shirts, and carried tote bags championing empathy, and leaned into discourse on its value. But it needed more teeth, more commitment, intention, and courage. This latest outcome is not a time to shy away from empathy, or its inherent value, or to see it as a weakness, even though it is meeting fierce resistance. Instead, this moment presents a valuable, if painful, reckoning. The wrong thing to do would be to double down on the status quo: to assume the solution lies in reinforcing an economic system that perpetuates inequality and that is failing the most vulnerable and most in need. This moment raises

229

questions about what empathy really means, and where it fails. It is not enough to talk of empathy with Trump supporters in a way that implies a patronising condescension to those who think differently, or are less educated, or less worldly. Instead, genuine action is required to understand how people are experiencing the world, and to engage with them and listen so as to design policies and solutions that can yield genuine, transformative change. This is not about pandering to Trump's base but returning to the values of democracy, equality, opportunity, fairness, and empowerment, armed with a richer knowledge of the hopes, fears, and aspirations of the American people, and the desire to write new stories about how to heal the divisions.

There is power in the distress of the present. Sometimes things need to break before they can be put back together. Sometimes it takes a reckoning to bring the essential process of change – just as in August 1963, when Martin Luther King reminded the American people, and the world, in his famous 'I have a dream' speech, of the 'fierce urgency of now'.[5]

This is not only a lesson for America. Around the world, as populism gains ground, and populist leaders are emboldened by the return of Donald Trump, we have to go beyond empathy as a means, to empathy as an end, to create politics where leaders who care are in power and where people feel seen, heard, engaged, and part of our political processes. We need to redefine the idea of the good life and good society.

We know enough, we have enough insight and wisdom to be able to make the changes. The problem is not knowledge or ability, it is our will and our courage. There are a number of ways we can realise this: by getting the basics right; putting people and well-being first; embracing imagination and innovation; and expanding our circle.

GETTING THE BASICS RIGHT

A weakness of our current politics is the tendency towards gimmick politics. Politics that responds to every trend and echoes popular moods without offering a longer-term and more sustainable vision. One way to address this is to get back to basics, and for politicians to gain a deeper understanding of what the core ingredients are for people to feel seen, heard, and cared for. Politicians need to listen to concerns and address the unnecessary frictions people face in their day to day, then offer a longer view.

First published in 1943, Abraham Maslow's hierarchy of needs is a familiar shortcut for understanding human motivations and priorities.[6] At its base sit basic physiological needs, for food, water, shelter, sleep, above that are the needs for safety and security. Then moving on to psychological needs, there are needs for relationships, love, and belonging, the fundamental elements of connection, of being seen and feeling a part of something. Related are the needs for esteem, feelings of accomplishment, and respect for self and others. Finally, at the top of the pyramid, is the need for self-actualisation, and the realisation of purpose, moral alignment, creativity, and a life of meaning and intent. The schema is not perfect, nor is it a rigid or static model, and Maslow updated it several times, but it offers a useful way of thinking about the core elements of what is needed for individuals in society.

In order to improve politics and society, we have to get the basics right. If politics can secure the essentials, providing the fundamentals needed to enable people to thrive, as well as the agency and freedoms for them to take and create opportunities, we will have the scaffolding for richer, more vibrant societies. There are some core building blocks.

People should have access to clean and safe drinking water. In 2024, over 4.4 billion people in low- and middle-income countries do not have access to clean water, almost double the estimated number in 2021.[7] This exposes people to preventable diseases like cholera, polio, and dysentery – a disease that causes the deaths of around a million people each year.[8] The struggle to get water can also have a physical impact, as it has to be carried, often over long distances, with associated health costs. There are critical economic and social implications too, as water scarcity or insecure supplies can present untold risks, and hinder people's productivity and livelihoods. It impedes people's ability to live well.

Yet clean water is also an issue for many so-called advanced economies. During the 2024 UK general election, a core concern for many voters was the quality of the nation's rivers and waterways, and the high levels of sewage and agricultural waste (such as from fertilisers and chicken farms) released into them by privatised water companies, which affected many of the country's beaches and tourist destinations around the coast. In Flint, Michigan, in the United States, ten years after the crisis in 2014 that revealed harmful levels of lead and bacteria in public water, causing a widespread public health crisis in the region, the water system is still not wholly fixed.[9] Such things are basic needs and rights for every citizen. They should be quick wins, 'no-brainer' policies.

Similarly, politics should prioritise clean air, with efforts to reduce pollution and create greener, safer spaces for people to live. Poor air quality has impacts on health and well-being, as well as the environment. According to the World Health Organization, air pollution is responsible for around 7 million premature deaths a year.[10] Measures to address air quality can have positive implications for respiratory diseases and other health conditions, and dramatically improve people's quality of life. It can also decrease health inequities, as those in the lowest-income areas tend to breathe the most polluted air.[11] This is a responsibility across many government departments – health, transport, industry, the environment, and economics.

More broadly, protection of our ecosystems, natural spaces, and national parks enables people to connect more with nature. There is substantial evidence that not only does this have positive benefits at a personal and collective level for well-being and mental, physical, and cognitive health, it also develops the eco-consciousnesses and care needed to sustain and protect our natural environments.[12]

Balancing these elements should involve a more holistic and sustainable approach to food systems and agricultural structures. Those who supply food while avoiding excessive waste and surplus, and without doing disproportionate harm to the environment through emissions or toxic residues, should be rewarded. There should be greater access to healthy, affordable, and nutritious food for more people.

Healthcare should be a universal right, with accessible, affordable options that put the patients first.

As an integral part of human life, reproductive health should prioritise the health and well-being of mother and child, ensuring sound and accessible medical support, regular check-ups and the freedom of women to choose what to do with their bodies so they are not forced to endure unnecessary physical, emotional, or psychological harms.

To cultivate healthy family life, there should be reforms to maternity and paternity leave, giving all parents time and support to enjoy the early stages of their new baby's life. Paid leave is correlated with improved child health and well-being, setting the right path for a child's future, and should be a standard option for any employment. Such a measure might have the connected benefit of addressing the declining fertility rates in many countries by addressing the anxieties of many women and men about being able to afford to raise children when the imperative is to return to work too quickly.

Opportunities for a good education should be available so that even if you did not have the chance, your children might be able to escape their circumstances and build a better future, with access to fair and just systems and opportunities. Education should encourage children to learn in creative environments, where play and social and emotional learning are as valuable as academic attainment. Play sparks curiosity, emotional intelligence, and social and developmental skills, helping children connect with others. Many Scandinavian countries are good at this. In Denmark children start school at 6 years old – later than in other countries – and are encouraged to get outside and be in nature. In any Danish town, you will regularly see crocodiles of children in outdoor gear on their way to an adventure, or getting wet and muddy. Community and cohesion are also a core part of Denmark's education system, encouraging independence at the same time as building a sense of communal responsibilities. There is a healthy culture of lifelong learning.[13]

Our economic systems should be fairer and more just and equitable, especially regarding taxation. Are people being rewarded fairly, and appropriately for their efforts? There remain absurd and disproportionate differentials between the salaries of CEOs and those of essential workers. It should not be right that CEOs can take home vast bonuses while frontline workers are losing their jobs and lacking basic benefits, such as pensions and parental leave.

Policy should prioritise work–life balance so people can find meaning outside of their jobs, and invest more time and energy in family, friends, community, and other aspects of their lives. A growing number of companies around the world are moving to a four-day week, and there is growing evidence of its benefits: allowing people time to rest, spend time with loved ones, and look after their health. Data from pilot schemes in Valencia, Spain, and the UK suggest a significant decrease in stress and positive environmental impacts, as well as an increase in productivity.[14]

Welfare should provide for people who find themselves in vulnerable positions, or at times of their lives where they need additional support. Welfare has been a contentious issue in recent years, but there needs to be concerted dialogues about how societies can strengthen their metaphorical safety nets and provide vital support.

Local infrastructure should be efficient and affordable. Urban planning and social initiatives can draw on empathy to aid in the design of cities, towns, and public spaces. Many such initiatives are already doing so. Barcelona offers an example of how cities are trying to carve out more green spaces, with evidence showing that even small areas of green in urban environments can have a benefit. The

Barcelona Superblocks are creating pedestrianised areas, to help people reconnect with their communities. They provide places for children to play, for local businesses to develop, and for people to use alternative modes of transport, and boost local ecosystems and bio-diversity. They are not perfect. There are concerns about the diversity of the neighbourhoods – they tend to attract older people and families rather than young people; there can be problems with noise and pollution in surrounding areas; and there can be a misplaced sense of safety due to the traffic systems. Nevertheless, they offer a model for redesigning cities with people and well-being as an integral priority.[15]

Getting the basics right will help rebuild our societies, going some way to remove the everyday frictions and frustrations that corrode trust and belief in the political system. This must be accompanied by enhancing standards of government, with politicians admitting shortcomings and demonstrating learning and awareness. Many of these initiatives require cross-party collaboration, focused on understanding and addressing the source of the problem, and not fixating on any one specific outcome.

Underpinning all of this should be a robust, transparent, and equitable legal framework, rooted in ideas of justice and the rule of law. Upheld as a core tenet of healthy democracies, it should guarantee the protection of our basic human rights and freedoms, while ensuring society is guided by stable and accountable institutions. It should limit excesses of power and abuses of authority, and protect the most vulnerable, while instilling norms and codes for civic responsibility and participation.

Political philosopher John Rawls's concepts of the 'original position' and the 'veil of ignorance' can help in this regard. They encourage people to consider what kind of society they would design if they were to start from scratch, and what principles they would prioritise if they did not know their position or role within that society.[16] Focused on ideas of justice and fairness, they offer a useful starting point for imagining the kind of society we might want to create.

THE GOOD SOCIETY: WHO WE WANT TO BE

Beyond the stories of who we are, and how we come together, there is a need to determine who we want to be, and what matters going forward. This means redirecting our focus.

Empathy situates care, understanding, and well-being at the centre of such a narrative. Yet our current political priorities are misplaced. 'It's the economy, stupid' has long been a fundamental tenet of what matters in politics and political campaigning – a phrase coined by Bill Clinton's strategist and advisor James Carville in 1992, during the election in which Clinton stood against George H.W. Bush. It has been replicated in multiple elections around the world, highlighting the importance of people's financial well-being. It is a valuable and necessary metric. However, too great an emphasis is placed on the economy and the market, guided by sets of data that purport to capture the quality of people's lives, such as GDP, at the expense of a richer picture. Wealth, status, power, and influence are celebrated and rewarded, but, in the process, we lose sight of the true quality of people's lives, and how secure, or free, or prosperous they feel. When the priorities of any government or society are profit, power, and sectional interests, in a narrow and extractive sense, then there are few incentives or benefits for them to engage with others to create more inclusive and collaborative approaches. If our ideas of what politics is, and what it can do, are too restrictive or cynical, it is harder to break out of those confines and imagine new ways of being and coexisting.

Too great a focus on growth in the economy, and related metrics of profit, GDP, and annual average incomes reduces people to statistics and rational actors. We create meaning from more than the health of our bank accounts. Other societal data on levels of depression, anxiety, and loneliness reveal a different picture. A country may be rich while its people are struggling.

There have been some prominent efforts to offer alternative metrics of success. Bhutan famously has a Gross National Happiness

Index. This term originated in the 1970s with King Jigme Singye Wangchuck, who declared it more important than GDP. It offers a more holistic measure of a society's prosperity, considering factors such as community vitality, education, living standards, psychological well-being, and ecological diversity and resilience.[17] However, it can also present a rosier picture than the reality might suggest.

Similarly, the *World Happiness Report* offers an annual survey of the world's levels of well-being, factoring in evaluations of quality of life, and how people are feeling about their circumstances.[18] It may be a subjective guide, but it shows how reducing people to economic agents also removes what else, apart from money, makes them feel rich, and where their self-worth comes from: that is, in their connection with others, in families, communities, and activities outside of work and production. The 2025 report offered a hopeful account of happiness and the importance of caring. Among its findings were the conclusion that societal well-being is dependent on perceptions of the benevolence of others – meaning that when we look for evidence of kindness, something we often underestimate in society, we can make a difference to our well-being. In addition, 'when society is more benevolent, the people who benefit most are those who are least happy. Happiness is more equally distributed in countries with higher levels of expected benevolence'.[19] This has positive and constructive implications for how we construct societies, and the ethos and norms which dominate. When thinking about the stories we tell, a more optimistic view of human kindness as a norm in society could go a long way.[20]

A critical way to transform who we can be is to reassess the economic systems and structures that shape our societies. The worth attributed to people needs to be redefined so it is less about their employment, wealth, or status, and more about something intrinsic to each of us. Such a shift would recognise people as equal members of society and reinforce the importance of dignity and recognition in politics as a way to overcome marginalisation and disconnection. In order to do so, sociologist Michèle Lamont emphasises the need to 'question negative portrayals and stigmas', and 'reconsider how we rank the sufferings of various groups'.[21] This is not, she advocates, about removing identity and themes of racism or sexuality from efforts to solve poverty or inequality. Instead, it is about viewing these themes as intrinsically linked. To solve inequality means understanding how ideas of worth – and unworthiness – which are shaped partly by social stigmas and structural barriers, determine social and political priorities, and impede people's ability to truly flourish.

Similarly seeking to get the basics right in politics and the economy, one powerful model can be found in the concept of the doughnut. Kate Raworth, the author of *Doughnut Economics*, describes how our existing system is failing and how current thinking can lead to flawed outcomes, and outlines a new approach that puts people first. She developed the doughnut concept during her time working at Oxfam in 2011, inspired by Earth-system science. Through it she offers a 'compass for guiding humanity'.[22] The O-shaped doughnut has an inner and outer ring. The inner ring marks the social foundations on which society rests, including the vital resources people need for well-being, and the safety nets for those in the most vulnerable conditions. The outer ring denotes the ecological ceiling, and the boundaries beyond which we overshoot and go beyond what is sustainable.[23] It is a powerful and valuable approach, which offers a 'sweet spot' for balancing how we engage with our environment and ecological systems, while also ensuring people's well-being needs are met. This emphasis on creating more sustainable and equitable economic systems is gaining traction.

During her time in office, New Zealand's Prime Minister Jacinda Ardern spoke powerfully about failures in existing approaches to prosperity. In January 2019, as part of a panel on 'More than GDP' at Davos, the annual meeting of the World Economic Forum, she highlighted her vision for societal as well as economic well-being. It was about moving beyond short-term cycles, to a longer-term view of politics through the lens of 'kindness, empathy and well-being'.[24]

In May of that year, she launched the world's first 'well-being budget'.[25] It was praised internationally as a progressive milestone.[26] Its priorities included 'tackling the mental health crisis, improving child well-being, supporting Māori and Pasifika aspirations, building a productive nation, transforming the economy, and investing in the country'. While it acknowledged the importance of economic growth and traditional fiscal measures of success, it also emphasised the need to recognise other metrics of the health of the nation – of the people, of communities, and of natural resources.[27] In her speech presenting the budget to Parliament, the prime minister highlighted one of the most pressing priorities – the mental health crisis and the growing rates of suicide in the country, especially among Māori men.[28] Care and empathy were front and centre.

However, the challenge with such ideas is they can be short-lived. They capture a moment, and an aspiration, but then do not always have staying power. Addressing mental health is critical, but for sustainable outcomes it requires not only support to frontline initiatives but a deeper unpicking of the conditions and societal context that contribute to mental illness. In New Zealand the idea of a well-being economy was quite top-down, rather than engaging with and empowering communities and civil society to help inform people and carry the initiative. A dramatic overhaul of an economy to prioritise well-being and care is still dependent on a strong economy and surplus capital. The vision of such a budget in New Zealand encountered Covid-19, and a global downturn in productivity, which derailed its intended vision and impact somewhat. Yet, while this episode offers lessons for the future about the balance between political vision and practical realities, the concept of well-being should not be disregarded. It is gaining ground, with civil society, non-state organisations, and other countries and leaders who are continuing to keep the idea alive.

That same year, in July 2019, Scotland's Prime Minister Nicola Sturgeon gave a TED Talk on why well-being should be a political priority: 'what we choose to measure as a country matters. It really matters, because it drives political focus, it drives public activity.'[29] It was welcome recognition for a country that has been leading the way.

The ideals of empathy and compassion are already mobilising these different forms of politics. Other countries and governments are exploring similar models. In Canberra, the Australian Capital Territory (ACT) state government's own Wellbeing Budget 2024–25 centres the quality of life of people in the capital both individually and as a community. Prioritising housing, physical and mental health, early years care, the cost of living, women's rights, and marginalisation, it introduces Wellbeing Impact Assessments (WIAs) to measure the success of policies, while recognising that such an approach is a longer-term investment unlikely to yield quick results.[30]

Katherine Trebeck is one of the leading international voices on well-being economics and an inspiring advocate for change. When we met in Canberra, she had just returned from time in Lismore, New South Wales, Australia, and had been energised to find enthusiasm there for a more community-based economy. This work has animated her for many years, since discovering the power to rethink our economic models to transform society. 'The biggest form of stress', she notes, 'is the gap between expectation and reality.'[31] She is motivated by a desire not only to alleviate the suffering caused by our economic problems, but to get to the root causes of how they came about. It is therefore not just about introducing measures to help people who are living on the street but understanding why and how they came to be there, and what interventions or initiatives might prevent that happening. Empathy and compassion are part of her approach, as she explains: the way to understand a problem is through noticing, understanding, and taking action.

She points out how, at times of crisis, we can tell who cares about people and community and who cares about profit. She recalls a recent instance of airport hotels raising their prices when planes were grounded and people were stuck, compared to during the pandemic when the whisky distillers in Scotland turned to making hand sanitiser to help the care effort.[32]

Well-being economics is about designing the economy so it better meets the needs of people and planet. This requires change at the local level (not least local ownership), in how tax systems are designed, in the sorts of firms that operate, in the measures of success that are used, and how the role of the economy is conceptualised. There is proof that different economic models can yield real change. Emilia-Romagna in northern Italy is one of the country's most prosperous regions. It is rich in tourism, culture, history, and amazing food. There are over 5,500 cooperatives there, responsible for around a third of the region's GDP, and constituting 5.7% of cooperatives across Italy.[33] Their ethos and origins can be found in intellectual thought from the eighteenth century on ethical economics, especially the work of Antonio Genovesi, which advocates 'an ethical and anthropological view of a market based on the promotion of the common good and societal well-being'.[34] They are heavily networked, both within and across sectors, which contributes to the resilience of the system, and ensures local communities, employment, and industry thrive. Critically, they have found ways to balance profit and employment, adjusting when times are harder to protect employees.[35]

Well-being economics in the round turns the lens away from sterile ideals of growth, which are insufficient and distortive metrics of life quality, to centre people and a richer understanding of what people need to feel and to have in order to live well. This emphasis on local communities and more circular or communal economies not only offers spaces for exchange and interaction but can also contribute to a deeper sense of belonging and meaning at a more local level. We get to feel part of something, and to contribute in turn, building trust, connection, and local resilience.

However, for this to transpire and become a reality, we need politics that embraces imagination, creativity, and the capacity to innovate and yield change.

INNOVATING CHANGE

Those in power have limited incentives to transform a system that serves them. Yet innovation is essential to keep politics dynamic and responsive. Politics cannot afford to become static, entrenched in the status quo. It has to adapt and change, responding to societal needs and developments.

Technology is going to be a critical domain that could undermine politics or re-energise it, offering us opportunities to connect in new ways. Already in the United Kingdom in 2024, an online avatar – of an older well-tailored male politician 'AI Steve' – was put forward as a candidate. It was rudimentary, but illustrative of the future potential. AI Steve was 'The only candidate who can have a conversation with 45,000 constituents at the same time and form policies based on what's just been discussed.'[36] It was an experiment in more expansive democracy. Yet it is also subject to similar problems of the media, as the algorithm guiding AI Steve and his outputs will reflect the biases and political preferences of its programmer.

There is some early evidence that perhaps AI can help us find common ground in debates around contentious issues.[37] A recent experiment involved researchers training a large language model called a Habermas Machine, which could then help mediate discussions of contentious issues – like immigration and Brexit – in the UK. They found that AI can help people find common ground through deliberative processes, and successfully incorporated dissenting views, while also adhering to the sentiments of the majority. In the experiments the Habermas Machine outperformed human mediators, it generated more consensus, and was able to incorporate more minority views to avoid people feeling excluded.[38] It has the potential to work alongside other participatory methods to enhance dialogue and overcome divides.

There can be a resistance to technology in democracies. And with just cause: there has been an expansion of government surveillance as well as the omniscience of big technology, tracking our every click and movement. Given the rise of misinformation and some of the social harms it does to mental health, well-being, and connection, especially – but not exclusively – to young people, there is good reason to be concerned about the societal impacts.

Innovation requires leadership: people who are able to countenance different approaches and shift the status quo. It incurs setbacks and false starts, which demand leaders and politicians, at all levels, who can tolerate a certain degree of failure in the process. It is dependent on vision and courage, and an ability to bring people along in the process.

Taiwan offers a fascinating example of how a country has welcomed innovation to facilitate people's engagement with government and increase transparency and accountability in politics and public institutions. Over the past few years, it has embraced the coexistence of technology and democracy, led by its former, and first, Digital Minister Audrey Tang. They offer a dynamic vision for technology and for how people engage with politics and claim greater agency within society. They want politics to be 'fast, fair and fun'.[39]

We stand at a crossroads. Technology could drive us apart, sowing chaos and conflict that bring down social order. It could suppress the human diversity that is its lifeblood, homogenizing us in a singular technical vision. Or it could dramatically enrich our diversity while strengthening the ties across it.[40]

During the pandemic, Audrey found there was a 'twin-demic' with the rise of misinformation and disinformation contributing to societal tensions. Mobilising the power of people, they created a public dashboard where people could share information, and they promoted the value of humour and memes to make light of the rumours being spread, and to encourage greater media awareness, in a more fun way.

Audrey's priority is for technology to align with societies, and not the other way around. Yet this also depends on a technologically literate population, and a government that trusts its citizens and gives them far greater agency within political processes. Audrey's strategy has been effective. In 2014 trust was at 9% in Taiwan; in 2024 it had risen to over 70%. This trust is not just a reflection of a society's confidence in government, it is seen as a critical asset, especially in its technology and software sectors, offering a unique advantage.[41]

As citizens, our capacity for engagement with the world should continue to expand. Technology, used wisely, can amplify empathy.[42] It affords us more opportunities to learn about, experience, and understand the world around us than ever before, and there is greater awareness of our responsibilities and our ability to effect change.

Virtual reality is just one among many increasingly useful tools that reveal the lived experiences of different people, bringing diverse worlds to our rooms and to exhibition spaces. Mexican director Alejandro G. Iñárritu, for example, has used virtual and immersive reality to reconstruct the experience of Mexican and Central American refugees in his Carne y Arena.[43] While there are dangers that such innovations may distort our perceptions or be used for propaganda, they can also elicit more care, more awareness and connection with the world around us and our role within it. Initial evidence suggests that virtual reality can shape voter behaviour.[44]

Tactile and sensory immersive experiences organised by creative organisations such as Empathy Action can make experiences more vivid and visceral, provoking emotional responses and helping people understand the implications and costs of policies.[45] Ben Solanky is the co-founder and director of this organisation, which leads initiatives on poverty traps and refugees, giving people vital insights into the dilemmas facing people in precarious situations. He has a background working in the humanitarian space, and speaks of it as inspiring his present commitment to change and his pragmatic optimism about the future. He has 'seen so much energy and good that has centred around passionate people who cared'.

I have not had the privilege of experiencing one of Empathy Action's immersive workshops in person, but via Zoom Ben walks me through 'Desperate Journeys', about the experiences of refugees trying to get across borders in treacherous circumstances. The staging is elaborate and convincing, progressively darker and more oppressive. He stops at each decision point – a tent where a family is gathering until conflict erupts, a legal checkpoint, a corrupt border guard, a smuggler. At each stage decisions become more urgent and more impossible. Through the screen alone my heart races, and I find myself searching for a different unobtainable and unrealistic option than the stark choices on offer. The experience offers debrief spaces, where people have time to catch their breath and reflect more on what they have witnessed and felt. These are what Ben terms 'sacred spaces' that contribute to deeper empathy and compassion.

In 2024, 3,000 people went through Empathy Action's experiences, held at different locations in the UK. Ben explains how a key part of the experience is 'the "stepping into" a liminal space of understanding. Or perhaps "stepping out" of our current corridor of understanding into a space where for the briefest of moments people can allow their imagination and skills of deep listening to be exercised with the people in the situations that attract too easily our judgements.' Such initiatives are important, giving people space to confront parts of life that they do not encounter every day, and to see, behind the headlines and the scare stories, the reality of what others are going through. 'The world doesn't need more charities like us', Ben notes. 'It does, however, need more people to be charitable in it.'[46]

In this way, too, artists, journalists, filmmakers, and storytellers are a critical part of the symbiotic relationship between government and society. They can shine a spotlight on the detrimental impact of different policies, on the suffering of people around the world, or on the ways in which we are more alike than different. They offer stories, experiences, and pictures that galvanise action, or make people think, becoming agents that foster empathy. Experiments suggest that empathy can improve perceptions of stigmatised groups.[47] In the process they widen the ambit of our concern.

EXPANDING THE CIRCLE

Originally published in 1981, philosopher and ethicist Peter Singer's book *The Expanding Circle* challenges the idea that we should care only for our closest family and community and instead posits that we have a choice to expand our circles of moral concern for more people, and even nonhumans. To achieve progress and realise our highest potential, we have to go beyond caring only for our closest communities to bring about real change.[48] This means moving away from self-interest and self-protection as the instinctive response and taking a wider perspective on what is good for society.

This involves breaking down the existing barriers to entry and widening the possibilities for participation. It is not only about political representation, but about the focus of political debates and the voices who can have a say. Too many political systems reward older, loyal voters who have been consistent taxpayers and have established interests in the status quo. More needs to be done to bring in the voices of younger voters, who may still be studying or building their lives, but who are deeply invested in the future. Some of the most inspiring people I meet are young people seeking change.

Fatou Jeng is one of them. Originally from the Gambia, she has done more in politics and climate activism than many twice her age. The World Wide Fund for Nature named her one of Africa's Top 100 Young Conservationists in 2022. She is a negotiator focusing on issues of gender and climate for her country at the United Nations Framework Convention on Climate Change (UNFCCC) and is a climate advisor to the United Nations' Youth Advisory Group.[49] Growing up in an agricultural family in the Gambia, she saw how her father's crops were depleted over time, how changes in the environment were having a direct impact on people's livelihoods.

She has a history of leadership, serving as head girl several times during her earlier education, and then becoming the first female president of the National Union of the Gambia's students, sitting on some of the most senior university councils alongside ministers. This experience helped her connect more with members of government and political leaders, and she learned how to communicate and engage with them in a way that could convey what was needed and why.

While the scale of the challenge is huge, Fatou is encouraged by how much more open politicians are to the perspectives of young people. She tells me about how, when senior politicians were invited to a Youth Conference in 2024, they remarked that it was an eye-opening experience to see the energy young people were investing in the nation's political future. As a result of this greater youth activism in the country, Fatou can see real shifts in how much more engaged young people are in politics and how more politicians are showing enthusiasm for and interest in their perspectives. Neither the government nor the many activist movements can do it alone, however. There has to be cooperation in order to achieve real change. This means getting yet more people on board and invested in the process.

To do this, a large part of the work she leads and is involved in develops literacy among younger people about politics and climate change. In the Gambia, as in many countries, there is still limited climate education. Increasing awareness and understanding of the issues helps people to realise their scale and importance, and prepares them for the necessary shifts in behaviour. The work of young people is vital: 'if we sit and leave it in the hands of older people ... [they] will do what is best for their own interests and not the greater good of the people'.[50]

She is unequivocal that young people should not be engaged with in a tokenistic way. Too often in politics, leaders can use engagement with youth initiatives as a performative aspect of their campaign or their image. Instead, such engagement should be sincere, meaningful, and mutually collaborative.[51] Young people may have the ideas, the imagination, and the energy, as well as the knowledge of how to engage across media platforms, yet they do not always have the power to really effect change in policy. We should change this.

Another person working across the local and international level to transform politics through youth activism is John Paul Jose. He is from Kerala in India, one of the greenest and lushest parts of the country, and grew up on a mountain where he would wake each day to the sunrise and birdsong. As a result he, too, was from early life very connected to nature, within a community traditionally engaged in agriculture and living on their inherited ancestral lands, acutely conscious of the impact of climate change on the livelihoods of him and those around him. This experience, his education, and the daily lived experience of coexisting with nature inform his approach. He wants to see understanding of nature itself to inform and guide climate solutions. He saw how social issues are often interconnected with the environment, rather than separate, and these two dimensions are what motivates him. He gradually became involved in social movements and sought to understand all he could about the issues, until this became an integral part of his life. This experience gave him insights into how change occurs and what is needed. 'Young people', he notes, 'are learning a lot, they are curious', and they have the energy to effect change.[52]

He emphasises the importance of grassroots initiatives, connecting policy and politics with the experiences of people on the ground, especially in rural areas, helping those directly affected by climate challenges. A large part of this involves listening to what people are actually experiencing and using that to guide policy solutions. There can be no one-size-fits-all approach, and he cautions against a tendency of external states to assume they have more knowledge or insight that can be imported to a particular region or other scenarios without understanding the place.

For both Fatou and John Paul, a common thread in their activism is the importance of political literacy, of raising awareness of the real challenges faced by people on the ground and generating awareness among people of their role and agency in politics. They are both engaged with other national and international activists, learning, sharing insights, and becoming involved in initiatives that are networked and global. While climate may be their guiding issue at present, it is not the only cause they care about. They also speak of justice, equity, humanitarian concerns, with a passion and determination that change is possible, but also unavoidable.

Young people are innovative in politics and consider power in different ways. They may be constrained to some extent by familial obligations, and lack of access to the highest decision-making offices, but they have a lot to share, and new ways of doing things that can strengthen our political imagination and perceptions of available options. In countries like Bangladesh they have been at the forefront of protests against the government.[53]

Many organisations are paying more attention to the power and importance of youth activism. The United Nations has a number of initiatives encouraging youth engagement, and offering training and toolkits for young people and youth parliaments.[54] In 2024, Transparency International partnered with youth groups around the world to call out corruption in climate action, and support the space and vibrancy of civil society at a time of increasing encroachment of vested and corporate interests.[55]

There needs to be a greater dialogue across generations, to understand the unique challenges people face, whether this means old age care and the vulnerability of ageing, or the precariousness that Generation Z is feeling at a time of economic crises, rising costs, and shrinking opportunities. Such intergenerational empathy can help yield new ideas to address problems in ways that can be mutually beneficial.

When we expand our circles of concern, empathy can be a tool for rethinking challenges and finding more creative approaches.

Empathy directed beyond humans is a feature of new climate action and environmentalism that emphasises sustainability and coexistence.[56] Given the scale and urgency of the climate crisis, and the imperative for leadership in this space, our empathy must extend to the wider world and natural environment in which we live. This 'biosphere consciousness' is important in enabling us to internalise our interconnectedness with the world around us,[57] building on the scientific thinking of Abraham Maslow, who argues against detached and distant objectivity, and figures such as Jane Goodall who approach nature with a 'caring objectivity'.[58]

Rather than seeing nature as something humans dominate, use, and exploit, there should be greater attunement to the world around us. Calls for such a shift come from multiple quarters. Climate leaders emphasise the importance of care and understanding for how we coexist with our natural environment. This means telling richer stories about our relationship with the ecosystems on which we depend.

There is also a lot to learn from Indigenous knowledge and insight – people who have lived on the land, and with the land, who know its stories and its secrets and how to care for it in a sustainable way, safeguarding it for future generations. Robin Wall Kimmerer is one of many advocates for such a shift. She is a member of the Potawatomi Nation (traditionally based in the Great Lakes region of North America), and is a botanist, author, and environmental activist. Her bestselling books like *Braiding Sweetgrass* and *The Serviceberry* articulate the value of Indigenous wisdom and experience in treating our environment with more reverence and respect. She encourages new ways of thinking about, and understanding, the land and respecting it as part of our ecosystem, and champions new ways of engaging with the world and each other that emphasise the importance of reciprocity, abundance, and the gift economy.[59]

Yet this is not just about stories and wisdom, but about finding legal and political mechanisms to safeguard and protect the environment and incentivise necessary change.

There are already signs of shifts. In March 2017, the Whanganui River in Aotearoa (New Zealand) became the first river to gain legal personhood, in recognition of its importance to the local peoples.[60] And in Mexico in December 2024, the government became the first country to sign protections for animal welfare into its constitution,[61] reflecting growing significance accorded to the topic in the region.

We should also give greater consideration to the future and to the sustainability of our politics. In the Indigenous philosophy of Northern America, the concept of responsibility to 'Seven Generations'[62] offers valuable insights about how we might take better care of future genera-tions and maintain our environment. Originating with the Great Law of Peace (Kaianere'ko:wa), which is dated to 1451 CE, though may have been earlier, it is an Iroquois idea, initiated by the journey of Ayenwahtha (commonly known as Hiawatha). He wanted to avenge the deaths of his family, but instead met Deganawida – the Great Peacemaker. They trav-elled together across what is now Ontario, Quebec, and New York State seeking to reconcile the tribes. Helped by the women elders, they created and maintained a federal model to aid unity, and those involved became collectively known as the Haudenosaunee (People of the Long House).[63] Their emphasis is on thinking not only of today, but of the lives of those seven generations into the future. Our actions reverberate through the ages, and we have responsibilities to those not yet born to protect the environment and consider the effects and sustainability of our actions.

*

There are, undoubtedly, difficult times ahead. Sweeping changes to our politics, some of which have been suggested in this book, are hard and take time, patience, and persistence. Looking to the future, and the scale of what is needed, the idea of a charismatic saviour can be appealing. It can feel easier to wait for someone to explain the source of our current problems and offer a vision for a better future.

However, waiting for such a figure removes our own agency, and exacerbates a sense of passivity and apathy in our politics. We cannot assume that things would be better if only we had better leaders, if only the people at the top exhibited certain qualities that we see only too rarely. Such an approach is risky. For those in leadership positions, it sets up unattainable ideals that no human can match. And it makes moving towards better politics, more inclusive societies, and more care, something transient, that lasts only so long as certain leaders retain power. This means it risks quickly coming undone once they leave office, as they should at the end of their democratic mandate.

Even when the present looks bleak or difficult, there are many grounds for hope. There is an opportunity to rethink our basic assumptions, to get back to basics, and to ask critical questions about how people are experiencing the world, and what tangible, practical measures are needed for change to occur. This requires politicians to hold less tightly to the status quo, and to connect with those who share similar values and ideas about what a good society should be, and why it is so important.

Embracing transformation and seeing the benefits of change requires courage, vision, and imagination. It involves expanding the circle, not shrinking it. It involves trusting that the more people that are invested and engaged in change, the more sustainable and responsive such change will be to the needs and aspirations of the people. We have to take risks, to imagine and explore more creative approaches that are rooted in community, in an idea of collective good and social benefit, and not just increasing personal profit or corporate interests.

Such innovation naturally incurs a chance of failure. Rather than fearing it, we should use it to learn, and iterate, and improve. This requires courageous leadership, and more honest conversations between politicians and people. This reaffirms the importance of participatory processes, that bring people on board early to contribute to and shape the change.

We are social beings, programmed to coexist with others, both for well-being and basic survival. We need to reconnect with each other, to strengthen community. There is no quick fix or easy short cut to genuine and lasting transformation. But done right, it will be worth the effort.

Conclusion

Transforming our politics is a process. It will take time and patience, and the investment and belief of people across society. However, to achieve it requires a reckoning – with history, with culture, with the challenges we face today, and with ourselves. The status quo cannot hold. It does not serve us, and we deserve better than the politics that plays to our base instincts or meets the bare minimum standards of a functioning democracy.

Empathy is a key part of this transformation. We cannot create better politics unless we understand how different people view the world, and what they need from it. We cannot build more vibrant democracies and healthier societies, unless we can work together to coexist and find common ground. Our ability to meet the challenges of the future is dependent on our capacity to find strength and connection with each other, and with a shared vision and story of who we are and what we are trying to create.

However, it is not enough to talk about empathy. Nor to promote listening and understanding if it is not matched by action. Empathy in politics should be empathy in action. It should be incorporated into how we design policy, in how we build deeper, more construc-tive connections between politicians and the people, in how we create civic spaces where people can feel a sense of belonging, and a part of community where they are more familiar and connected with their neighbours and those around them.

Rather than pushing for a political system where we all think alike, and coalesce around narrow ideas of interests and identities, empathy compels a deeper, more inclusive approach that both respects and embraces our differences. It invites us to go beyond the surface level to the underlying causes. In the process, it offers to reinvigorate democracy, by putting people (and their intrinsically messy complexity) at the heart of politics.

Nevertheless, empathy and politics is a vast topic. This book has only scratched the surface. Although it began as a study of leaders and leadership, the limitations of empathy in this space and the visible and manifold ways that it is constrained by systems and structures expanded this book's focus and made the imperative for empathy to be a part of politics at all levels more urgent. In the process, by giving a more global take on empathy in politics, it has enabled an exploration of the concept and its role in different contexts, countries, and diverse political systems. This reveals its universality, as a vital part of human relations and a means by which we create change in our societies. However, it also comes at the expense of a deeper appreciation of specific leaders and politicians, or of how it works in any one country, and the more nuanced factors that might facilitate or impede it in practice. It is just one contribution in a much bigger conversation.

Empathy is variable and imperfect, like anything human. That does not make it any less important or essential. Calling for more empathy comes with inevitable tensions and limitations. For even as it should be a core part of healthy and cooperative democratic societies, boundaries and standards must be taken into consideration.

As we have seen, it can be used as a means of connection and motivation by politicians on the left and right, and not always with the best outcomes. It can be used rhetorically, as an integral part of

discourses that resonate with the mood of the moment and the interests of specific audiences, with little changing at the level of policy.
Populist leaders may use it to cultivate a strong in-group following
and a sense of national identity among a people, at the expense of
those they consider undeserving or outside their core group. Similarly,
politicians on the left may champion it as a core part of progressive
politics but not necessarily apply it equally to those with whom they
disagree.

The task now, therefore, is to move beyond using the language of
empathy as a means in politics without the substance and the power
to back it up. For empathy to be transformative, it needs to be a
central part of the political ends we seek – that is, more vibrant,
inclusive, pluralistic societies, in which more people feel engaged and
invested. This requires a restoration of trust, in our politics, our institutions, and in each other.

We need leaders who are not just empathetic and can put people
first, but who demonstrate courage, vision, integrity, and an ability to
build bridges across parties, and across political affiliations. If too
little empathy can leave people feeling disconnected, but empathy
wrongly applied can fuel polarisation, then it is imperative to have
leaders who can marshal it wisely, who can identify its benefits for
connection, but also explain the value of embracing, not excluding,
others. We need leaders who can communicate effectively to reach
broader groups of people, and tell a new, more hopeful, inclusive
story of the future, and of who we are as societies, through weaving a
narrative that recognises how intertwined our fates are.

However, empathy is more than a leadership quality or trait. We
should not rely on empathic individuals alone. Instead, empathy
should be a fundamental part of our political ecosystem, of how we
think about the problems we face, and be a means by which we explore
more creative solutions. In the process, as empathy empowers more
people to be a part of our political processes, it has to coexist with, and
enhance, vital democratic principles, such as fundamental freedoms,

the right to expression, association, and movement, the rule of law, and the freedom of our media.

This presents a unique task for our politicians and political leaders. They need not only to listen, but to act, and to address the systemic and structural barriers that prevent people from being able to thrive or from expressing their democratic rights. There is a need for humility and a willingness to learn and adapt. This requires bigger, more fundamental questions to be asked about the core assumptions driving our vision of society: What does a 'good society' really look like? Where are we going wrong? What must change? And how can we create and achieve better outcomes for citizens, and for our communities?

Empathy exposes the failings of politics, by opening and enabling conversations about people's grievances, their mistrust, and their frustrations. It offers insights into how people feel they have been let down by a system and those who represent them.

Empathy therefore has to be matched by courage. Creating necessary change compels a step into the discomfort of uncertainty and unpopularity, and hard conversations. It entails the long, difficult process of doing the work to address present failings. It will not be easy, nor quick. But it is essential.

In its ideal form, empathy in politics and leadership is rooted in the collective emotional power of hope, of care for others, and respect and dignity. Power is to be found in what we can achieve together, for each other, rather than something imposed for the general good. What is the purpose of power if tightly held at the expense of society's well-being? At the heart of politics, there needs to be care, connection, and respect for others. It should be integral to our way of being that we relate to others with dignity and respect, that we seek to understand before we judge, and that we do not intentionally dehumanise or demean others.

Nevertheless, it is not enough to seek hope and action solely from our politicians. We cannot look to them for better visions of the future and wait for them to create it. We have to be proactive in supporting the conditions and environment that make them capable of delivering on it, and to claim the power we have, as citizens and communities, to make such change a reality.

Over the course of writing this book, the people I met with and spoke to, who gave their time and wisdom, consistently inspired me and gave me hope that this is already happening.

Even with the scale of the challenge ahead, there are so many grounds for growth and optimism. Movements are afoot around the world to create positive change and empower citizens. From climate action in Kerala or the Gambia, to community incubators in Denmark, to new media initiatives in the Middle East and Africa, and innovative crowd-sourced technological solutions in Taiwan, consensus is growing that we can do more and create better political systems that serve us and foster a vital sense of belonging. People who have not traditionally seen themselves in politics are finding their voice and the energy to make change. And they are finding each other. In communities, in online spaces, in schools and universities and town halls, they are united by a vision and a desire for deeper connection, for more inclusion, understanding, equity, and opportunities.

Hope is the well-spring for this transformation and change, courage gives it substance and energy, and empathy is how we come together to tell a richer story and make it a reality.

A Plan for Action

This book has explored ideas and examples of how empathy is being incorporated into politics at various levels. But we can go further. Below are some practical ideas to bring empathy into the heart of politics, into leadership, and into our communities to aid the momentum for change.

NATIONAL

Reframe the Problem

The problems we are facing are about the economy, security, welfare, and many other critical issues, yet they are also about connection, community, resilience, and general well-being. Our politics needs to look more creatively at the underlying causes of current frustrations and find more innovative, human-centred solutions. Continuing with the status quo will not work. We need different frames of reference that put people first, and more creative means of looking at issues – beyond growth, security, and budgets – to gain a richer view of society and what is needed.

A PLAN FOR ACTION

Engage in Genuine Dialogue

Dialogue involves an interest in speaking with people and listening to their perspectives in order to bring change to society. However, too often when people call for dialogue it can be in name but not in content. For genuine dialogue, politicians and citizens alike have to actively listen to different voices, to be curious about what they have to say, including any critique, and be willing to engage in ongoing conversations. It is an iterative process, involving listening and learning and feeding back.

Speak Across the Divide

Politicians need to speak to people beyond their immediate supporters, to represent a wider proportion of their country and listen to and seek to understand their needs, hopes, and concerns. This involves moving beyond narrow partisan interests. They cannot afford to ignore or diminish the needs of those who vote for other parties. Instead, more politicians should be able to acknowledge and reflect on how their politics might impact those beyond their base and seek points of commonality, accommodating a diversity of views and – critically – legitimising the normality of difference.

Foster Bipartisanship on Common Issues of Concern

To realise change, we need politicians who can work across the floor with other parties and groups on common issues; who can build alliances on climate change, on health, on tax, and on transport; who can find people who share similar visions of the outcome, even if they have alternative approaches to the process. This will inevitably involve dialogue, compromise, and courage, but it will help to create more long-term, sustainable policies that last beyond an electoral term and that have greater investment at the legislative level. We need more politicians who have constructive cross-party working relationships that bridge the divides in government and model the potential for cooperation in the political sphere.

Enhance Public Engagement

Politicians should invest more time and energy in supporting and engaging with the public through participatory democracy, citizens' assemblies, and other forms of outreach. Engagement facilitates dialogue and supports trust building. It also reveals new insights and perspectives that can help strengthen the design and delivery of policy initiatives. It enhances the connection between politics and the people and helps policy become more iterative, enabling people to feel more involved in matters of state.

Escape the Bubble

Politicians have to leave the bubble of the political capital regularly. The world often looks very different in the regions from the political centre. By getting out and meeting more people, listening to how the centre looks from different parts of the country, and how policy is translated to the frontline, they will be better equipped to adjust accordingly.

Restore Trust

Trust is essential for effective politics and healthy democracies. Politicians, political leaders, and institutions need to earn back the trust that has been lost. They need to address corruption, limit the disproportionate and distortive influence of big money and lobby groups, and create more integrity and honesty in politics, with accountability and transparency measures. Those in politics at all levels have to demonstrate they are trustworthy, earn that title, and work with the public more constructively.

Change the Political Environment

Toxic workplaces can impede empathy and sap energy, whether in an office, a government department, or a legislative institution. The political work environment must be transformed to offer more support and enable people to do their best, delivering on their commitment to constituents without burning out. A better balance must be found between incentives to stand and the standards of the profession, to increase the chance that we get the right people in office.

Increase Representation and Diversity

Our politics will not change until it reflects the societies it serves. We need to drastically increase representation of all groups in political office, through initiatives, mentoring, and creating a more conducive environment. This involves identifying barriers to entry and removing impediments to the job.

Develop Emotional Literacy and Read the Room

Emotional literacy is an asset for effective leadership. We need politicians who can demonstrate care and manage their emotions. They should be aware and literate in how emotions shape decision-making and the interpretations of events. They should be attuned and responsive to public moods, and able to reassure and guide the people, especially at times of crisis and division. Although training can help, it also involves normalising emotions in the public space.

Deliver Training for Politicians

Develop more training for politicians to help them adapt to life in the public eye and the demands of our political systems. Provide support and mentoring and offer opportunities for continued development as careers progress.

Centre Empathy in Policymaking

Policymaking should engage with citizens and consider how those who use the services designed by governments, or who are on the receiving end of initiatives, experience policy. Service users should be brought in earlier and connected with frontline service providers.

Policymakers should be trained in empathy and given the space and time to think more creatively about the problems they are trying to solve. What is the real-world impact of a catchy idea? Does it help those who need it most? What are its long-term implications?

Trust Citizens More

Give people more agency and more opportunities to voice their ideas for solutions to the problems affecting their communities and daily lives. Policy does not have to be centralised; it can be shared. Much can be learned from those already on the frontline. Start from a position of trust and see it reciprocated.

Lower the Voting Age

As part of efforts to connect more people with politics, governments should lower the voting age. If 16-year-olds can pay taxes, get married, raise a child, join the military, or drive a car, then they should be able to have a say on how their country is run. Lowering the voting age will help energise younger people who feel disenchanted or let down by older generations and help deepen engagement in politics from a young age.

Invest in Culture and the Arts

Culture and the arts are often on the chopping block when budgets are tight, yet in the long term, investment in culture and the arts benefit society.[1] We learn who we are through music, theatre, art, and the humanities. As much as data and science are integral to our modern world, we also need to connect with our intrinsic humanness, to create new stories and weave new meanings through creativity, which encourages people to think and feel about themselves and others in different ways.

COLLECTIVE AND COMMUNAL

Be a Good Citizen

Just as we have rights within society, we also have responsibilities to our neighbours and community. We should keep each other safe, check in with those who may be the most vulnerable in our community, look after shared spaces such as parks and squares, support local infrastructure like local shops, libraries, sports centres, and community halls. That is, we should all cultivate community.

Be Active in Your Community

Get involved in local community activities. Volunteer, join clubs and associations, get to know people different from yourself but interested in similar hobbies or passions. This will help you find connections outside of your comfort zone and help develop a deeper sense of belonging.

Find an Issue You Are Passionate About

Whether it is climate change, tax equality, access to healthcare, or the rights of animals, find something that you are interested in and care about, and learn more. If you want to be more active, join a community who are putting ideas into action. Politics can appear vast, but focus on what matters to you, to facilitate the small, necessary, steps for change.

Participate in Local Politics and Citizens' Assemblies

There are increasing opportunities to get involved in participatory democracy and to take an active part in debating pressing issues at a local and national level. Organisations like DemocracyNext offer resources and guidance on how to get involved, and how to run such debates and assemblies.[2] If you want more sustained commitment, you could become a member of a local school board or a local councillor, or get involved with an issue you care about in your community.

Develop Civics Education

Bring empathy into schools and develop greater political and emotional literacy and the ability to participate in political debates. Help people engage with politics from a young age, so they understand their rights and responsibilities, as well as the complexities of political change. Encourage people to understand their agency and start training the practice of democracy early.

Hold the Media to Account

We have to become more media literate and hold what is published to higher standards focused on truthful, honest, and balanced reporting. The media should tell richer and more complex stories that inform us of the challenges ahead, convey the complexity and different sides of stories, but also give more of a human face to current affairs so we get a deeper understanding of the implications of events and policy decisions. We should hold all forms of media to account for misreporting and spreading misinformation, highlight instances where bias is leading to a distortion of events, and ensure that fact-checking is used to substantiate stories.

PERSONAL STEPS

Be Curious and Listen

So often when we speak with people, we do not truly listen to what they have to say, but spend that time anticipating what we might say in return. Ask more questions, be curious. If you don't understand their perspective, ask follow-up questions, don't assume you know what they mean. Suspend judgement. Consider not only how they think, but also how things feel. What is not being said? What is it difficult for them to say?

Practise Being Uncomfortable

We cannot create smooth lives where we never encounter resistance or difficulties. We will confront ideas and ways of living that make little sense to us, and some conversations will be more trying than others. Some may force you to consider how your own perspective is not complete. Lean into the discomfort and get curious about why you feel that way.

Understand and Own Your Biases

We will never truly be impartial. Our own political views can feel instinctive and sometimes visceral parts of our identities, but we can get better at understanding, owning and acknowledging our own biases. We can engage in self-reflection to learn more about how we view the world. We can seek input on how to navigate our biases, and endeavour to speak with others with respect and dignity wherever possible, in recognition that their viewpoint is as real to them as ours is to us.

Increase Your Emotional Literacy

We are often bad at truly understanding what we feel and how that shapes how we interpret and respond to the world. We need to invest more in what Susan David calls 'Emotional Agility',[3] a capacity to interpret emotions and not hold them too closely, conscious of their transient nature and role in shaping our perspectives. Marc Brackett suggests the RULER method to enhance your emotional intelligence – 'Recognizing, Understanding, Labeling, Expressing, and Regulating'.[4] The more we talk about emotions as assets, not weaknesses, in public discourse, the easier this becomes.

Consume a Varied Media Diet

We all have our go-to outlets that speak our language and prioritise the issues that matter most to us. Read around more, watch different news channels. Look at how they frame a topic differently, what they focus on, what this reveals about how other people think, and where there are points of connection. Break out of your echo chamber and confuse your algorithms. At the same time, try to limit the time spent on social media and be more conscious of how it occupies the hours of your day and distracts your attention, in order to be more intentional and present when determining how and when you consume information.

Set Boundaries as Kindly as Possible

Disagreement is an inherent part of democracy, yet empathy does not mean you have to accept bad behaviour or offensive views. When you encounter such behaviour, if possible, try to set a boundary kindly. This is easier said than done, but rather than escalate it, in a contest neither side is likely to win, be firm, but fair, while true to your own ideals and values. Ask for the topic to change, state firmly that you disagree and do not want to discuss the matter. Let them know such language or terminology is unacceptable. Try to avoid demeaning them in return.

Call People In, Not Out

At a time of 'cancel culture', and platforms where people can be called out for their views, their actions, their pasts, we need to call people in. In the words of Loretta Ross, this means 'instead of using anger, blaming and shaming as your method of achieving accountability, you use love, grace and respect'.[5] This opens pathways for deeper understanding and connection by not invalidating or demeaning the other person.

Recognise Your Positionality and Privilege

Some of these steps may be less risky for some members of society than others. It is far easier to push back against insults or harm when you occupy a privileged position in society. Not everyone enjoys such benefits. Stand with those who risk more to share their voice. Be an ally.

Practise Grace

There will always be some bad actors who want to disrupt and break things with little disregard for others because they find power in it. Yet the majority of people are not bad actors. Some people are struggling with things we cannot know, some have been shaped politically by bad, traumatic, or challenging past experiences. You do not have to like them, or agree with them, but, whenever possible, leave the conversation with grace, without needing to make the other person feel small or insignificant.

Notes

Introduction

1. Elon Musk on *The Joe Rogan Experience* podcast, 28 February 2025.
2. Gad Saad, *Suicidal Empathy*, forthcoming. Gad Saad, 'The Parasitic Mind and Suicidal Empathy', *The Saad Truth* podcast, 16 December 2024.
3. Quoted in Hannah Knowles, Marianna Sotomayor, and Mariana Alfaro, 'Some GOP lawmakers start to call out DOGE', *Washington Post*, 25 February 2025, https://www.washingtonpost.com/politics/2025/02/25/doge-gop-lawmakers-concerns-musk/
4. Adam Tooze, 'Elon Musk's first principles', *Foreign Policy*, 25 March 2025, https://foreignpolicy.com/2025/03/25/elon-musk-trump-doge-physics-principles/
5. Walter Isaacson, Musk's biographer, noted his lack of empathy: Walter Isaacson, *Elon Musk*, Simon & Schuster, 2023. This features in Paulo Confino, 'One of Elon Musk's favorite video games taught him the "life lesson" that "empathy is not an asset." It's the opposite of what most CEOs preach', *Fortune*, 12 September 2023, https://fortune.com/2023/09/12/elon-musk-walter-isaacson-book-empathy-video-games-life-lessons-management/
6. Allie Beth Stuckey, *Toxic Empathy: How Progressives Exploit Christian Compassion*, Sentinel, 2024.
7. Joe Rigney, *The Sin of Empathy: Compassion and its Counterfeits*, Canon Press, 2025.
8. David French, 'Behold the strange spectacle of Christians against empathy', *New York Times*, 13 February 2025, https://www.nytimes.com/2025/02/13/opinion/trump-usaid-evangelicals.html
9. L.A. Santos, J.G. Voelkel, R. Willer, and J. Zaki, 'Belief in the utility of cross-partisan empathy reduces partisan animosity and facilitates political persuasion', *Psychological Science* 33:9 (2022): 1557–1573, https://doi.org/10.1177/09567976221098594. Stanford psychologist and prominent expert on empathy Jamil Zaki has been vocal on this too; see Sarah McCamon, 'Can empathy be a bad thing? New thinking on the right says "yes" ', NPR, 31 March 2025, https://www.wbur.org/hereandnow/2025/03/31/empathy-conservative

268

10. Carolyn Pedwell, *Affective Relations: The Transnational Politics of Empathy*, Palgrave Macmillan, 2014.
11. Rebecca Solnit, *The Faraway Nearby*, Penguin Random House, 2014.
12. Martin Buber, *I and Thou*, Simon & Schuster, 1996.
13. See for example, Thomas Kohut, *Empathy and the Historical Understanding of the Human Past*, Routledge, 2020.
14. Claire Yorke, 'The significance and limitations of empathy in strategic communications', *Defence Strategic Communications* 2:2 (2017): 137–160.
15. Charles Taylor, 'The politics of recognition', in John Arthur and Amy Shapiro (eds), *Campus Wars*, Routledge, 1995, pp. 249–263.
16. Taylor, 'The politics of recognition', p. 250.
17. Frans de Waal, *Age of Empathy*, Souvenir Press, 2019.
18. W.T. Tucker, 'Max Weber's Verstehen', *Sociological Quarterly* 6:2 (1965): 157–165, https://doi.org/10.1111/j.1533-8525.1965.tb01649.x
19. For great insights into emotional literacy, see: Lisa Feldman Barrett, *How Emotions are Made: The Secret Life of the Brain*, Pan Macmillan, 2017, and Susan David, *Emotional Agility: Get Unstuck, Embrace Change, and Thrive in Work and Life*, Penguin, 2016.
20. Pedwell, *Affective Relations*; A. Lobb, 'Critical empathy', *Constellations: An International Journal of Critical and Democratic Theory* 24:4 (2017): 594–607.
21. Elisabeth Porter, 'Can politics practice compassion?', *Hypatia* 21:4 (2006): 97–123, https://doi.org/10.1111/j.1527-2001.2006.tb01130.x
22. Compassion in Politics, https://www.compassioninpolitics.com/about_us
23. Author interview with Jennifer Nadel, online, 2 April 2025.
24. Martha C. Nussbaum, *Upheavals of Thought: The Intelligence of Emotions*, Cambridge University Press, 2008, pp. 301–302.
25. Zachary Shore, *A Sense of the Enemy: The High Stakes History of Reading Your Rival's Mind*, Oxford University Press, 2014; Allison Abbe, 'Understanding the adversary: Strategic empathy and perspective taking in national security', *US Army War College Quarterly: Parameters* 53:2 (2023): 9.
26. Claire Yorke, 'Is empathy a strategic imperative? A review essay', *Journal of Strategic Studies* 46 (2022): 1–21.
27. H.R. McMaster, *Battlegrounds: The Fight to Defend the Free World*, William Collins, 2020.
28. Ralph K. White, 'Empathizing with the rulers of the USSR', *Political Psychology* 4:1 (1983): 121–137.
29. Jamil Zaki, *The War for Kindness: Building Empathy in a Fractured World*, Robinson, 2019.
30. Ernst and Young, 'Authentic Empathy', https://www.ey.com/en_us/consulting/authentic-empathy and Ernst and Young, 'New EY Consulting survey confirms 90% of US workers believe empathetic leadership leads to higher job satisfaction and 79% agree it decreases employee turnover', 14 October 2021, https://www.ey.com/en_us/news/2021/09/ey-empathy-in-business-survey
31. Helen Demetriou and Bill Nicholl, 'Empathy is the mother of invention: Emotion and cognition for creativity in the classroom', *Improving Schools* 25:1 (2022): 4–21, https://doi.org/10.1177/1365480221989500
32. Michael Ventura, *Applied Empathy: The New Language of Leadership*, Touchstone, 2019.

33. Kaitlin Ugolik Phillips, *The Future of Feeling: Building Empathy in a Tech-Obsessed World*, Little A, 2020.

34. A lot of recent work has focused particularly on former US President Barack Obama and former New Zealand Prime Minister Jacinda Ardern. See also: Colleen J. Shogan, 'The contemporary presidency: The political utility of empathy in presidential leadership', *Presidential Studies Quarterly* 39:4 (2009): 859–877; Eric Leake, 'Empathizer-in-chief: The promotion and performance of empathy in the speeches of Barack Obama', *Journal of Contemporary Rhetoric* 6 (2016); Uri Friedman, 'New Zealand's prime minister may be the most effective leader on the planet', *Atlantic*, 19 April 2020, https://www.theatlantic.com/politics/archive/2020/04/jacinda-ardern-new-zealand-leadership-coronavirus/610237/

35. Michael E. Morrell, *Empathy and Democracy: Feeling, Thinking, and Deliberation*, Penn State Press, 2010.

36. Zaki, *The War for Kindness*, p. 37.

37. Roman Krznaric, *Empathy: A Handbook for Revolution*, Random House, 2014.

38. Neta C. Crawford, 'Institutionalizing passion in world politics: Fear and empathy', *International Theory* 6:3 (2014): 535–557, p. 544.

39. Elizabeth Segal, *Social Empathy: The Art of Understanding Others*, Columbia University Press, 2018; Peter Bazalgette, *The Empathy Instinct: How to Create a More Civil Society*, John Murray, 2017; Anita Nowak, *Purposeful Empathy: Tapping Our Hidden Superpower for Personal, Organizational, and Social Change*, Broadleaf, 2023.

40. Zaki, *The War for Kindness*.

41. Crawford, 'Institutionalizing passion in world politics'.

42. Antonin Lacelle-Webster, 'Democratic politics and hope: An Arendtian perspective', *European Journal of Political Theory* 23:4 (2024): 477–498. Thank you to Antonin Lacelle-Webster for speaking with me about his ideas and research during a visit to Canberra in October 2024.

43. This is based on my doctoral methodology and the criteria I used. It has been published elsewhere.

44. Avivah Wittenberg-Cox, 'What do countries with the best coronavirus responses have in common? Women leaders', *Forbes*, 13 April 2020, https://www.forbes.com/sites/avivahwittenbergcox/2020/04/13/what-do-countries-with-the-best-coronavirus-reponses-have-in-common-women-leaders/?sh=2e4132803dec. Others also made this connection with gender, and we will discuss this further in Chapter 7.

45. Richard V. Reeves, *Of Boys and Men: Why the Modern Male is Struggling, Why It Matters, and What to Do About It*, Brookings Institution Press, 2022.

1 Empathy and Politics

1. Adrian Leftwich, *What is Politics? The Activity and Its Study*, John Wiley & Sons, 2015.

2. Ben Ansell, *Why Politics Fails: The Five Traps of the Modern World and How to Escape Them*, Random House, 2023.

3. These themes of a good life and political society are central to his writings: Aristotle, *Nicomachean Ethics*, Penguin Classics, 2004, and Aristotle, *The Politics*, Penguin, 1982.

4. Matthias Strolz, Austrian politician, Love Politics website, in German, https://www.lovepolitics.net/ausbildung

5. Morrell, *Empathy and Democracy*.

6. Yana Gorokhovskaia, Adrian Shahbaz, and Amy Slipowitz, 'Marking 50 years in the struggle for democracy', Freedom House, 2023, https://freedomhouse.org/report/freedom-world/2023/marking-50-years

7. Economist Intelligence Unit, Democracy Index 2024, February 2025, https://services.eiu.com/campaigns/democracy-index-2024/

8. Corruption Perceptions Index 2022, Transparency International, https://www.transparency.org/en/cpi/2022

9. IPSOS Global Trustworthiness Index 2022, p. 3, https://www.ipsos.com/sites/default/files/ct/news/documents/2022-07/Global%20trustworthiness%202022%20Report.pdf

10. Author interview with Monica Brezzi from OECD, online, 5 November 2024. Supported by additional research by the OECD, including Mariana Prats, Sina Smid, and Monica Ferrin, 'Lack of trust in institutions and political engagement: An analysis based on the 2021 OECD Trust Survey', OECD Working Papers on Public Governance 75, 2024, https://doi.org/10.1787/83351a47-en

11. For good discussions of capitalism and its failings see: Thomas Piketty, *Capital in the 21st Century*, Harvard University Press, 2014; and Kate Raworth, *Doughnut Economics: Seven Ways to Think Like a 21st-Century Economist*, Penguin, 2018.

12. 'New Surgeon General Advisory raises alarm about the devastating impact of the epidemic of loneliness and isolation in the United States', U.S. Department of Health and Human Services, https://www.hhs.gov/about/news/2023/05/03/new-surgeon-general-advisory-raises-alarm-about-devastating-impact-epidemic-loneliness-isolation-united-states.html

13. Surgeon General Advisory, *Our Epidemic of Loneliness and Isolation*, U.S. Department of Health and Human Services, 2023, https://www.hhs.gov/sites/default/files/surgeon-general-social-connection-advisory.pdf

14. A. Goldsworthy, L. Osborne, and A. Chesterfield, *Poles Apart: Why People Turn Against Each Other, and How to Bring Them Together*, Penguin, 2022.

15. Levi Boxell, Matthew Gentzkow, and Jesse M. Shapiro, 'Cross-country trends in affective polarization', *Review of Economics and Statistics* 106:2 (2022): 557–565, https://doi.org/10.1162/rest_a_01160

16. Shanto Iyengar, Yphtach Lelkes, Matthew Levendusky, Neil Malhotra, and Sean J. Westwood, 'The origins and consequences of affective polarization in the United States', *Annual Review of Political Science* 22 (2019): 129–146.

17. Elizabeth N. Simas, Scott Clifford, and Justin H. Kirkland, 'How empathic concern fuels political polarization', *American Political Science Review* 114:1 (2020): 258–269.

18. Pew Research Center, 'Americans' dismal views of the nation's politics', 19 September 2023, https://www.pewresearch.org/politics/2023/09/19/americans-dismal-views-of-the-nations-politics/

19. Morrell, *Empathy and Democracy*.

20. Naomi Head, 'Costly encounters of the empathic kind: A typology', *International Theory* 8:1 (2016): 171–199, https://doi.org/10.1017/S1752971915000238

21. Ralph K. White, 'Empathizing with Saddam Hussein', *Political Psychology* 12:2 (1991): 291–308.
22. Krznaric, *Empathy*.
23. Paul Bloom, *Against Empathy: The Case for Rational Compassion*, Random House, 2017.
24. Bloom, *Against Empathy*.
25. Fritz Breithaupt, *The Dark Sides of Empathy*, Cornell University Press, 2019.
26. Carolyn Pedwell, 'Empathy's entanglements', in Francesca Mezzenzana and Daniela Peluso (eds), *Conversations on Empathy: Interdisciplinary Perspectives on Imagination and Radical Othering*, Routledge/Taylor & Francis, 2023, pp. 279–288.
27. Lauren Berlant, *Cruel Optimism*, Duke University Press, 2011, p. 5.
28. This is a prominent theme in the academic literature on healthcare and nursing.
29. C.D. Batson, J.G. Batson, R.M. Todd, B.H. Brummett, L.L. Shaw, and C.M.R. Aldeguer, 'Empathy and the collective good: Caring for one of the others in a social dilemma', *Journal of Personality and Social Psychology* 68:4 (1995): 619–631, https://doi.org/10.1037/0022-3514.68.4.619
30. For a good book on this see: Carolyn Calloway-Thomas (ed.), *Empathy in the Global World: An Intercultural Perspective*, Sage, 2010.
31. Doron Shulztiner and Guy E. Carmi, 'Human dignity in national constitutions: Functions, promises and dangers', *American Journal of Comparative Law* 62:2 (2014): 461–490, https://doi.org/10.5131/AJCL.2013.0003
32. Steven Pinker, 'The stupidity of dignity', *New Republic*, 28 May 2008, https://newrepublic.com/article/64674/the-stupidity-dignity
33. Michèle Lamont, *Seeing Others: How Recognition Works – And How It Can Heal a Divided World*, Simon & Schuster, 2023.
34. Across multiple disciplines including art, literature, pedagogy, and healthcare and nursing, there are diverse approaches and mediums for teaching empathy. See for example: Erika Weisz and Jamil Zaki, 'Empathy building interventions: A review of existing work and suggestions for future directions', in E.M. Seppälä, E. Simon-Thomas, S.L. Brown, M.C. Worline, C.D. Cameron, and J.R. Doty (eds), *The Oxford Handbook of Compassion Science*, Oxford University Press, 2017, pp. 205–217.
35. Karina Schumann, Jamil Zaki, and Carol S. Dweck, 'Addressing the empathy deficit: Beliefs about the malleability of empathy predict effortful responses when empathy is challenging', *Journal of Personality and Social Psychology* 107:3 (2014): 475.
36. Carol Dweck, *Mindset: The New Psychology of Success*, Ballantine Books, 2008.
37. Zaki, *The War for Kindness*, p. 15.
38. Segal, *Social Empathy*.
39. Segal, *Social Empathy*.
40. Anthony M. Clohesy, *Politics of Empathy: Ethics, Solidarity, Recognition*, Routledge, 2013, p. viii.
41. Minouche Shafik, *What We Owe Each Other: A New Social Contract for a Better Society*, Princeton University Press, 2021.
42. Abeba Birhane, 'Descartes was wrong: "A person is a person through other persons"', Aeon, 7 April 2017, https://aeon.co/ideas/descartes-was-wrong-a-person-is-a-person-through-other-persons

43. Jonathan Mercer, 'Emotional beliefs', *International Organization* 64:1 (2010): 1–31, https://doi.org/10.1017/S0020818309990221

44. Martha Nussbaum, *Political Emotions: Why Love Matters for Justice*, Belknap Press, 2013, p. 2.

45. Krznaric, *Empathy*, p. 56.

46. See Sara Ahmed, *The Cultural Politics of Emotion*, Routledge, 2012, and Andrew A.G. Ross, *Mixed Emotions: Beyond Fear and Hatred in International Conflict*, University of Chicago Press, 2019.

47. Ross, *Mixed Emotions*, p. 3.

48. Matthew Smith, 'Net favourability towards Israel reaches new lows in key Western European countries', YouGov, 3 June 2025, https://yougov.co.uk/international/articles/52279-net-favourability-towards-israel-reaches-new-lows-in-key-western-european-countries

49. David, *Emotional Agility*.

50. Emma Hutchison and Roland Bleiker, 'Emotions in the War on Terror', in Alex J. Bellamy, Roland Bleiker, Sara E. Davies, and Richard Devetak (eds), *Security and the War on Terror*, Routledge, 2007, p. 57.

51. Author interview with Janet Rice, former Australian senator and Green Party leader, Canberra, 5 November 2024.

52. Author interview with the Rt Hon Johnny Mercer, former British Conservative politician and military veteran, phone, 29 July 2021.

53. Clohesy, *Politics of Empathy*; see also Stephen G. Morris, 'Empathy and the liberal–conservative political divide in the US', *Journal of Social and Political Psychology* 8:1 (2020): 8–24.

54. Y. Hasson, M. Tamir, K.S. Brahms, J.C. Cohrs, and E. Halperin, 'Are liberals and conservatives equally motivated to feel empathy toward others?', *Personality and Social Psychology Bulletin* 44:10 (2018): 1449–1459, https://doi.org/10.1177/0146167218769867

55. Bloom, *Against Empathy*.

56. President George W. Bush, 'President promotes compassionate conservatism', President George W. Bush Archives, The White House, 30 April 2002, https://georgewbush-whitehouse.archives.gov/news/releases/2002/04/20020430-5.html

57. Patrick T. Brown, 'The failure of "compassionate conservatism" offers lessons for the Trumpian right', *Politico*, 14 June 2022, https://www.politico.com/news/magazine/2022/06/14/trump-populists-compassionate-conservatism-00039136

58. William McKenzie, 'President George W. Bush on compassionate conservatism: A conversation with President George W. Bush', *The Catalyst* 12 (Fall 2018), https://www.bushcenter.org/catalyst/opportunity-road/george-w-bush-on-compassionate-conservatism

59. Jesse Norman and Janan Ganesh, *Compassionate Conservatism: What It Is, Why We Need It*, Policy Exchange, 2006, https://www.policyexchange.org.uk/wp-content/uploads/2016/09/compassionate-conservatism-june-06.pdf

60. Author interview with Alastair Masser, former UK Government Special Advisor under Prime Minister David Cameron, online, 28 November 2024.

61. Author interview with Alastair Masser.

62. Irin Carmon, 'Donald Trump's worst offense? Mocking disabled reporter, poll finds', NBC News, 11 August 2016, https://www.nbcnews.com/

politics/2016-election/trump-s-worst-offense-mocking-disabled-reporter-poll-finds-n627736

63. I spent some time in the US in the months ahead of the election in 2016. During several weeks in California almost all the local people I met in Orange County mentioned how much they liked Trump's straight-talking manner, even if he was often uncouth or offensive.

64. Peter Coleman, *The Five Percent: Finding Solutions to Seemingly Impossible Conflicts*, Public Affairs, 2011.

2 The Art of Leadership

1. Transcript of the Address by the Prime Minister of Barbados, the Honourable Mia Amor Mottley, QC, MP, at the United Nations General Assembly 73rd Session, 28 September 2018, https://www.youtube.com/watch?v=ygDuLa1adok

2. Mary Robinson on *What Makes Us Human*, Mary Robinson Foundation for Climate Justice, posted 11 June 2013, https://www.mrfcj.org/resources/what-makes-us-human/

3. The first survey by EY, 'EY empathy in business survey 2021', was during the period of the pandemic and the associated Great Resignation when people were leaving their jobs in high numbers as a result of being dissatisfied in the workplace. The most recent survey is from 2023: 'Authentic empathy: The key to your organization's business success', EY LLP (Americas), 30 March 2023, https://www.ey.com/en_us/consulting/authentic-empathy. These surveys reveal that although a high number want to see empathy, and value it, some people see it as disingenuous if not authentic. The survey shows that people want to see it embedded at all levels of the workplace.

4. Archie Brown, *The Myth of the Strong Leader: Political Leadership in the Modern Age*, Basic Books, 2014.

5. This term was used in S. Cooper and A. Wakelam, 'Leadership of resuscitation teams: "Lighthouse Leadership"', *Resuscitation* 42:1 (1999): 27–45, https://doi.org/10.1016/s0300-9572(99)00080-5, PMID: 10524729. It is increasingly used in management and leadership parlance. A range of consultancies and leadership training courses for businesses offer insights into this concept.

6. James MacGregor Burns, *Leadership*, Harper Collins, 1978; Open Road Media kindle edn, 2012.

7. Henry Kissinger, *Leadership: Six Studies in World Strategy*, Penguin, 2022.

8. Doris Kearns Goodwin, *Leadership: In Turbulent Times*, Simon & Schuster, 2019.

9. Brown, *The Myth of the Strong Leader*.

10. Burns, *Leadership*.

11. Bernard M. Bass, 'Two decades of research and development in transformational leadership', *European Journal of Work and Organizational Psychology* 8:1 (1999): 9–32, at p. 9, https://doi.org/10.1080/135943299398410

12. James MacGregor Burns, *Transforming Leadership: A New Pursuit of Happiness*, Grove Press, 2003.

13. Chielozona Eze, 'Nelson Mandela and the politics of empathy: Reflections on the moral conditions for conflict resolutions in Africa', *African Conflict and Peacebuilding Review* 2:1 (2012): 122–135.

14. Nussbaum, *Political Emotions*, p. 2.
15. From IISS (International Institute of Strategic Studies), *The Military Balance 2022*; Angela Dewan, 'Ukraine and Russia's militaries are David and Goliath: Here's how they compare', CNN, 25 February 2022, https://edition.cnn.com/2022/02/25/europe/russia-ukraine-military-comparison-intl/index.html
16. Sharon Braithwaite, 'Zelensky refuses US offer to evacuate, saying "I need ammunition, not a ride"', CNN, 26 February 2022, https://edition.cnn.com/2022/02/26/europe/ukraine-zelensky-evacuation-intl/index.html
17. Afiq Fitri, 'How President Zelensky's approval ratings have surged', *New Statesman*, 1 March 2022, https://www.newstatesman.com/chart-of-the-day/2022/03/how-president-zelenskys-approval-ratings-have-surged
18. Anna Myroniuk, 'I did not vote for Ukraine's president. His courage has changed my mind and inspired millions', *Washington Post*, 27 February 2022, https://www.washingtonpost.com/opinions/2022/02/27/ukraine-russia-zelensky-president-changed-my-mind-inspired-millions/
19. Reuters, 'Full transcript of Zelenskyy's emotional appeal to Russians', NBC News, 24 February 2022, https://www.nbcnews.com/news/world/full-transcript-zelenskyys-emotional-appeal-russians-rcna17485
20. Simon Shuster, 'Volodymyr Zelensky: 2022 TIME Person of the Year', *Time*, 7 December 2022, https://time.com/person-of-the-year-2022-volodymyr-zelensky/
21. Burns, *Transforming Leadership*.
22. Author interview with Sir Nick Harvey, former MP, online, August 2024.
23. For more information see the Malala Fund, https://malala.org/malalas-story
24. The DRC has experienced multiple periods of conflict and armed activity, with the First Congo War in 1996–97, and the Second Congo War from 1998 to 2002. There are no exact figures of the scale of the violence, although approximately 6 million people have died since 1996. Rape has been one of the horrific weapons of war wielded against women, children, and men. The majority of victims were women (73%) and children (25%). For an explainer of the history of conflict in the DRC, see Global Conflict Tracker: Conflict in the Democratic Republic of Congo, Council of Foreign Relations, Center for Preventive Action, 20 March 2025, https://www.cfr.org/global-conflict-tracker/conflict/violence-democratic-republic-congo. A briefing by the European Parliament gives a shocking but useful overview of the scale of sexual violence in the country: 'At a glance', European Parliament, November 2014, https://www.europarl.europa.eu/EPRS/EPRS-AaG-542155-Sexual-violence-in-DRC-FINAL.pdf
25. Fatma Tanis, 'He fights sexual violence. He's won a Nobel and now a $1 million honor. Is he hopeful?', NPR, 10 May 2024, https://www.npr.org/sections/goatsandsoda/2024/05/10/1248112056/aurora-prize-nobel-denis-mukwege-sexual-violence#:~:text=In%202018%20Dr.,unrelenting%20campaign%20against%20sexual%20violence
26. In an American context see Anand Giridharadas, *The Persuaders: Winning Hearts and Minds in a Divided Age*, Random House, 2022.
27. Michael Ventura, *Applied Empathy: The New Language of Leadership*, Hachette UK, 2019.
28. Katharine Murphy, 'Bob Hawke, the typical Australian who enjoyed extraordinary popularity as a public figure', *Guardian*, 16 May 2019, https://www.

theguardian.com/australia-news/2019/may/16/bob-hawke-former-australian-prime-minister-dies-aged-89

29. Lech Blaine, '83 top blokes: The larrikin myth, class and power', *Quarterly Essay* 83 (2021).

30. C.J. Coventry, 'Sedimentary layers: Bob Hawke's beer world record and ocker chic', *Journal of Australian Studies* 47:3 (2023): 478–496.

31. 'Let's Stick Together', Labour campaign advert, 1987, https://laborhistory.org.au/lets-stick-together-1987-election-ad/

32. Colleen J. Shogan, 'The contemporary presidency: The political utility of empathy in presidential leadership', *Presidential Studies Quarterly* 39:4 (2009): 859–877.

33. Bill Clinton's 'I feel your pain moment', 1992 Presidential Town Hall Debate, https://www.c-span.org/video/?c4842764/user-clip-clintons-feel-pain-moment. This example is also used in Claire Yorke, 'Will empathy win the day?', *The World Today*, 5 October 2020, https://www.chathamhouse.org/publications/the-world-today/2020-10/will-empathy-win-day

34. Claire Yorke, 'The significance and limitations of empathy in strategic communications', *Defence Strategic Communications* 2:2 (2017): 137–160.

35. Prime Minister Jacinda Ardern, 'Jacinda Ardern: "It takes strength to be an empathetic leader"', BBC News, 14 November 2018, https://www.bbc.com/news/av/world-asia-46207254

36. Doris Kearns Goodwin, *Team of Rivals: The Political Genius of Abraham Lincoln*, Simon & Schuster, 2006.

37. G. Tremlett, 'José Mujica: Is this the world's most radical president?', *Guardian*, 18 September 2014, https://www.theguardian.com/world/2014/sep/18/-sp-is-this-worlds-most-radical-president-uruguay-jose-mujica

38. Jack Nicas, 'How to be truly free: Lessons from a philosopher president', *New York Times*, 23 August 2024, https://www.nytimes.com/2024/08/23/world/americas/pepe-mujica-uruguay-president.html

39. Emir Kusturica (director), *El Pepe: A Supreme Life*, documentary film, released September 2018.

40. Eve Fairbanks, 'Jose Mujica was every liberal's dream president. He was too good to be true', *New Republic* via the Pulitzer Center, 6 February 2015, https://pulitzercenter.org/stories/jose-mujica-was-every-liberals-dream-president-he-was-too-good-be-true

41. Fairbanks, 'Jose Mujica was every liberal's dream president'.

42. US President Joe Biden, 'Victory speech: Full transcript', ABC Australia, 8 November 2020, https://www.abc.net.au/news/2020-11-08/us-president-elect-joe-biden-victory-speech-full-transcript/12861698?utm_campaign=abc_news_web&utm_content=link&utm_medium=content_shared&utm_source=abc_news_web

43. Biden, Victory speech.

44. Biden, Victory speech.

45. Charlotte Alter, 'Joe Biden's empathy offensive', *Time*, 2 June 2020; Peter Wehner, 'Biden may be just the person America needs', *Atlantic*, 2 November 2020, https://www.theatlantic.com/ideas/archive/2020/11/joe-bidens-super-power/616957/

46. Some later pointed to inaccuracies in these stories, and mismatches on dates, but this idea of being 'Average Joe' remained the central message.

47. John Hendrickson, 'What Joe Biden can't bring himself to say', *Atlantic*, January/February 2020, https://www.theatlantic.com/magazine/archive/2020/01/joe-biden-stutter-profile/602401/

48. Joe Biden, Tweet, 16 April 2020, https://twitter.com/JoeBiden/status/1250585 968664600582?s=20

49. Aaron Blake, 'This photo of Trump's notes captures his empathy deficit better than anything', *Washington Post*, 21 February 2018, https://www.washington-post.com/news/the-fix/wp/2018/02/21/this-photo-of-trumps-notes-captures-his-empathy-problem-better-than-anything/

50. Jared McDonald, 'Who cares? Explaining perceptions of compassion in candidates for office', *Political Behavior* 43:4 (2021): 1371–1394, https://doi.org/10.1007/s11109-020-09592-8

51. Richard Reeves, *President Nixon: Alone in the White House*, Simon & Schuster, 2001, p. 21.

52. This notebook was found randomly in files at the Nixon Library, Yorba Linda, in 2016. It was not catalogued correctly, but photos were taken.

53. Richard Nixon, *Leaders: Profiles and Reminiscences of Men Who Have Shaped the Modern World*, Simon & Schuster, 2013.

54. Marlise Simons, 'Former Bosnian leader begins his defense at genocide trial', *New York Times*, 16 October 2012, https://www.nytimes.com/2012/10/17/world/europe/radovan-karadzic-former-bosnian-leader-begins-his-genocide-defense.html. This was cited in Björn Krondorfer's *Unsettling Empathy: Working with Groups in Conflict*, Rowman & Littlefield, 2020.

3 Navigating Crises

1. Global Terrorism Index 2019, https://www.visionofhumanity.org/wp-content/uploads/2020/11/GTI-2019-web.pdf

2. This is also discussed in Claire Yorke, 'Making the connection: The role of empathy in communicating policy', Global Relations Forum, https://www.gif.org.tr/files/MakingTheConnection.pdf

3. The Christchurch Call, https://www.christchurchcall.com; France Diplomacy, 'Christchurch call to eliminate terrorist and violent extremist content online', 15 May 2019, https://id.ambafrance.org/IMG/pdf/christchurch_call_to_action_final11may.pdf?4216/00b690f19c790562d9117a81b663d413bf0738ba

4. Breithaupt, *The Dark Sides of Empathy*; Head, 'Costly encounters of the empathic kind' Bloom, *Against Empathy*.

5. For more pro-social accounts of human behaviour at times of crisis, see: Nicholas A. Christakis, *Blueprint: The Evolutionary Origins of a Good Society*, Little, Brown Spark, 2019; Rutger Bregman, *Humankind: A Hopeful History*, Bloomsbury, 2020.

6. A whole range of news articles highlighted her handling of the crisis, supported by a growing body of academic work: Uri Friedman, 'New Zealand's prime minister may be the most effective leader on the planet', *Atlantic*, 19 April 2020,

https://www.theatlantic.com/politics/archive/2020/04/jacinda-ardern-new-zealand-leadership-coronavirus/610237/; 'Coronavirus: How New Zealand relied on science and empathy', BBC News, 21 April 2020, https://www.bbc.com/news/world-asia-52344299; Andreea Voina and Mihnea S. Stoica, 'Reframing leadership: Jacinda Ardern's response to the Covid-19 pandemic', *Media and Communication* 11:1 (2023): 139–149; Geoffrey Craig, 'Kindness and control: The political leadership of Jacinda Ardern in the Aotearoa New Zealand COVID-19 media conferences', *Journalism and Media* 2:2 (2021): 288–304, https://doi.org/10.3390/journalmedia2020017; A.V. Simpson, A. Rego, M. Berti, S. Clegg, and M. Pina e Cunha, 'Theorizing compassionate leadership from the case of Jacinda Ardern: Legitimacy, paradox and resource conservation', *Leadership* 18:3 (2022): 337–358, https://doi.org/10.1177/17427150211055291

7. Jennifer Summers, Hao-Yuan Cheng, Hsien-Ho Lin, Lucy Telfar Barnard, Amanda Kvalsvig, Nick Wilson, and Michael G. Baker, 'Potential lessons from the Taiwan and New Zealand health responses to the COVID-19 pandemic', *Lancet Regional Health–Western Pacific* 4 (2020).

8. Timothy Rich, 'How much has President Tsai benefited from public views of COVID-19 policies, and what are the implications for 2024?', Global Taiwan Institute, 8 February 2023, https://globaltaiwan.org/2023/02/how-much-has-president-tsai-benefited-from-public-views-of-covid-19/

9. Vanessa L. Deane and Jason Ramel, 'Crisis leadership in Barbados during the initial response to the COVID-19 pandemic', Natural Hazards Center, University of Boulder, Colorado, 2022, https://hazards.colorado.edu/quick-response-report/crisis-leadership-in-barbados-during-the-initial-response-to-the-covid-19-pandemic

10. Mia Mottley, Transcript of an Address to the Nation, 29 April 2020, https://pmo.gov.bb/2020/04/29/pm-announces-phased-re-opening/

11. C. Daryl Cameron, 'Compassion collapse: Why we are numb to numbers', in Seppälä, Simon-Thomas, Brown, Worline, Cameron, and Doty (eds), *The Oxford Handbook of Compassion Science*, pp. 261–271.

12. Michael Bang Petersen, Magnus Storm Rasmussen, Marie Fly Lindholt, and Frederik Juhl Jørgensen, 'Pandemic fatigue and populism: The development of pandemic fatigue during the Covid-19 pandemic and how it fuels political discontent across eight western democracies', *PsyArXiv*, 2021, psyarxiv.com/y6wm4

13 George Mitchell speaking to Alison Beard, 'George Mitchell on Effective Negotiation', *HBR IdeaCast* podcast, episode 468, June 2015, https://hbr.org/podcast/2015/06/george-mitchell-on-effective-negotiation

14. 'Mo Mowlam in Maze Prison 1998', RTÉ Archives, 2018, https://www.rte.ie/archives/2018/0108/931726-mo-mowlam-visits-maze/

15. 'The H-Blocks', Prison Memory Archive, https://prisonsmemoryarchive.com/pma-for-education/the-h-blocks/

16. 'Appointment an opportunity for peace', RTÉ news report by David Power, broadcast 3 May 1997, RTÉ Archives, https://www.rte.ie/archives/2017/0502/871861-mo-mowlam-secretary-of-state-for-northern-ireland/

17. 'Mo Mowlam in Maze Prison 1998'.

18. 'Mo Mowlam in Maze Prison 1998'.

19. For a detailed account of the history see, for example, Paul Bew, *Ireland: The Politics of Enmity 1789–2006*, Oxford University Press, 2007.

20. As well as pointing to empathy's rising popularity in response to failures in the neoliberal order, critiques of empathy also highlight how it too has sometimes been co-opted by neoliberal thinking. Tammy Amiel Houser, 'The rise and fall of empathy in an era of financial crisis: Rethinking the neoliberal imaginary', *Journal for Cultural Research* 24:4 (2020): 269–285, https://doi.org/10.1080/147 97585.2020.1820305

21. 'The global crisis: causes, responses and challenges', Geneva, International Labour Office, 2011, https://www.ilo.org/sites/default/files/wcmsp5/groups/public/@dgreports/@dcomm/@publ/documents/publication/wcms_155824.pdf

22. Commission on Presidential Debates, 'October 15, 1992 Second half debate transcript', 15 October 1992, http://www.debates.org/index.php?page=october-15-1992-second-half-debate-transcript

23. Anjela Taneja, Anthony Kamande, Chandreyi Guharay Gomez, Dana Abed, Max Lawson, and Neelanjana Mukhia, 'Takers not makers: The unjust poverty and unearned wealth of colonialism', Oxfam, 20 January 2025, https://www.oxfam.org/en/research/takers-not-makers-unjust-poverty-and-unearned-wealth-colonialism. The full report is available at: https://oi-files-d8-prod.s3.eu-west-2.amazonaws.com/s3fs-public/2025-01/English%20-%20Davos%20Full%20Report%202025.pdf

24. Alan Berube and Bruce Katz, 'Katrina's window: Confronting concentrated poverty across America', Brookings Institution, 1 October 2005, https://www.brookings.edu/articles/katrinas-window-confronting-concentrated-poverty-across-america/ For an update, see: Alan Berube and Natalie Holmes, 'Concentrated poverty in New Orleans 10 years after Katrina', Brookings Institution, 27 August 2015, https://www.brookings.edu/articles/concentrated-poverty-in-new-orleans-10-years-after-katrina/

25. George W. Bush, 'President outlines Hurricane Katrina relief efforts', President George W. Bush Archives, The White House, 31 August 2005, https://georgewbush-whitehouse.archives.gov/news/releases/2005/08/20050831-3.html

26. Colleen J. Shogan, 'The contemporary presidency: The political utility of empathy in presidential leadership', *Presidential Studies Quarterly* 39:4 (2009): 859–877, http://www.jstor.org/stable/41427426.

27. Nick Wing, 'Bush admits Katrina Air Force One photo was "huge mistake"', *Huffington Post*, updated 25 May 2011, https://www.huffingtonpost.co.uk/entry/bush-katrina-photo-mistake_n_779527

28. Pew Research Center, 'Two-in-three critical of Bush's relief efforts', 8 September 2005, https://www.pewresearch.org/politics/2005/09/08/two-in-three-critical-of-bushs-relief-efforts/

29. Joanne B. Ciulla, 'Being there: Why leaders should not "fiddle" while Rome burns', *Presidential Studies Quarterly* 40:1 (2010): 38–56.

30. Alasdair Pal, 'Leader of resource-rich Western Australia resigns due to burnout', Reuters Asia Pacific, 29 May 2023, https://www.reuters.com/world/asia-pacific/western-australia-state-leader-resigns-2023-05-29/

31. Jonathan Powell, *Talking to Terrorists: How to End Armed Conflicts*, Random House, 2014.

32. Bethany Bell and Nick Thorpe, 'Austria's migrant disaster: Why did 71 die?', BBC News, 25 August 2016, https:// www.bbc.com/news/world-europe-37163217

33. 'Welcome refugees and reject racism, Merkel says after rallies', Reuters, 31 December 2014, https://www. reuters.com/article/us-germany-merkel/welcome-refugees-and-reject-racism-merkel-says-after-rallies-idUSKBN0K90GL20141231

34. UNHCR, 'The Dublin Regulation: Overview', https://www.unhcr.org/4a9d1 3d59.pdf

35. Eurostat, 'Asylum and first-time asylum applicants by citizenship, age and sex – Annual aggregated data (rounded)', http://appsso.eurostat.ec.europa.eu/nui/show.do?dataset=migr_asyappctza&lang=en

36. Chancellor Angela Merkel, 'Sommerpressekonferenz von Bundeskanzlerin Merkel', 31 August 2015, https://www.bundesregierung.de/breg-de/aktuelles/pressekonferenzen/sommerpressekonferenz-von-bundeskanzlerin-merkel-848300

37. 'Merkel warns that refugee crisis tests Europe's core ideals', DW, 31 August 2015, https://p.dw.com/p/1GOaJ

38. Niamh McIntyre, Mark Rice-Oxley, Niko Kommenda, and Pablo Gutiérrez, 'It's 34,361 and rising: How the List tallies Europe's migrant bodycount', Guardian, 20 June 2018, https://www.theguardian.com/world/2018/jun/20/the-list-europe-migrant-bodycount

39. 'Merkel's refugee policy divides Europe', Spiegel Online, 21 September 2015, https://www.spiegel.de/international/germany/refugee-policy-of-chancellor-merkel-divides-europe-a-1053603.html

40. Janosch Delcker, 'The phrase that haunts Angela Merkel', Politico, 19 August 2016, https://www.politico.eu/article/the-phrase-that-haunts-angela-merkel/

41. This example appears in a report I wrote: Yorke, 'Making the connection'.

42. For a more detailed account of this see former US Secretary of Defence Robert McNamara's account of the crisis in James G. Blight and Janet M. Lang, The Fog of War: Lessons from the Life of Robert S. McNamara, Rowman & Littlefield, 2005; see also Office of the Historian, 'The Cuban Missile Crisis, October 1962', https://history.state.gov/milestones/1961-1968/cuban-missile-crisis#:~:text=The%20Cuban%20Missile%20Crisis%20of,in%20the%20foreign%20policy%20process

43. Nik Gowing, 'Skyful of Lies' and Black Swans, Reuters Institute for the Study of Journalism, Department of Politics and International Relations, University of Oxford, 2009.

44. Stephanie Dolamore, Darrell Lovell, Haley Collins, and Angela Kline, 'The role of empathy in organizational communication during times of crisis', Administrative Theory & Praxis 43:3 (2021): 366–375.

45. David, Emotional Agility.

46. Claire Yorke, 'Reading the mood: Atmospherics and counterterrorism', RUSI Journal 165:1 (2020): 64–73.

47. 'Leadership in a crisis: Responding to the coronavirus outbreak and future challenges', McKinsey, 16 March 2020, https://www.mckinsey.com/capabilities/people-and-organizational-performance/our-insights/leadership-in-a-crisis-responding-to-the-coronavirus-outbreak-and-future-challenges

48. Britain's Mood Measured Weekly, YouGov, https://yougov.co.uk/topics/politics/trackers/britains-mood-measured-weekly

49. Kissinger, Leadership.

50. Her Majesty's Government, *Securing Britain in an Age of Uncertainty: The Strategic Defence and Security Review*, October 2010, Her Majesty's Stationery Office, https://assets.publishing.service.gov.uk/government/uploads/system/up loads/attachment_data/file/62482/strategic-defence-security-review. pdf

51. For interesting work on trauma and its role in politics and collective identities, see: Adam B. Lerner, *From the Ashes of History: Collective Trauma and the Making of International Politics*, Oxford University Press, 2022; and Lara A. Tcholakian, Svetlana N. Khapova, Erik Van De Loo, and Roger Lehman, 'Collective traumas and the development of leader values: A currently omitted, but increasingly urgent, research area', *Frontiers in Psychology* 10 (2019)' https://pmc.ncbi.nlm.nih.gov/articles/PMC6509438/

4 From Power Over to Power With

1. Dacher Keltner, 'Don't let power corrupt you', *Harvard Business Review*, October 2016, https://hbr.org/2016/10/dont-let-power-corrupt-you

2. S.T. Fiske and E. Dépret, 'Control, interdependence and power: Understanding social cognition in its social context', *European Review of Social Psychology* 7:1 (1996): 31–61, https://doi.org/10.1080/14792779443000094

3. Moises Naim, *The End of Power: From Boardrooms to Battlefields and Churches to States: Why Being in Charge Isn't What It Used to Be*, Hachette, 2014.

4. There is a distinction between power and authority. Authority is the legitimacy to act, often associated with certain positions. A prime minister, a president, a secretary general, or a community leader typically has authority because of the position they occupy that is invested with the ability to act on behalf of others. It might also be that someone's expertise and knowledge confer on them an authority to make decisions, or guide action for others, which can give them power to shape debate and outcomes. Certainly, people can have authority without power, and power without authority. They might occupy positions of authority and be unable to effect change or lack the credibility and/or ability to enact that power or inspire others to follow them.

5. J.-T. Martelli and C. Jaffrelot, 'Do populist leaders mimic the language of ordinary citizens? Evidence from India', *Political Psychology* 44 (2023): 1141–1160, https://doi.org/10.1111/pops.12881

6. Bloom, *Against Empathy*.

7. Project 2025: Presidential Transition Project, https://www.project2025.org

8. Prime Minister Keir Starmer, PM remarks at Immigration White Paper press conference: 12 May 2025, https://www.gov.uk/government/speeches/pm-remarks-at-immigration-white-paper-press-conference-12-may-2025

9. Antonio Gramsci's ideas are articulated in his *Prison Notebooks*. For an overview of his ideas see, for example, Thomas R. Bates, 'Gramsci and the theory of hegemony', *Journal of the History of Ideas* 36:2 (1975): 351–366, https://doi.org/10.2307/2708933

10. Hannah Arendt, *Eichmann in Jerusalem: A Report on the Banality of Evil*, Penguin Classics, 2022.

11. Carolyn Pedwell, 'Economies of empathy: Obama, neoliberalism and social justice', *Environment and Planning D: Society and Space* 30 (2012): 280–297. See also Pedwell, *Affective Relations*.

12. Larry Buchanan, Quoctrung Bui, and Jugal K. Patel, 'Black Lives Matter may be the largest movement in U.S. history', *New York Times*, 3 July 2020, https://www.nytimes.com/interactive/2020/07/03/us/george-floyd-protests-crowd-size.html

13. Robin Willardt and Petra C. Schmid, 'The threat of powerlessness: Consequences for affect and (social) cognition', *Journal of Experimental Social Psychology* 111 (2024), 104576, https://www.sciencedirect.com/science/article/pii/S0022103123001336

14. Martin Luther King Jr, 'Pilgrimage to nonviolence', Archives at the King Institute at Stanford University, 13 April 1960, https://kinginstitute.stanford.edu/king-papers/documents/pilgrimage-nonviolence. For his India trip see 'India Trip', 3 February 1959 to 18 March 1959, online archives at the King Institute at Stanford University, https://kinginstitute.stanford.edu/india-trip

15. King, 'Pilgrimage to nonviolence'.

16. William Jefferson Clinton, 'Honoring Rosa Parks with the Congressional Gold Medal', 15 June 1999, American Rhetoric, https://www.americanrhetoric.com/speeches/wjclintonrosaparksmedalofhonor.htm

17. Clinton, 'Honoring Rosa Parks with the Congressional Gold Medal'.

18. 'Transcript: Greta Thunberg's speech at the U.N. Climate Action Summit', NPR, 23 September 2019, https://www.npr.org/2019/09/23/763452863/transcript-greta-thunbergs-speech-at-the-u-n-climate-action-summit

19. James Baldwin and Raoul Peck, *I Am Not Your Negro: A Companion Edition to the Documentary Film Directed by Raoul Peck*, Vintage, 2017.

20. Hannah Arendt, *The Human Condition*, University of Chicago Press, 1998, p. 44.

21. Efforts to achieve women's suffrage in the United States were growing at this time, and although some states gave women some rights in the latter part of the 1800s and early 1900s, it was not until 1919 that the Nineteenth Amendment was signed, granting women the right to vote. However, while many white women were then able to vote from 1920, non-white women and First Nations women were not given the same rights. And even when the right to vote was granted to First Nations women in 1924, they continued to face obstacles and restrictions. Black and Latina women did not have the right to vote until as late as 1965.

22. D. Melé and J.M. Rosanas, 'Power, freedom and authority in management: Mary Parker Follett's "power-with"', *Philosophy of Management* 3 (2003): 35–46, at p. 45, https://doi.org/10.5840/pom20033221

23. Mary Parker Follett, *Creative Experience*, Left of Brain Books, 2021, p. 189.

24. Melé and Rosanas, 'Power, freedom and authority in management'.

25. Melé and Rosanas, 'Power, freedom and authority in management, p. 38.

26. Follett, *Creative Experience*, p. 192.

27. There is extensive research that reveals how gender biases shape our world. Caroline Criado Perez, *Invisible Women*, Random House, 2019.

28. Australian Human Rights Commission, 'Bringing them home: Report of the National Inquiry into the Separation of Aboriginal and Torres Strait Islander Children from Their Families', April 1997, https://humanrights.gov.au/our-work/projects/bringing-them-home-report-1997

29. Parliament of Australia, 'Apology to Australia's Indigenous Peoples', 13 February 2008, https://www.aph.gov.au/Visit_Parliament/Art/Icons/Apology_to_Australias_Indigenous_Peoples

30. For a good overview of this history and continued efforts to tell a richer story see Thomas Mayo, *Always Was Always Will Be*, Hardie Grant Explore, 2024.

31. J. Decety and K.J. Yoder, 'Empathy and motivation for justice: Cognitive empathy and concern, but not emotional empathy, predict sensitivity to injustice for others', *Social Neuroscience* 11:1 (2016): 1–14, https://doi.org/10.1080/17470919.2015.1029593

32. This is a topic worthy of another book and far deeper analysis, and so it is dealt with only briefly here.

33. Bloom, *Against Empathy*; Breithaupt, *The Dark Sides of Empathy*.

34. I am grateful to Naaman Kranz, a legal expert, for his kindness and intellect in discussing these topics and helping me refine my thinking.

35. Christian Bason, *Leading Public Design: Discovering Human-Centred Governance*, Bristol University Press, 2017, https://doi.org/10.2307/j.ctt1t88xq5

36. Kit Collingwood-Richardson, 'Empathy and the future of policy making', Medium, 14 May 2018, foreword, https://medium.com/foreword/empathy-and-the-future-of-policy-making-7d0bf38abc2d

37. HMRC Corporate Report, 'HMRC: Public sector equality duty compliance 2020 to 2021', 22 March 2022, https://www.gov.uk/government/publications/hmrc-compliance-with-the-public-sector-equality-duties-2020-to-2021/hmrc-public-sector-equality-duty-compliance-2020-to-2021

38. Author interview with Andrew Clark-Jones, online, December 2024.

39. Author interview with Olli-Pekka Heinonen, online, November 2024.

40. Author interview with Olli-Pekka Heinonen.

41. Mikko Annala, Juha Leppänen, Silva Mersola, and Charles F. Sabel, *Humble Government: How to Realize Ambitious Reforms Prudently*, Demos, 14 December 2020, https://demoshelsinki.fi/publication/the-more-complex-and-uncertain-a-policy-issue-is-the-more-useful-it-is-to-approach-it-through-humility/

42. Collingwood-Richardson, 'Empathy and the future of policy making'.

5 Telling Richer Stories

1. President Nelson Mandela, 'Nelson Mandela's inauguration speech as President of SA', 10 May 1994, SA News, published online 10 May 2018, https://www.sanews.gov.za/south-africa/read-nelson-mandelas-inauguration-speech-president-sa

2. Wilmot James, 'How Mandela – and a cup of tea – smoothed the way for South Africans learning to live with one another', *Daily Maverick*, 5 May 2024, https://www.dailymaverick.co.za/article/2024-05-05-how-mandela-and-a-cup-of-tea-stole-an-afrikaner-generals-heart/

3. Charles Tilly, *Stories, Identities, and Political Change*, Rowman & Littlefield, 2002, p. 27.

4. Francis Fukuyama, *Identity: The Demand for Dignity and the Politics of Resentment*, Farrar, Straus & Giroux, 2018.

5. See, for example, Joshua Greene, *Moral Tribes: Emotion, Reason, and the Gap Between Us and Them*, Penguin, 2014.

6. David Livingstone Smith, *Less Than Human: Why We Demean, Enslave, and Exterminate Others*, St Martin's Press, 2011, p. 13.

7. Cynthia Kroet, 'Viktor Orbán: Migrants are "a poison"', *Politico*, 27 July 2016, https://www.politico.eu/article/viktor-orban-migrants-are-a-poison-hun garian-prime-minister-europe-refugee-crisis/

8. United Nations High Commissioner for Refugees Filippo Grandi, cited in 'Why the language we use to talk about refugees matters', Amnesty International, 5 March 2020, https://www.amnesty.org/en/latest/news/2020/03/why-the-language-we-use-to-talk-about-refugees-matters/

9. 'Rwanda jails man who preached genocide of Tutsi "cockroaches"', BBC News, 15 April 2016, https://www.bbc.com/news/world-africa-36057575

10. Chris Hedges, *War Is a Force that Gives Us Meaning*, Anchor, 2003.

11. Jennifer N. Gutsell and Michael Inzlicht, 'Intergroup differences in the sharing of emotive states: Neural evidence of an empathy gap', *Social Cognitive and Affective Neuroscience* 7:5 (June 2012): 596–603, https://doi.org/10.1093/scan/nsr035

12. F. Pratto and D.E. Glasford, 'Ethnocentrism and the value of a human life', *Journal of Personality and Social Psychology* 95 (2008): 1411–1428.

13. Greene, *Moral Tribes*.

14. I am grateful to my friend Pablo de Orellana, an expert in identity politics and populism, for this framing and for being happy to discuss this issue at length.

15. Heineken Advert, 'Worlds apart: An experiment', https://www.youtube.com/watch?v=etIqln7vT4w

16. 'How does this Heineken beer commercial reduce toxic polarization?', Builders, 21 February 2024, https://startswith.us/2024/02/21/how-does-this-heineken-beer-ad-reduce-toxic-polarization/

17. Author involvement in Human Library Session, Copenhagen, Denmark, 2021.

18. The Human Library, https://humanlibrary.org

19. Author interview with Jo Berry, online, 13 November 2024.

20. 'Patrick Magee: The IRA Brighton bomber', BBC News, 22 June 1999, http://news.bbc.co.uk/2/hi/uk_news/301223.stm

21. Richard English, *Armed Struggle: The History of the IRA*, Pan Books, 2012.

22. This well-known quote is attributed to Nelson Mandela, and St Augustine, and a number of other sources.

23. Desmond Tutu, *No Future without Forgiveness*, Penguin, 2012.

24. Confrontation here implies an emotional and psychological challenge from being confronted with diverse perspectives, rather than physical conflict.

25. 'Colombia's final steps to the end of war', International Crisis Group, 7 September 2016, https://www.crisisgroup.org/latin-america-caribbean/andes/colombia/colombia-s-final-steps-end-war

26. See the talk Santos gave at Columbia University, 2022, https://www.sipa. columbia.edu/news/ball-professor-juan-manuel-santos-challenges-students-lead-empathy

27. President Santos, talk at Columbia University.

28. Author interview with His Excellency Mauricio Rodríguez Múnera, online, 13 November 2024.

29. Author interview with His Excellency Mauricio Rodríguez Múnera.

30. Adam Isacson, 'A long way to go: Implementing Colombia's peace accord after five years', WOLA, 23 November 2021, https://www.wola.org/analysis/a-long-way-to-go-implementing-colombias-peace-accord-after-five-years/

31. 'Colombia peace deal: Historic agreement is signed', BBC News, 27 September 2016, https://www.bbc.com/news/world-latin-america-37477202

32. A. Phelan, 'Engaging insurgency: The impact of the 2016 Colombian Peace Agreement on FARC's political participation', *Studies in Conflict & Terrorism* 42:9 (2018): 836–852, https://doi.org/10.1080/1057610X.2018.1432027

33. Juan Manuel Santos, *The Battle for Peace: The Long Road to Ending a War with the World's Oldest Guerrilla Army*, University Press of Kansas, 2021, pp. 356–359.

34. Santos, *The Battle for Peace*, pp. 364–366.

35. Author interview with His Excellency Mauricio Rodríguez Múnera.

36. E. Bruneau, A. Casas, B. Hameiri, et al., 'Exposure to a media intervention helps promote support for peace in Colombia', *Nature Human Behaviour* 6 (2022): 847–857, https://doi.org/10.1038/s41562-022-01330-w

37. Author interview with His Excellency Mauricio Rodríguez Múnera.

38. Alessandro Rampietti, 'The photographer who exposed Colombia's invisible war', Al Jazeera, 4 October 2019, https://www.aljazeera.com/news/2019/10/4/the-photographer-who-exposed-colombias-invisible-war

39. Björn Krondorfer, *Unsettling Empathy: Working with Groups in Conflict*, Rowman & Littlefield, 2020, p. 89.

40. 'Colombia: Is "total peace" back on track?', International Crisis Group, 4 October 2023, https://www.crisisgroup.org/latin-america-caribbean/andes/colombia/colombia-total-peace-back-track

41. D.R. Revelo and C.E. Sottilotta, 'Barriers to peace? Colombian citizens' beliefs and attitudes *vis-à-vis* the government–FARC–EP agreement', *Studies in Conflict & Terrorism* 46:1 (2020): 46–67, https://doi.org/10.1080/1057610X.2020.1752008

42. Thank you to Thomas Mayo, who also spoke about this in the context of how to heal Australia after the Indigenous Voice referendum in 2023. Author interview with Thomas Mayo, Sydney, October 2024.

43. The National Dialogues Model, https://kansallisetdialogit.fi/en/about-national-dialogues/the-national-dialogues-model/

44. Statement of Intent of the 2024 Government of National Unity, https://www.anc1912.org.za/statement-of-intent-of-the-2024-government-of-national-unity-2/; reiterated in: https://www.thepresidency.gov.za/annual-address-president-cyril-ramaphosa-national-council-provinces-parliament-cape-town

45. State of the Nation 2025, 'National Dialogue', https://www.stateofthenation.gov.za/national-dialogue

46. Klaus Kotzé, 'The National Dialogue Pathway to a People's Plan for South Africa', Occasional Paper 8, Inclusive Society, August 2024, https://www.inclusivesociety.org.za/post/the-national-dialogue-pathway-to-a-people-s-plan-for-south-africa

47. Chris Spies, 'Why the proposed national dialogue risks becoming a missed opportunity', *Mail and Guardian*, 6 December 2024, https://mg.co.za/thought-leader/opinion/2024-12-06-why-the-proposed-national-dialogue-risks-becoming-a-missed-opportunity/

48. Annette Kämmerer, 'The scientific underpinnings and impacts of shame', *Scientific American* 9 (August 2019), https://www.scientificamerican.com/article/the-scientific-underpinnings-and-impacts-of- shame/#:~:text=Shame%20is%20the%20uncomfortable%20sensation,behavior%20is%20not%20self%2Devident; M.S. Treeby, C. Prado, S.M. Rice, and S.F. Crowe, 'Shame, guilt, and facial emotion processing: Initial evidence for a positive relationship between guilt-proneness and facial emotion recognition ability', *Cognition and Emotion* 30:8 (2016): 1504–1511, https://doi.org/10.1080/02699931.2015.1072497

49. M. Silfver, 'Coping with guilt and shame: A narrative approach', *Journal of Moral Education* 36:2 (2007): 169–183, https://doi.org/10.1080/0305724070 1325274

50. Xuechunzi Bai, Miguel R. Ramos, and Susan T. Fiske, 'As diversity increases, people paradoxically perceive social groups as more similar', *Proceedings of the National Academy of Sciences* 117:23 (2020): 12741–12749.

51. See, for example, Paul Litt, *Trudeaumania*, UBC Press, 2016, and Robert Wright, *Trudeaumania: The Rise to Power of Pierre Elliott Trudeau*, Harper Collins, 2016.

52. Gerald Clark, 'Trudeau without the Trudeaumania', *New York Times*, 25 January 1970, https://www.nytimes.com/1970/01/25/archives/trudeau-without-the-trudeaumania-canadas-pm-is-not-a-simple-swinger.html

53. Pierre Trudeau, Speech to the Ukrainian-Canadian Congress, Winnipeg, 9 October 1971.

54. Appendix of Canadian Culture, House of Commons Debates, 28th Parliament, 3rd Session: Vol. 8, Library of Parliament / Bibliothèque du Parlement, https://parl.canadiana.ca/view/oop.debates_HOC2803_08

55. Clark, 'Trudeau without the Trudeaumania'.

56. Government of Canada/Gouvernement de Canada, Canadian Multiculturalism Act, R.S.C., 1985, c. 24 (4th Supp.), 1988, c. 31, assented to 21 July, 1988, https://laws-lois.justice.gc.ca/eng/acts/C-18.7/page-1.html

57. Canadian Prime Minister Justin Trudeau, Statement by the Prime Minister on the 50th anniversary of Canada's multiculturalism policy, 8 October 2021, https://www.pm.gc.ca/en/news/statements/2021/10/08/statement-prime-minister-50th-anniversary-canadas-multiculturalism

58. Government of Canada, 'Welcoming Week toolkit', https://www.ircc.canada.ca/ftp/immigration-matters-toolkit/welcoming-week.asp

59. J.A. Banks, 'Diversity and citizenship education in multicultural nations', *Multicultural Education Review* 1:1 (2009): 1–28, https://doi.org/10.1080/2377 0031.2009.11102861

6 Creating a Healthy Ecosystem

1. Hegel on Montesquieu, in Michael E. Brint, *A Genealogy of Political Culture*, Routledge, 2021, p. 12.

2. Gabriel Abraham Almond and Sidney Verba, *The Civic Culture: Political Attitudes and Democracy in Five Nations*, Princeton University Press, 2015. See also John Street, 'Political culture: From civic culture to mass culture', *British Journal of Political Science* 24:1 (1994): 95–113.
3. Brint, *A Genealogy of Political Culture*.
4. Author interview with Jennifer Nadel, online, April 2025, and Compassion in Politics, https://www.compassioninpolitics.com
5. Author interview with Sir Nick Harvey.
6. Author interview with Brendan Smyth, Canberra, 18 October 2024.
7. 'Fact Sheet: President Biden's Unity Agenda for the Nation', The White House Archives, 8 March 2024, https://bidenwhitehouse.archives.gov/briefing-room/statements-releases/2024/03/08/fact-sheet-president-bidens-unity-agenda-for-the-nation/ and Steve Benen, 'Why has Biden managed to put together so many bipartisan wins?', MSNBC, 15 December 2022, https://www.msnbc.com/rachel-maddow-show/maddowblog/biden-managed-put-together-many-bipartisan-wins-rcna61883
8. Laurel Harbridge-Yong, Craig Volden, and Alan E. Wiseman, 'The bipartisan path to effective lawmaking', *Journal of Politics* 85:3 (2023): 1048–1063, https://www.journals.uchicago.edu/doi/10.1086/723805
9. Author interview with Sir Nick Harvey.
10. For a fascinating graphic of this shift, see Casey Briggs, Ben Spraggon, Simon Elvery, and Julian Fell, 'Over five decades, here's how voters have shifted away from the major parties', ABC, 24 April 2025, https://www.abc.net.au/news/2025-04-24/election-data-rise-independents-major-party-drift/105144918
11. Nicholas Wheeler, 'Investigating diplomatic transformations', *International Affairs* 89:2 (2003): 477–496, https://ciaotest.cc.columbia.edu/journals/riia/v89i2/f_0028338_23056.pdf
12. Edelman Trust Barometer, https://www.edelman.com/trust/trust-barometer
13. Such data gives helpful insights, but a noted problem with metrics such as this barometer is that the objective is to reinforce the importance of business to society, and the failure of political institutions. Edelman Trust Barometer 2022, https://www.edelman.com/trust/2022-trust-barometer and Edelman Trust Barometer 2023, https://www.edelman.com/trust/2023/trust-barometer
14. OECD, *Building Trust to Reinforce Democracy: Main Findings from the 2021 OECD Survey on Drivers of Trust in Public Institutions*, 13 July 2022, https://www.oecd-ilibrary.org/sites/b407f99c-en/index.html?itemId=/content/publication/b407f99c-en
15. OECD, *Building Trust to Reinforce Democracy*.
16. Apparently Churchill never said this, although he is often cited as having done so. His work showed a far more positive impression of the average voter. Michael Richards, *Red Herrings: Famous Quotes Churchill Never Said*, International Churchill Society, 9 June 2013, https://winstonchurchill.org/publications/finest-hour/finest-hour-141/red-herrings-famous-quotes-churchill-never-said/
17. The Respect Agenda was based on polling with over 4,000 people. https://www.moreincommon.org.uk/our-work/research/the-agenda/
18. OECD, 'Trust in government', https://www.oecd.org/en/topics/trust-in-government.html

19. Author interview with Monica Brezzi, OECD, online, 5 November 2024.
20. World Bank Group, 'Worldwide governance indicators', https://www.world-bank.org/en/publication/worldwide-governance-indicators/interactive-data-access
21. OECD, 'OECD Survey on Drivers of Trust in Public Institutions 2024 Results – Country Notes: Switzerland', https://www.oecd.org/en/publications/oecd-survey-on-drivers-of-trust-in-public-institutions-2024-results-country-notes_a8004759-en/switzerland_b0df7353-en.html
22. Lars P. Feld and Gebhard Kirchgässner, 'Direct democracy, political culture, and the outcome of economic policy: A report on the Swiss experience', *European Journal of Political Economy* 16:2 (2000): 287–306, https://doi.org/10.1016/S0176-2680(00)00003-3
23. Feld and Kirchgässner, 'Direct democracy, political culture, and the outcome of economic policy'.
24. Benjamin Jansen and Alois Stutzer, 'Affective Partisan Polarization and Citizens' Attitudes and Behavior in Swiss Democracy', WWZ Working Paper 2024/04 (2024), and https://www.swissinfo.ch/eng/swiss-politics/political-rifts-are-less-deep-in-switzerland-than-elsewhere/78305484
25. Author interview with Monica Brezzi.
26. Author interview with Monica Brezzi.
27. M. Evans, L. Dare, R. Tanton, Y. Vidyattama, and J. Seaborn, *Trust in Australian Regional Public Services: Citizens not Customers – Keep it Simple. Say What You Do and Do What You Say*, APS Reform Report, November 2019, https://www.apsreform.gov.au/research/trust-australian-regional-public-services/findings/what-trust-means-australian-citizens
28. Amnesty International, 'Gun violence', https://www.amnesty.org/en/what-we-do/arms-control/gun-violence/
29. Rory Stewart, *Politics on the Edge: A Memoir from Within*, Jonathan Cape/Random House, 2023.
30. More in Common, https://www.moreincommon.org.uk
31. Compassion in Politics, Campaign to 'Stop the Nastiness', https://www.compassioninpolitics.com/stop_the_nastiness
32. More in Common, https://www.moreincommon.org.uk
33. Mostafa Rachwani, 'Andrew Laming ordered into empathy training by Scott Morrison after downplaying apology', *Guardian*, 27 March 2021, https://www.theguardian.com/australia-news/2021/mar/27/andrew-laming-liberal-mps-facebook-page-removed-after-he-downplayed-apology
34. 'Nationals MPs to undergo empathy training to improve workplace culture', SBS Australia, 28 March 2021, https://www.sbs.com.au/news/article/nationals-mps-to-undergo-empathy-training-to-improve-workplace-culture/bpeon1xo2
35. Michael Koziol, 'We took 5 politicians to empathy training – here's what happened', *Sydney Morning Herald*, 4 April 2021, https://www.smh.com.au/politics/federal/we-took-five-politicians-to-empathy-training-here-s-what-happened-20210401-p57fzr.htm.
36. Author interview with Katherine Teh, Melbourne, 25 October 2024.
37. Sue Williamson, 'Andrew Laming: Why empathy training is unlikely to work', *The Conversation*, 29 March 2021, https://theconversation.com/andrew-laming-why-empathy-training-is-unlikely-to-work-158050

38. Marco Peña, 'A new political leadership for the twenty-first century', CSIS (Center for Strategic and International Studies), December 2021, https://www.csis.org/analysis/new-political-leadership-twenty-first-century
39. Katherine Murphy, 'The political life is no life at all', *Meanjin*, Winter 2017, https://meanjin.com.au/essays/political-life/
40. Love Politics, https://www.lovepolitics.net
41. Author interview with Sonja Jöchtl, co-founder of Love Politics, online, October 2024.
42. Author interview with Sonja Jöchtl.
43. Discussion with Sonja Jöchtl, Love Politics, 19 October 2024.
44. Jeremy Paxman, *The Political Animal*, Penguin, 2007, and Isabel Hardman, *Why We Get the Wrong Politicians*, Atlantic Books, 2022.
45. Author interview with Sonja Jöchtl.
46. Robert Bosch Foundation, https://www.bosch-stiftung.de/en/project/programs-political-decision-makers/details
47. Author interview with Susanne Zels, online, November 2024.
48. Author interview with Susanne Zels.
49. For a detailed account on the gaps in our political knowledge and how we can address them, see Arthur Lupia, *Uninformed: Why People Know So Little About Politics and What We Can Do About It*, Oxford University Press, 2016.
50. Lupia, *Uninformed*.
51. Richard Haas, 'Why we need civics', *Atlantic*, 22 January 2023, https://www.theatlantic.com/ideas/archive/2023/01/american-identity-democracy-civics-education-requirement/672789/
52. Julia Butler, 'Better civic education will help Australians respond in challenging times', *The Strategist*, ASPI, 4 May 2020, https://www.aspistrategist.org.au/better-civic-education-will-help-australians-respond-in-challenging-times/
53. Diana Owen, 'Political knowledge and the development of civic dispositions and skills', paper presented at the American Political Studies Association Teaching and Learning Conference, 'Teaching to Empower Students', Albuquerque, New Mexico, 2020, https://preprints.apsanet.org/engage/api-gateway/apsa/assets/orp/resource/item/5e3b2bfc889eb900192b0421/original/political-knowledge-and-the-development-of-civic-dispositions-and-skills.pdf
54. Franklin D. Roosevelt, 'Message for American Education Week', 27 September 1938, https://www.presidency.ucsb.edu/documents/message-for-american-education-week
55. Marin Lessenski, 'Media Literacy Index 2022', OSCE, 6 December 2022, https://www.osce.org/files/f/documents/0/4/534146.pdf
56. Author interview with Dr Eenariina Hämäläinen, teacher and author, online, November 2024.
57. Michael E. Morrell, 'Empathy and democratic education', *Public Affairs Quarterly* 21:4 (2007): 381–403, http://www.jstor.org/stable/40441496
58. Empathy Studios, https://www.empathystudios.com
59. Slum Soccer, https://www.slumsoccer.org
60. 'One week of empathy lessons may significantly improve emotional awareness', Empathy Studios and the University of Cambridge, https://news.educ.cam.ac.uk/230216-empathy-week

61. 'One term of empathy training measurably improved classroom behaviour', University of Cambridge, 28 August 2024, https://www.cam.ac.uk/research/news/one-term-of-empathy-training-measurably-improved-classroom-behaviour

62. Author interview with Ed Kirwan, filmmaker, storyteller, and CEO and founder of Empathy Studios, online, December 2024.

63. H. Demetriou and B. Nicholl, 'Empathy is the mother of invention: Emotion and cognition for creativity in the classroom', *Improving Schools* 25:1 (2022): 4–21, https://doi.org/10.1177/1365480221989500; M. Steponavičius, C. Gress-Wright, and A. Linzarini, 'Social and emotional skills: Latest evidence on teachability and impact on life outcomes', OECD Working Papers 34, November 2023, https://doi.org/10.1787/ba34f086-en

64. Author interview with Ed Kirwan.

65. Author interview with Ed Kirwan.

7 Embracing More Inclusive Politics

1. Reuters Staff, 'Here's how Norway is reassuring children over COVID-19 fears', 17 March 2020, https://www.weforum.org/agenda/2020/03/norway-pm-tells-kids-it-is-ok-to-feel-scared-during-coronavirus

2. Jacinda Ardern, 'Tooth fairy and Easter bunny are essential workers', BBC News, 6 April 2020, https://www.bbc.com/news/av/world-asia-52189013

3. Wittenberg-Cox, 'What do countries with the best Coronavirus responses have in common?'. https://doi.org/?

4. R.A. Renstrom and V.C. Ottati, ' "I feel your pain": The effect of displaying empathy on political candidate evaluation', *Journal of Social and Political Psychology* 8:2 (2020): 767–787, https://doi.org/10.5964/jspp.v8i2.1292

5. Jennifer J. Jones, 'Talk "like a man": The linguistic styles of Hillary Clinton, 1992–2013', *Perspectives on Politics* 14:3 (2016): 625–642, https://doi.org/10.1017/S1537592716001092

6. This can be seen in some of the arguments and initiatives put forward by members of the current Republican administration. See also, for example, Stuckey, *Toxic Empathy*.

7. Julia Gillard and Ngozi Okonjo-Iweala, *Women and Leadership: Real Lives, Real Lessons*, MIT Press, 2022, p. 10.

8. Julia Gillard, 'Motions', House Hansard, page 11581, 9 October 2012, https://parlinfo.aph.gov.au/parlInfo/search/display/display.w3p;query=Id%3A%22chamber%2Fhansardr%2F5a0ebb6b-c6c8-4a92-ac13-219423c2048d%2F0039%22

9. Lisa Feldman Barrett, *How Emotions Are Made: The Secret Life of the Brain*, Pan Macmillan, 2017, p. 226, and Madeline Albright, *Madam Secretary: A Memoir*, Miramax Books, 2003.

10. Rebecca Traister, *Good and Mad: The Revolutionary Power of Women's Anger*, Simon & Schuster, 2018.

11. Andrew Roberts, 'Winston wept: The extraordinary lachrymosity and romantic imagination of Winston Churchill', *Finest Hour* 174 (Autumn 2016): 34, https://winstonchurchill.org/publications/finest-hour/finest-hour-174/winston-

wept-the-extraordinary-lachrymosity-and-romantic-imagination-of-winston-churchill/

12. From Martin Gilbert, *Churchill: A Life*, vol. 8, Henry Holt, 1991, p. 675, quoted in Roberts, 'Winston wept', p. 34.

13. 'Trudeau becomes emotional remembering Guy Lafleur: "He was a hero"', Global News, 22 April 2022, https://globalnews.ca/video/8778309/trudeau-becomes-emotional-remembering-guy-lafleur-he-was-a-hero

14. 'Justin Trudeau cries over death of tragically hip frontman', NBC News, 18 October 2017, https://www.nbcnews.com/video/justin-trudeau-cries-over-death-of-gord-downie-of-tragically-hip-1076212291754

15. The White House, 'Remarks by the President in Eulogy for the Honorable Reverend Clementa Pinckney', 26 June 2015, https://obamawhitehouse.archives.gov/the-press-office/2015/06/26/remarks-president-eulogy-honorable-reverend-clementa-pinckney; James Fallows, 'Obama's grace', *Atlantic*, 27 June 2015, https://www.theatlantic.com/politics/archive/2015/06/grace/397064/

16. Charlotte Alter, 'Obama's approval rating cracks 50%', *Time*, 30 June 2015, https://time.com/3941331/barack-obama-approval-rating-poll/

17. Others have commented on her being part of a conspiracy around the Great Reset: see Daisy Cousens, 'Jacinda Ardern quickly becoming the Great Reset's high priestess as the movement's slow march towards big government control rumbles on', Sky News, 19 October 2022, https://www.skynews.com.au/world-news/jacinda-ardern-quickly-becoming-the-great-resets-high-priestess-as-the-movements-slow-march-towards-big-government-control-rumbles-on/news-story/0066bd636f7aa11daf54088c8a817014

18. Statement by Sanna Marin, Sky News, 25 August 2022, https://www.skynews.com.au/australia-news/i-am-human-finnish-pm-sanna-marin-tearfully-defends-private-life-after-party-videos-and-photos-leaked/news-story/2969efe5b9e4d38786abab2973d3df7a

19. Statement by Sanna Marin.

20. Charlotte Alter, 'Brazilian politician tells congresswoman she's "not worthy" of sexual assault', *Time*, 11 December 2014, https://time.com/3630922/brazil-politics-congresswoman-rape-comments/

21. Emma Graham-Harrison, 'Women pushed even further from power in Xi Jinping's China', *Guardian*, 22 October 2022, https://www.theguardian.com/world/2022/oct/22/where-are-the-women-at-the-top-of-chinese-politics

22. Minglu Chen, 'Where are the women in Chinese politics?', *East Asia Forum*, 2023, https://eastasiaforum.org/2023/05/25/where-are-the-women-in-chinese-politics/

23. Leta Hong Fincher, *Betraying Big Brother: The Feminist Awakening in China*, Verso Books, 2021.

24. Shan Huang and Wanning Sun, '#Metoo in China: Transnational feminist politics in the Chinese context', *Feminist Media Studies* 21:4 (2021): 677–681.

25. Hannah June Kim and Chungjae Lee, 'The 2022 South Korean presidential election and the gender divide among the youth', *Pacific Affairs*, 95:2 (June 2022): 285–308, https://doi.org/10.5509/2022952285

26. For interesting data on the disparity, see Cecilia Hyunjung Mo and Soosun You, 'The fight over gender equality in South Korea', Carnegie Endowment

report, 16 April 2025, https://carnegieendowment.org/research/2025/04/the-fight-over-gender-equality-in-south-korea?lang=en

27. Jung Han Wool, 'A new variation of modern prejudice: Young Korean men's anti-feminism and male-victim ideology', *Frontiers in Psychology* 14 (2023), https://doi.org/10.3389/fpsyg.2023.1230577

28. Hannah Roberts, 'How Giorgia Meloni thinks', *Politico*, 23 September 2023, https://www.politico.eu/article/how-giorgia-meloni-thinks-brothers-of-italy-election-salvini-mario-draghi-silvio-berlusconi/

29. Barbie Latza Nadeau, 'Femme fascista: How Giorgia Meloni became the star of Italy's far right', *World Policy Journal* 35:2 (2018): 14–21, muse.jhu.edu/article/701256

30. Amy Kazmin, 'Giorgia Meloni: The far-right firebrand poised to be Italy's next premier', *Financial Times*, 24 September 2022, https://www.ft.com/content/ce6835e6-823c-47bb-8ab3-ff8779174b04

31. 74,222,958 to be precise.

32. Ruth Igielnik, Scott Keeter, and Hannah Hartig, 'Behind Biden's 2020 victory', Pew Research Center, 30 June 2021, https://www.pewresearch.org/politics/2021/06/30/behind-bidens-2020-victory/

33. Carter Sherman, '2024 US elections takeaways: How female voters broke for Harris and Trump', *Guardian*, 7 November 2024, https://www.theguardian.com/us-news/2024/nov/06/election-trump-harris-women-voters

34. Dominik Geppert, 'Emotions and gender in Margaret Thatcher and Helmut Kohl's Cold War', *Diplomacy & Statecraft* 32:4 (2021): 766–788, https://doi.org/10.1080/09592296.2021.1996719

35. Shirley Chisholm and mae dell, 'Interview: Sister Shirley says', *Off Our Backs* 4:4 (1974): 9–25, http://www.jstor.org/stable/25783809

36. Kiana Cox, 'Black Americans' mistrust of the U.S. political system', Pew Research Center, 15 June 2024, https://www.pewresearch.org/race-and-ethnicity/2024/06/15/black-americans-mistrust-of-the-u-s-political-system/

37. MeToo Movement, https://metoomvmt.org/get-to-know-us/history-inception/

38. Naomi Alderman, *The Power*, Hachette, 2017.

39. Elliot Kennedy, 'Rwanda's legislature is majority female. Here's how it happened', *National Geographic*, 15 October 2019, https://www.nationalgeographic.com/culture/graphics/graphic-shows-women-representation-in-government-around-the-world-feature

40. World Economic Forum, *Gender Gap Report 2022*, 13 July 2022, https://www.weforum.org/reports/global-gender-gap-report-2022/in-full

41. Katherine Schaeffer, 'Key facts about women's suffrage around the world, a century after U.S. ratified 19th Amendment', Pew Research Center, 5 October 2020, https://www.pewresearch.org/fact-tank/2020/10/05/key-facts-about-womens-suffrage-around-the-world-a-century-after-u-s-ratified-19th-amendment/

42. Rwandan Parliament, 'Women's Representation', https://www.parliament.gov.rw/women-representation

43. Annie Barbara Chikwanha and Theresa Moyo, 'The Motivation for Women in Politics: The Contemporary Politics of Women's Participation and Representation in Africa', Report by IDEA International, 2024, https://www.

idea.int/publications/catalogue/html/motivation-women-politics-contempo
rary-politics-womens-participation

44. Venice Commission, 'Report on the Impact of Electoral Systems on Women's
Representation in Politics', Study 482/2008, https://www.venice.coe.int/web
forms/documents/default.aspx?pdffile=CDL-AD(2009)029-e p.7

45. European Parliament, 'Differential impact of electoral systems on female
political representation', March 1997, https://www.europarl.europa.eu/work
ingpapers/femm/w10/2_en.htm

46. Michelle K. Ryan and S. Alexander Haslam, 'The glass cliff: Evidence that
women are over-represented in precarious leadership positions', *British Journal
of Management* 16:2 (2005): 81–90.

47. It features in S.K. Grogan, 'Charles Fourier and the nature of women', in Susan
K. Grogan (ed.), *French Socialism and Sexual Difference*, Palgrave Macmillan,
1992, pp. 20–41.

48. 'Emma Watson: Gender equality is your issue too', UN Women, 20 September
2014, https://www.unwomen.org/en/news/stories/2014/9/emma-watson-gender-
equality-is-your-issue-too

49. He for She, https://www.heforshe.org/en

50. United Nations, 'United Nations General Assembly Platform of Women
Leaders', 20 September 2022, https://www.un.org/pga/77/unga-platform-
of-women-leaders/

51. 'Reprogramming power: Audrey Tang is bringing hacker culture to the state',
apolitical, 18 October 2018, https://apolitical.co/solution-articles/en/repro-
gramming-power-audrey-tang-is-bringing-hacker-culture-to-the-state

52. Criado Perez, *Invisible Women*.

53. Reeves, *Of Boys and Men*.

54. Thank you to Shannon Zimmerman, an expert on gender and politics, for her
insights and expertise on this.

8 Transforming the Media Landscape

1. The Uluru Statement, 2017, https://ulurustatement.org/the-statement/view-
the-statement/

2. For the official statements of each side, you can read this document by the
Australian Electoral Commission: https://www.aec.gov.au/referendums/files/
pamphlet/your-official-yes-no-referendum-pamphlet.pdf

3. See https://www.abc.net.au/news/2023-05-22/peter-dutton-says-indigenous-
voice-will-re-racialise-the-country/102378700, and in opposition to it, see
Michael Bachelard, 'Dutton's claim the Voice will "re-racialise" Australia is
wrong. Here's why', *Sydney Morning Herald*, 27 May 2023, https://www.smh.
com.au/politics/federal/dutton-s-claim-the-voice-will-re-racialise-australia-
is-wrong-here-s-why-20230525-p5db7i.html

4. Author interview with Thomas Mayo, Sydney, October 2024. That so many
young people voted Yes – over 60% – suggests the future may be different.

5. 'Vast majority of voters still think First Nations Australians should have a voice',
Australian National University, November 2023, https://www.anu.edu.au/
news/all-news/vast-majority-of-voters-still-think-first-nations-australians-
should-have-a-voice

6. Malcolm Turnbull and Sharan Burrow, 'Sky News spreading fear and false-hoods on Indigenous voice is an affront to Australian democracy', *Guardian*, 25 July 2023, https://www.theguardian.com/commentisfree/2023/jul/25/indige-nous-voice-to-parliament-sky-news-falsehoods-referendum

7. Denis Muller, 'How did the media perform on the Voice referendum? Let's talk about truth-telling and impartiality', *The Conversation*, 15 October 2023, https://theconversation.com/how-did-the-media-perform-on-the-voice-referendum-lets-talk-about-truth-telling-and-impartiality-214961#:~:text=During%20the%20Voice%20debate%2C%20for,statement%20or%20the%20proposed%20Voice

8. Denis Muller, 'Journalists reporting on the Voice to Parliament do voters a disservice with "he said, she said" approach', *The Conversation*, 1 May 2023, https://theconversation.com/journalists-reporting-on-the-voice-to-parliament-do-voters-a-disservice-with-he-said-she-said-approach-204361

9. Stan Grant, 'For years I've been a media target for racism and paid a heavy price. For now, I want no part of it – I'm stepping away', *ABC News*, 19 May 2023, https://www.abc.net.au/news/2023-05-19/stan-grant-media-target-racist-abuse-coronation-coverage-enough/102368652

10. Stan Grant, 'Stan Grant's impassioned Q+A leaving speech: "I feel like I'm part of the problem" – video', *Guardian*, 23 May 2023, https://www.theguardian.com/australia-news/video/2023/may/23/stan-grants-impassioned-qa-leaving-speech-i-feel-like-im-part-of-the-problem-video

11. Grant, 'For years I've been a media target for racism'.

12. Zaki, *The War for Kindness*, p. 97.

13. Social Media and News Fact Sheet, Pew Research Center, November 2023, https://www.pewresearch.org/journalism/fact-sheet/social-media-and-news-fact-sheet/

14. Michael Schudson, *Why Democracies Need an Unlovable Press*, Polity, 2008, p. 12.

15. Susan Sontag, *Regarding the Pain of Others*, Penguin, 2004.

16. C. Wright Mills, *The Sociological Imagination*, Oxford University Press, 2000 [1959].

17. Kareem Khadder, Abeer Salman, Eyad Kourdi, and Pauline Lockwood, 'UN says no food has entered northern Gaza since start of October, putting 1 million people at risk of starvation', CNN, 11 October 2024, https://edition.cnn.com/2024/10/11/middleeast/food-northern-gaza-starvation-un-intl/index.html

18. See, for example, the criticism of CNN's handling of the war coverage: Chris McGreal, 'CNN staff say network's pro-Israel slant amounts to "journalistic malpractice"', *Guardian*, 4 February 2024, https://www.theguardian.com/media/2024/feb/04/cnn-staff-pro-israel-bias; Al Jazeera Staff, 'Failing Gaza: Pro-Israel bias uncovered behind the lens of Western media', Aljazeera, 5 October 2024, https://www.aljazeera.com/news/2024/10/5/failing-gaza-pro-israel-bias-uncovered-behind-the-lens-of-western-media

19. Shanto Iyengar and Donald R. Kinder, *News that Matters: Television and American Opinion*, University of Chicago Press, 2010.

20. Bernard Cecil Cohen, *The Press and Foreign Policy*, Princeton University Press, 2016 [1963], p. 13.

21. Cohen, *The Press and Foreign Policy*, p. 13.
22. Thanks to Sir Nick Harvey for this point.
23. James Curran, *Media and Power*, Routledge, 2022, p. 6.
24. Christabel Ligami, 'Social media helping younger adults combat HIV stigma', *Lancet HIV* 10:5 (2023): e280–e281.
25. Adam Smith, *The Theory of Moral Sentiments*, Penguin, 2010.
26. For an interesting account of its themes, see Stuart A. Thompson, 'I traded my news apps for Rumble, the right-wing YouTube. Here's what I saw', *New York Times*, 13 December 2024, https://www.nytimes.com/interactive/2024/12/13/business/rumble-trump-bongino-kirk.html
27. Bloom, *Against Empathy*.
28. See Jon Ronson, *So You've Been Publicly Shamed*, Riverhead Books, 2016.
29. Rebecca Solnit, 'Turns out the zombie apocalypse isn't as fun as they said it would be – Rebecca Solnit on our dangerously disconnected world', *Guardian*, 16 November 2024, https://www.theguardian.com/society/2024/nov/16/zombie-apocalypse-dangerously-disconnected-world-rebecca-solnit
30. A.J. Martingano, S. Konrath, S. Zarins, and A.A. Okaomee, 'Empathy, narcissism, alexithymia, and social media use', *Psychology of Popular Media* 11:4 (2022): 413–422, https://doi.org/10.1037/ppm0000419
31. Byung-Chul Han, *In the Swarm: Digital Prospects*, vol. 3, MIT Press, 2017.
32. Sherry Turkle, *Reclaiming Conversation: The Power of Talk in a Digital Age*, Penguin, 2016; Sherry Turkle, *Alone Together: Why We Expect More from Technology and Less from Each Other*, Hachette, 2017.
33. The Offline Club, https://www.theoffline-club.com
34. Off the Radar, https://www.offtheradar.nl
35. The topic of empathy, AI, and the impact of the confluence of these for our media environment and news consumption is a far larger topic than there is space for here. However, there is a growing body of work examining the intersection. See, for example, Phillips, *The Future of Feeling*.
36. McDonald, 'Who cares? Explaining perceptions of compassion in candidates for office'.
37. Franklin D. Roosevelt, 'March 12, 1933: Fireside Chat 1: On the Banking Crisis', The Miller Center: Presidential Speeches Archive, https://millercenter.org/the-presidency/presidential-speeches/march-12-1933-fireside-chat-1-banking-crisis
38. Roosevelt, 'March 12, 1933: Fireside Chat 1: On the Banking Crisis'.
39. Jeremi Suri, 'How presidential empathy can improve politics', *Washington Post*, 12 March, 2019, https://www.washingtonpost.com/outlook/2019/03/12/how-presidential-empathy-can-improve-politics/
40. NCC Staff, 'How the Kennedy–Nixon debate changed the world of politics', National Constitution Center, 26 September 2017, https://constitutioncenter.org/blog/the-debate-that-changed-the-world-of-politics
41. 'The Kennedy–Nixon debates', *History*, 21 October 2010, https://www.history.com/articles/kennedy-nixon-debates
42. James McCandless, 'How a bacon sandwich derailed Ed Miliband's UK political career', *Huffington Post*, 12 October 2018, https://www.huffpost.com/entry/ed-miliband-bacon-sandwich_n_5bbe27b0e4b01470d0580898.   Hadley

Freeman, 'Ed Miliband: "If I went on *Strictly*, it would make the bacon sandwich look elegant"', *Guardian*, 3 July 2017, https://www.theguardian.com/lifeand-style/2017/jul/03/ed-miliband-if-i-went-on-strictly-it-would-make-the-bacon-sandwich-look-elegant

43. One of many articles critiquing her clothes in 2002: Hadley Freedman, 'Look at those shoes', *Guardian*, 9 October 2002, https://www.theguardian.com/world/2002/oct/09/gender.fashion. Many years later people were still debating her sartorial choices: Sarah Rainey, 'What Theresa's shoes reveal about her march to power', *Daily Mail*, 2 November 2016, https://www.dailymail.co.uk/femail/article-3895698/What-Theresa-s-shoes-reveal-march-power-PM-s-choice-footwear-carefully-chosen-match-political-message.html

44. During a photoshoot for the *Sun-Herald*, the media made much of the empty fruit bowl: see for example Josephine Tovey, 'Gillard's fruit bowl runneth over', *Sydney Morning Herald*, 24 June 2010, https://www.theage.com.au/politics/federal/gillards-fruit-bowl-runneth-over-20100624-z0cv.html; 'Gillard bares all', *Sydney Morning Herald*, 24 January 2005, https://www.smh.com.au/national/gillard-bares-all-20050124-gdkjww.html

45. Megan Garber, 'How Alexandria Ocasio-Cortez's plain black jacket became a controversy', *Atlantic*, 16 November 2018, https://www.theatlantic.com/entertainment/archive/2018/11/alexandria-ocasio-cortezs-clothes-a-tedious-backlash/576064/

46. Vanessa Friedman, 'A very French tempest in a turtleneck', *New York Times*, 11 October 2022, https://www.nytimes.com/2022/10/11/style/emmanuel-macron-turtleneck-energy.html

47. Jack Moore, 'Get a load of young Justin Trudeau, everyone', *GQ*, 1 March 2017, https://www.gq.com/story/young-trudeau

48. Antonia Noori Farzan, 'Five years ago, Obama was blasted for wearing a tan suit', *Washington Post*, 28 August 2019, https://www.washingtonpost.com/nation/2019/08/28/tan-suit-scandal-obama-trump/

49. Hacked Off: Campaign for a Free and Accountable Press, https://hackinginquiry.org

50. Jonathan Haidt, *The Anxious Generation: How the Great Rewiring of Childhood is Causing an Epidemic of Mental Illness*, Random House, 2024.

51. Philipp J. Schneider and Marian-Andrei Rizoiu, 'The effectiveness of moderating harmful online content', *Proceedings of the National Academy of Sciences* 120:34 (2023): e2307360120.

52. Jonathan Stempel, Diane Bartz, and Nate Raymond, 'Meta's Instagram linked to depression, anxiety, insomnia in kids – US states' lawsuit', Reuters, 25 October 2023, https://www.reuters.com/legal/dozens-us-states-sue-meta-platforms-harming-mental-health-young-people-2023-10-24/

53. Steven Barclay, Steven Barnett, Martin Moore, and Judith Townend, 'News Deserts in the UK', report by the Joseph Rowntree Trust, Charitable Journalism Project, 21 June 2022, https://camri.ac.uk/blog/articles/news-deserts-in-the-uk/

54. *Bristol Cable*, https://thebristolcable.org

55. Author interview with Eliz Mizon, journalist and Strategy Lead, *Bristol Cable*, October 2024.

56. Edward Said wrote of how the West orientalises the Middle East. Edward W. Said, *Orientalism: Western Conceptions of the Orient*, Penguin, 2016 [1978].
57. Egab, https://www.egab.co
58. Reyya Mozhami, 'Yemeni women become mobile phone technicians to curb sextortion', *El País*, 20 April 2024, https://english.elpais.com/society/2024-04-20/yemeni-women-become-mobile-phone-technicians-to-curb-sextortion.html
59. Author interview with Dina Aboughazala, CEO of Egab, online, September 2024.
60. Author interview with Dina Aboughazala.
61. Report for the World, https://reportfortheworld.org
62. Author interview with Preethi Nallu, journalist, storyteller, and executive director of Report for the World, online, April 2025.
63. Author interview with Preethi Nallu.
64. Maria Ojala, Ashlee Cunsolo, Charles A. Ogunbode, and Jacqueline Middleton, 'Anxiety, worry, and grief in a time of environmental and climate crisis: A narrative review', *Annual Review of Environment and Resources* 46:1 (2021): 35–58; Ashlee Cunsolo, Sherilee L. Harper, Kelton Minor, Katie Hayes, Kimberley G. Williams, and Courtney Howard, 'Ecological grief and anxiety: The start of a healthy response to climate change?', *Lancet Planetary Health* 4:7 (2020): e261–e263.

9 Engaging Society

1. Barack Obama, 'Obama to graduates: Cultivate empathy', speech at Northwestern University, 19 June 2006, https://englishdocs.eu/wp-content/uploads/2022/03/OBAMA-TO-GRADUATES-CULTIVATE-EMPATHY.pdf
2. Barack Obama, *Dreams from My Father*, Canongate Books, 2008.
3. Obama, 'Obama to graduates: Cultivate empathy'.
4. See Priya Parker, *The Art of Gathering*, Penguin, 2018.
5. America in One Room, https://helena.org/projects/america-in-one-room
6. Emily Badger and Kevin Quealy, 'These 526 voters represent all of America: And they spent a weekend together', *New York Times*, 2 October 2019, https://www.nytimes.com/interactive/2019/10/02/upshot/these-526-voters-represent-america.html
7. Emily Badger and Kevin Quealy, 'These Americans tried to listen to one another. A year later here's how they're voting', *New York Times*, 24 October 2020, https://www.nytimes.com/interactive/2020/10/24/upshot/these-526-voters-a-year-later.html?referringSource=articleShare
8. Braver Angels, https://braverangels.org. See also 'Two Americans talk across the political divide', *Financial Times*, 30 May 2022, https://www.ft.com/content/dae86868-7bd2-4280-8e57-287717f0f9dc
9. Braver Angels on Education, https://braverangels.org/braver-education/
10. Braver Angels on Faith, https://braverangels.org/braver-faith/
11. BridgeUSA, https://www.bridgeusa.org/about-us/
12. Author interview with Manu Meel, BridgeUSA, Zoom, 19 November 2021.
13. BridgeUSA, https://bridgeusa.org/how-it-works/
14. More in Common, https://www.moreincommon.com/about-us/our-dna/

15. Pew Research Center, 'Trust and Distrust in America', July 2019, https://www.pewresearch.org/politics/2019/07/22/the-state-of-personal-trust/
16. This word is incredibly difficult to say as in Danish the 'd' sounds like an 'l' to English speakers.
17. Meik Wiking, *The Little Book of Hygge: Danish Secrets to Happy Living*, HarperCollins, 2017. And for some academic reflections on the cultural translation of the concept, see Malene Breunig and Shona Kallestrup, 'Translating hygge: A Danish design myth and its anglophone appropriation', *Journal of Design History* 33 (2020): 158–174.
18. There is also a downside to hygge – as it can mean more isolationism, a closing in of a group for safety.
19. L.L. Elbek and P. Starke, 'Registers of security: The concept of *tryghed* in Danish politics', *Security Dialogue* 55:2 (2024): 216–234, https://doi.org/10.1177/09670106231223121
20. Martin Krasnik, 'Tryghed, lighed og broderskab', Weekendavisen, 27 October 2022, https://www.weekendavisen.dk/2022-43/ideer/tryghed-lighed-og-broderskab
21. 'Trust: A cornerstone of Danish culture', Denmark.dk, 4 April 2023, https://denmark.dk/people-and-culture/trust
22. M. Kate Berardi, Annie M White, Dana Winters, Kaila Thorn, Mark Brennan, and Pat Dolan, 'Rebuilding communities with empathy', *Local Development & Society* 1:1 (2020): 57–67, https://doi.org/10.1080/26883597.2020.1794761
23. Gordon W. Allport, *The Nature of Prejudice*, Addison-Wesley, 1954.
24. Jacob R. Brown, Ryan D. Enos, James Feigenbaum, and Soumyajit Mazumder, 'Childhood cross-ethnic exposure predicts political behavior seven decades later: Evidence from linked administrative data', *Science Advances* 7:24 (2021): eabe8432.
25. Robert Putnam identified this years ago, in relation to US society: Robert D. Putnam, *Bowling Alone: The Collapse and Revival of American Community*, Simon & Schuster, 2000. And although he does not capture the complete picture, or new ways of organising, in many countries these civic spaces have shrunk further.
26. Running for Resilience, https://www.runningforresilience.com
27. Life in Mind, Australian Bureau of Statistics, Causes of Death, 2023, https://lifeinmindaustralia.imgix.net/assets/src/uploads/ABS_COD_2023/LiM_State_and_territory_suicide_data_summary_2023_Final.pdf
28. Sager der Samler, http://sagerdersamler.dk/sager/
29. I visited this organisation and interviewed Paul Natorp, one of the founders, in December 2021.
30. Author interview with Paul Natorp, entrepreneur and founder of Sager der Samler, Aarhus, Denmark, December 2021.
31. Author interview with Michele Alena, innovator, community leader, and author, Zoom, 9 February 2022. His book on civic imagination is currently available only in Italian. He has since become Deputy Mayor of San Lazzaro di Savena, Bologna and the Coordinator of Participatory Processes of the Emilia-Romagna region.
32. Author interview with Michele Alena.

33. Jon Alexander, with Ariane Conrad, *Citizens: Why the Key to Fixing Everything is All of Us*, Canbury Press, 2022.
34. Alexander, with Conrad, *Citizens*.
35. Baratunde Thurston, *How to Citizen* podcast, https://www.howtocitizen.com//
36. Author interview with Jon Alexander, strategist, storyteller, and connector, online, December 2022.
37. Author interview with Sir Nick Harvey.
38. 'Who are the gilets jaunes and what do they want?', *Guardian*, 3 December 2018, https://www.theguardian.com/world/2018/dec/03/who-are-the-gilets-jaunes-and-what-do-they-want
39. Agence France Press, 'Macron's ratings fall further after month of gilets jaunes protests', *Guardian*, 16 December 2018, https://www.theguardian.com/world/2018/dec/16/macrons-ratings-fall-further-after-month-of-gilets-jaunes-protests
40. Letter from M. Emmanuel Macron to the French people (en français), 13 January 2019, https://www.elysee.fr/admin/upload/default/0001/03/0090173c1bc9aaa87f21995ae3b88a55f1fda3d0.pdf
41. Letter from M. Emmanuel Macron to the French people (English translation), 13 January 2019, https://www.elysee.fr/en/emmanuel-macron/2019/01/13/letter-to-the-french-people-from-emmanuel-macron
42. Le Grand Débat National, https://granddebat.fr
43. 'French President Macron's ratings creep up amid town hall meetings', France24, 25 January 2019, https://www.france24.com/en/20190125-france-macron-ratings-national-debate-yellow-vests-opinion-polls-policy-economy-taxes
44. Emily Kasriel, *Deep Listening: Transform Your Relationships with Family, Friends, and Foes*, eBook, Thorsons, 2025.
45. Author interview with Cormac Russell, author and expert on community renewal and development, online, October 2024.
46. Author interview with Cormac Russell,
47. Author interview with Cormac Russell.
48. Author interview with Cormac Russell.
49. Author interview with Cormac Russell.
50. Author interview with Cormac Russell; see also Cormac Russell and John McKnight. *The Connected Community: Discovering the Health, Wealth, and Power of Neighborhoods*, Penguin Australia, 2022.
51. Author interview with Cormac Russell.
52. The Irish Citizens' Assembly Project, http://www.citizenassembly.ie/work/
53. The criteria for inclusion in the database is that they were commissioned by public authorities, lasted at least one full day, involved a diverse engagement and demographic profile of participants, and had to evaluate a range of information and perspectives to reach a shared decision. OECD Deliberative Democracy Database, 2023, https://airtable.com/appP4czQlAU1My2M3/shrX048tmQLl8yzdc/tblrttW98WGpdnX3Y/viwX5ZutDDGdDMEep
54. Mary F. Scudder, 'Beyond empathy: Strategies and ideals of democratic deliberation', *Polity* 48:4 (2016): 524–550.
55. Author interview with Janet Rice.
56. DemocracyNext, https://demnext.org

57. DemocracyNext, https://demnext.org

58. Author interview with Claudia Chwalisz, founder and CEO of DemocracyNext, online, January 2023.

59. Author interview with Laurie Drake, community leader and Builder, online, 30 January 2023.

60. The Global Assembly, 'Report of the 2021 Global Assembly: Giving everyone a seat at the global governance table', November 2022, https://globalassembly. org/resources/downloads/GlobalAssembly2021-FullReport.pdf

61. Executive Summary, Global Assembly Report 2021, p. 7.

62. Author interview with Nicole Curato, academic and expert on participatory and deliberative democracy, online, March 2025.

63. Global Assembly Report 2021.

64. Global Assembly Report 2021, p. 135.

65. Author interview with Nicole Curato.

66. Author interview with Nicole Curato.

67. Author interview with Nicole Curato.

68. Author interview with Nicole Curato.

69. Sonia Phalnikar, 'France's citizen climate assembly: A failed experiment?', *Deutsche Welle*, 16 February 2021, https://www.dw.com/en/frances-citizen-climate-assembly-a-failed-experiment/a-56528234

70. 'End of life citizens' assembly concludes with 92% consensus, delivers recommendations to Macron', DemocracyNext, 4 April 2023, https://www.demnext. org/news/democracy-in-france-end-of-life-citizens-assembly-concludes-with-92-consensus-delivers-recommendations-to-macron

71. Béatrice Jérôme, 'French citizens' convention supports active assistance in dying using different models', *Le Monde*, 2 April 2023, https://www.lemonde.fr/ en/france/article/2023/04/02/french-citizens-convention-supports-active-assistance-in-dying-using-different-models_6021469_7.html

72. Finland's Digital Compass, 2022, https://julkaisut.valtioneuvosto.fi/bitstream/ handle/10024/164472/VN_2022_72.pdf?sequence=1&isAllowed=y

73. Ministry of Justice (1999, latest amendments in 2018), The Constitution of Finland, 731/1999, Ministry of Justice, Helsinki, https://www.finlex.fi/en/laki/ kaannokset/1999/en19990731.pdf. See also 'Finland – Citizen's Initiative to the Parliament', https://www.coe.int/en/web/human-rights-and-biomedicine/-/ finland-citizen-s-initiative-to-the-parliament-2012-

10 The Case for Empathy

1. Allison Pecorin and Meredith Deliso, 'Bernie Sanders blasts Democratic Party following Kamala Harris loss', *ABC News*, 7 November 2024, https://abcnews. go.com/Politics/bernie-sanders-response-presidential-election/story?id= 115582079

2. Stephen Collinson, 'Biden may have handed Trump a big assist with his "garbage" gaffe', CNN, 30 October 2024, https://edition.cnn.com/2024/10/30/ politics/biden-garbage-gaffe-analysis/index.html

3. Katie Reilly, 'Read Hillary Clinton's "basket of deplorables" remarks about Donald Trump supporters', *Time*, 10 September 2016, https://time. com/4486502/hillary-clinton-basket-of-deplorables-transcript/bernie

4. The White House, 'President Trump highlights victories for Americans, sets path for next 100 days', 4 May 2025, https://www.whitehouse.gov/articles/2025/05/president-trump-highlights-victories-for-americans-sets-path-for-next-100-days/

5. Martin Luther King Jr, 'I have a dream' speech, *Talk of the Nation*, NPR, 16 January 2023, https://www.npr.org/2010/01/18/122701268/i-have-a-dream-speech-in-its-entirety

6. A.H. Maslow, 'A theory of human motivation', *Psychological Review* 50:4 (1943): 370–396, https://doi.org/10.1037/h0054346

7. E. Greenwood, T. Lauber, J. van den Hoogen, A. Donmez, R.S. Bain, R. Johnston, et al., 'Mapping safe drinking water use in low- and middle-income countries', *Science* 385:6710 (2024): 784–790, https://www.science.org/doi/10.1126/science.adh9578

8. 'Drinking water: Fact sheet', World Health Organization, 13 September 2023, https://www.who.int/news-room/fact-sheets/detail/drinking-water

9. Hilary Beaumont, 'Flint residents grapple with water crisis a decade later: "If we had the energy left, we'd cry"', *Guardian*, 25 April 2024, https://www.theguardian.com/us-news/2024/apr/25/flint-michigan-water-crisis

10. 'Resources and news on air pollution', World Health Organization, https://www.who.int/health-topics/air-pollution#tab=tab_2

11. Jyoti Madhusoodanan, 'Fixing air pollution could dramatically improve health disparities', *Nature*, 621 (20 September 2023): S30–S34, https://www.nature.com/articles/d41586-023-02614-5

12. K.E. Schertz and M.G. Berman, 'Understanding nature and its cognitive benefits', *Current Directions in Psychological Science* 28:5 (2019): 496–502, https://doi.org/10.1177/0963721419854100

13. This was a key observation from my two years living in Denmark, and is a theme in Helen Russell's great account of the country: Helen Russell, *The Year of Living Danishly: Uncovering the Secrets of the World's Happiest Country*, Icon Books, 2015.

14. Douglas Broom, 'Four-day work week trial in Spain leads to healthier workers, less pollution', World Economic Forum, 25 October 2023, https://www.weforum.org/stories/2023/10/surprising-benefits-four-day-week/

15. K. Pérez, L. Palència, M.J. López, et al., 'Environmental and health effects of the Barcelona superblocks', *BMC Public Health* 25:634 (2025), https://doi.org/10.1186/s12889-025-21835-z

16. Daniel Chandler, *Free and Equal: What Would a Fair Society Look Like?*, Penguin, 2023.

17. OECD, Bhutan's Gross National Happiness, 23 August 2024, https://www.oecd.org/en/publications/well-being-knowledge-exchange-platform-kep_93d45d63-en/bhutan-s-gross-national-happiness-gnh-index_ff75e0a9-en.html

18. J.F. Helliwell, H. Huang, M. Norton, L. Goff, and S. Wang, 'World happiness, trust and social connections in times of crisis', in *World Happiness Report 2023*, Sustainable Development Solutions Network, 2023, chapter 2.

19. J.F. Helliwell, R. Layard, J.D. Sachs, J.-E. De Neve, L.B. Aknin, and S. Wang (eds), *World Happiness Report 2025*, Wellbeing Research Centre, University of Oxford, 2025, https://worldhappiness.report

20. Bregman, *Humankind*.

21. Lamont, *Seeing Others*, p. 8.
22. Raworth, *Doughnut Economics*, p. 44.
23. Raworth, *Doughnut Economics*.
24. There are videos of her speech, but an overview can be found here: 'New Zealand will have a new "well-being budget", says Jacinda Ardern', World Economic Forum, 23 January 2019, https://www.weforum.org/stories/2019/01/new-zealand-s-new-well-being-budget-will-fix-broken-politics-says-jacinda-ardern/
25. New Zealand Treasury, 'The Wellbeing Budget', May 2019, https://www.treasury.govt.nz/sites/default/files/2019-06/b19-wellbeing-budget.pdf
26. Charlotte Graham-McLay, 'New Zealand's next liberal milestone: A budget guided by "well-being"', *New York Times*, 22 May 2019, https://www.nytimes.com/2019/05/22/world/asia/new-zealand-wellbeing-budget.html
27. New Zealand Treasury, 'The Wellbeing Budget'.
28. Te Whatu Ora/Health New Zealand, 'Numbers and rates of suicide deaths in Aotearoa New Zealand', version published 30 October 2024, https://tewhatuora.shinyapps.io/suicide-web-tool/
29. Nicola Sturgeon, 'Why governments should prioritise well-being', TED, July 2019, https://www.ted.com/talks/nicola_sturgeon_why_governments_should_prioritize_well_being/transcript
30. ACT Government, 'Budget 2024–25: Wellbeing Budget Statement', https://www.treasury.act.gov.au/__data/assets/pdf_file/0010/2513674/Budget-2024-25-Wellbeing-Statement.pdf
31. Author interview with Katherine Trebeck, well-being economist, Canberra, April 2025.
32. Author interview with Katherine Trebeck.
33. Júlia Martins Rodrigues, Karen Miner, and Sonja Novkovic, 'Complex cooperative networks case study: Emilia-Romagna – All roads lead to Bologna: Italian cooperative networks', a report of the International Centre for Cooperative Management at Saint Mary's University, 2024, https://www.smu.ca/webfiles/EMILIAROMAGNACASESTUDY.pdf
34. Rodrigues, Miner, and Novkovic, 'Complex cooperative networks case study: Emilia Romagna'.
35. See, for example, this study: Guido Caselli, Michele Costa, and Flavio Delbono, 'What do cooperative firms maximize, if at all? Evidence from Emilia⊠Romagna in the pre⊠Covid decade', *Annals of Public and Cooperative Economics* 93:4 (2022): 821–847.
36. AI Steve was part of the British general election, https://www.ai-steve.co.uk/#
37. Michael Henry Tessler, Michiel A Bakker, Daniel Jarrett, Hannah Sheahan, Martin J. Chadwick, Raphael Koster, et al., 'AI can help humans find common ground in democratic deliberation', *Science* 386:6719 (2024), https://doi.org/10.1126/science.adq2852
38. Tessler et al., 'AI can help humans find common ground in democratic deliberation'.
39. *How to Citizen* podcast, Season 3, episode 6, with Audrey Tang, https://www.howtocitizen.com//
40. E. Glen Weyl, Audrey Tang, and the Plurality Community, *Plurality: The Future of Collaborative Technology and Democracy*, GitHub, 2023.

41. Evan A. Feigenbaum and Jacob Feldgoise, 'Why trust is Taiwan's pivotal competitive advantage', Carnegie Endowment, 7 March 2022, https://carnegieendowment.org/posts/2022/03/why-trust-is-taiwans-pivotal-competitive-advantage?lang=en

42. Weyl et al., *Plurality*, p. 327.

43. Carne y Arena, https://phi.ca/en/carne-y-arena/

44. W. Weber, F. Dingerkus, S.I. Fabrikant, M. Zampa, M. West, and O. Yildirim, 'Virtual reality as a tool for political decision-making? An empirical study on the power of immersive images on voting behavior', *Frontiers in Communication* 7:842186 (2022), https://doi.org/10.3389/fcomm.2022.842186

45. Empathy Action, https://www.empathyaction.org

46. Author interview with Ben Solanky, CEO of Empathy Action, online, June 2025.

47. C. Daniel Batson, Marina P. Polycarpou, Eddie Harmon-Jones, Heidi J. Imhoff, Erin C. Mitchener, Lori L. Bednar, et al., 'Empathy and attitudes: Can feeling for a member of a stigmatized group improve feelings toward the group?', *Journal of Personality and Social Psychology* 72:1 (1997): 105.

48. Peter Singer, *The Expanding Circle: Ethics, Evolution, and Moral Progress*, Princeton University Press, 2011.

49. United Nations Climate Action, 'The Second Youth Advisory Group on Climate Change', 2023, https://www.un.org/en/climatechange/youth-in-action/youth-advisory-group

50. Author interview with Fatou Jeng, youth climate activist, online, 28 November 2024.

51. Author interview with Fatou Jeng.

52. Author interview with John Paul Jose, youth climate activist, online, November 2024.

53. Youths were key actors in protests in 2024, which resulted in a change of government in Bangladesh: see Steven Liller, 'Youth leading the way to good governance in Bangladesh', UNDP blog, 21 October 2024, https://www.undp.org/blog/youth-leading-way-good-governance-bangladesh

54. UNICEF, 'The Youth-led Action Initiative', https://www.unicef.org/youthledaction/initiative; UNDP (United Nations Development Programme), 'Youth Parliament Toolkit', https://www.undp.org/asia-pacific/publications/youth-parliament-toolkit-effective-platforms-future-leaders

55. Transparency International, 'International Anti-Corruption Day 2024: Time to tackle the murky world of climate negotiations', 6 December 2024, https://www.transparency.org/en/news/international-anti-corruption-day-2024-time-to-tackle-the-murky-world-of-climate-negotiations

56. Katrina Brown, W. Neil Adger, Patrick Devine-Wright, John M. Anderies, Stewart Barr, François Bousquet, et al., 'Empathy, place and identity interactions for sustainability', *Global Environmental Change* 56 (2019): 11–17.

57. Jeremy Rifkin, *The Empathic Civilization: The Race to Global Consciousness in a World in Crisis*, Polity, 2010.

58. Rifkin, *The Empathic Civilization*, pp. 593–616.

59. Robin Wall Kimmerer, *Braiding Sweetgrass: Indigenous Wisdom, Scientific Knowledge and the Teachings of Plants*, Milkweed Editions, 2013; and Robin Wall Kimmerer, *The Serviceberry*, Simon & Schuster, 2024.

60. 'Change-maker – the Whanganui River', He Tohu – The New Zealand National Library, https://natlib.govt.nz/he-tohu/learning/social-inquiry-resources/cultural-interaction/cultural-interaction-supporting-activities-and-resources/change-maker-whanganui-river#:~:text=In%20March%202017%2C%20the%20Whanganui,the%20story%20of%20this%20river

61. Sam Delgado, 'Mexico just put animal welfare into its national constitution', *Vox*, 7 December 2024, https://www.vox.com/future-perfect/390144/mexico-constitution-reform-animal-rights

62. Linda Clarkson, Vern Morrissette, and Gabriel Régallet, *Our Responsibility to the Seventh Generation: Indigenous Peoples and Sustainable Development*, International Institute for Sustainable Development, 1992, https://www.iisd.org/system/files/publications/seventh_gen.pdf

63. For the Haudenosaunee Confederacy, see https://www.haudenosauneeconfederacy.com/who-we-are/ and for the Haudenosaunee Great Law of Peace, see https://contensis.uwaterloo.ca/sites/sandboxes/admin/testCopy-1205/lecture-content/module-3/3c.aspx

A Plan for Action

1. Bazalgette, *The Empathy Instinct*.
2. DemocracyNext, https://www.demnext.org
3. David, *Emotional Agility*.
4. Marc Brackett, The RULER Method, https://marcbrackett.com/ruler/
5. Loretta Ross, 'What if we called people in, rather than calling them out?', NPR, 3 December 2021, https://www.npr.org/transcripts/1061209084

Further Reading

Empathy

Abbe, Allison, 'Understanding the adversary: Strategic empathy and perspective taking in national security', *US Army War College Quarterly: Parameters* 53:2 (2023): 19–38.

Batson, C.D., Batson, J.G., Todd, R.M., Brummett, B.H., Shaw, L.L., and Aldeguer, C.M.R., 'Empathy and the collective good: Caring for one of the others in a social dilemma', *Journal of Personality and Social Psychology* 68:4 (1995): 619–631, https://doi.org/10.1037/0022-3514.68.4.619

Batson, C. Daniel, Polycarpou, Marina P., Harmon-Jones, Eddie, Imhoff, Heidi J., Mitchener, Erin C., Bednar, Lori L., et al., 'Empathy and attitudes: Can feeling for a member of a stigmatized group improve feelings toward the group?', *Journal of Personality and Social Psychology* 72:1 (1997): 105–118.

Bazalgette, Peter, *The Empathy Instinct: How to Create a More Civil Society*, Hachette, 2017.

Blight, James G. and Lang, Janet M., *The Fog of War: Lessons from the Life of Robert S. McNamara*, Rowman & Littlefield, 2005.

Bloom, Paul, *Against Empathy: The Case for Rational Compassion*, Random House, 2017.

Breithaupt, Fritz, *The Dark Sides of Empathy*, Cornell University Press, 2019.

Calloway-Thomas, Carolyn (ed.), *Empathy in the Global World: An Intercultural Perspective*, Sage, 2010.

Clohesy, Anthony M., *Politics of Empathy: Ethics, Solidarity, Recognition*, Routledge, 2013.

Decety, J. and Yoder, K.J., 'Empathy and motivation for justice: Cognitive empathy and concern, but not emotional empathy, predict sensitivity to injustice for others', *Social Neuroscience* 11:1 (2016): 1–14, https://doi.org/10.1080/17470919.2015.1029593

De Waal, Frans, *The Age of Empathy: Nature's Lessons for a Kinder Society*, Crown, 2010.

Demetriou, H. and Nicholl, B., 'Empathy is the mother of invention: Emotion and cognition for creativity in the classroom', *Improving Schools* 25:1 (2022): 4–21, https://doi.org/10.1177/1365480221989500

Goldie, Peter and Coplan, Amy (eds), *Empathy: Philosophical and Psychological Perspectives*, Oxford University Press, 2011.

Gutsell, Jennifer N. and Inzlicht, Michael, 'Intergroup differences in the sharing of emotive states: Neural evidence of an empathy gap', *Social Cognitive and Affective Neuroscience* 7:5 (2012): 596–603, https://doi.org/10.1093/scan/nsr035

Hasson, Y., Tamir, M., Brahms, K.S., Cohrs, J.C., and Halperin, E., 'Are liberals and conservatives equally motivated to feel empathy toward others?', *Personality and Social Psychology Bulletin* 44:10 (2018): 1449–1459, https://doi.org/10.1177/0146167218769867

Head, Naomi, 'Costly encounters of the empathic kind: A typology', *International Theory*, 8:1 (2016): 171–199, https://doi.org/10.1017/S1752971915000238

Kohut, Thomas A., *Empathy and the Historical Understanding of the Human Past*, Routledge, 2020.

Krondorfer, Björn, *Unsettling Empathy: Working with Groups in Conflict*, Rowman & Littlefield, 2020.

Krznaric, Roman. *Empathy: A Handbook for Revolution*, Random House, 2014.

Mezzenzana, Francesca and Peluso, Daniela, *Conversations on Empathy: Interdisciplinary Perspectives on Imagination and Radical Othering*, Routledge/Taylor & Francis, 2023.

Morrell, Michael E., *Empathy and Democracy: Feeling, Thinking, and Deliberation*, Penn State Press, 2010.

Nowak, Anita, *Purposeful Empathy: Tapping Our Hidden Superpower for Personal, Organizational, and Social Change*, Broadleaf, 2023.

Pedwell, Carolyn, *Affective Relations: The Transnational Politics of Empathy*, Palgrave Macmillan, 2014.

Pedwell, Carolyn, 'Economies of empathy: Obama, neoliberalism and social justice', in *Affective Relations: Thinking Gender in Transnational Times*, Palgrave Macmillan, 2014, https://doi.org/10.1057/9781137275264_2

Phillips, Kaitlin Ugolik, *The Future of Feeling: Building Empathy in a Tech-Obsessed World*, Little A, 2020.

Porter, Elisabeth, 'Can politics practice compassion?', *Hypatia* 21:4 (2006): 97–123, https://doi.org/10.1111/j.1527-2001.2006.tb01130.x

Rifkin, Jeremy, *The Empathic Civilization: The Race to Global Consciousness in a World in Crisis*, Polity, 2010.

Schumann, Karina, Zaki, Jamil, and Dweck, Carol S., 'Addressing the empathy deficit: Beliefs about the malleability of empathy predict effortful responses when empathy is challenging', *Journal of Personality and Social Psychology* 107:3 (2014): 475–493.

Scudder, Mary F., *Beyond Empathy and Inclusion: The Challenge of Listening in Democratic Deliberation*, Oxford University Press, 2020.

Segal, Elizabeth, *Social Empathy: The Art of Understanding Others*, Columbia University Press, 2018.

Shore, Zachary, *A Sense of the Enemy: The High Stakes History of Reading Your Rival's Mind*, Oxford University Press, 2014.

Smith, David Livingstone, *Less Than Human: Why We Demean, Enslave, and Exterminate Others.*, St Martin's Press, 2011.

Ventura, Michael. *Applied Empathy: The New Language of Leadership*, Touchstone, 2019.

White, Ralph K., 'Empathizing with the rulers of the USSR', *Political Psychology* 4:1 (1983): 121–137.

White, Ralph K., 'Empathizing with Saddam Hussein', *Political Psychology* 12:2 (1991): 291–308.

Yorke, Claire, 'Is empathy a strategic imperative? A review essay', *Journal of Strategic Studies* 46 (2022): 1–21.

Yorke, Claire, 'The significance and limitations of empathy in strategic communications', *Defence Strategic Communications* 2:2 (2017): 137–160.

Zaki, Jamil, *The War for Kindness: Building Empathy in a Fractured World*, Robinson, 2019.

Emotions

Ahmed, Sara, *The Cultural Politics of Emotion*, Routledge, 2013.

Barrett, Lisa Feldman, *How Emotions are Made: The Secret Life of the Brain*, Pan Macmillan, 2017.

Brackett, Marc, The RULER Method, https://marcbrackett.com/ruler/

Christakis, Nicholas A., *Blueprint: The Evolutionary Origins of a Good Society*, Little, Brown, 2019.

Damasio, Antonio R., *Descartes' Error*, Random House, 2006.

David, Susan, *Emotional Agility: Get Unstuck, Embrace Change, and Thrive in Work and Life*, Penguin, 2016.

Elbek, L.L. and Starke, P., 'Registers of security: The concept of *tryghed* in Danish politics', *Security Dialogue* 55:2 (2024): 216–234, https://doi.org/10.1177/0967 0106231223121

Greene, Joshua, *Moral Tribes: Emotion, Reason, and the Gap Between Us and Them*, Atlantic Books, 2014.

Helliwell, J.F., Huang, H., Norton, M., Goff, L., and Wang, S., 'World happiness, trust and social connections in times of crisis', in *World Happiness Report 2023*, Sustainable Development Solutions Network, 2023.

Hicks, Donna, *Dignity: Its Essential Role in Resolving Conflict*, Yale University Press, 2021.

Hutchison, Emma and Bleiker, Roland, 'Emotions in the War on Terror', in Bellamy, Alex J., Bleiker, Roland, Davies, Sara E., and Devetak, Richard (eds), *Security and the War on Terror*, Routledge, 2007, pp. 56–70.

IPSOS Global Trustworthiness Index 2022, https://www.ipsos.com/sites/default/files/ct/news/documents/2022-07/Global%20trustworthiness%202022%20 Report.pdf p.3

Kämmerer, Annette, 'The scientific underpinnings and impacts of shame', *Scientific American*, 9 August 2019, https://www.scientificamerican.com/article/the-scientific-underpinnings-and-impacts-of-shame/#:~:text=Shame%20is%20 the%20uncomfortable%20sensation,behavior%20is%20not%20self%2Devident

Lerner, Adam B., *From the Ashes of History: Collective Trauma and the Making of International Politics*, Oxford University Press, 2022.

FURTHER READING

Nussbaum, Martha C., *Political Emotions*, Harvard University Press, 2013.

Nussbaum, Martha C., *Upheavals of Thought: The Intelligence of Emotions*, Cambridge University Press, 2008.

OECD, *Building Trust to Reinforce Democracy: Main Findings from the 2021 OECD Survey on Drivers of Trust in Public Institutions*, 13 July 2022, https://www.oecd-ilibrary.org/sites/b407f99c-en/index.html?itemId=/content/publication/b407f99c-en

OECD, *Trust in Government*, https://www.oecd.org/en/topics/trust-in-government.html

Ronson, Jon, *So You've Been Publicly Shamed*, Riverhead Books, 2016.

Rosen, Michael, *Dignity: Its History and Meaning*, Harvard University Press, 2012.

Ross, Andrew A.G., *Mixed Emotions: Beyond Fear and Hatred in International Conflict*, University of Chicago Press, 2019.

Smith, Adam, *The Theory of Moral Sentiments*, Penguin, 2010.

Surgeon General Advisory, *Our Epidemic of Loneliness and Isolation*, U.S. Department of Health and Human Services, 2023, https://www.hhs.gov/sites/default/files/surgeon-general-social-connection-advisory.pdf

Taylor, Charles, 'The politics of recognition', in Arthur, John and Shapiro, Amy (eds), *Campus Wars*, Routledge, 1995, pp. 249–263.

Leadership

Brown, Archie, *The Myth of the Strong Leader: Political Leadership in the Modern Age*, Basic Books, 2014.

Burns, James MacGregor, *Leadership*, HarperCollins, 1978.

Burns, James MacGregor, *Transforming Leadership: A New Pursuit of Happiness*, Grove Press, 2003.

Ciulla, Joanne B., 'Being there: Why leaders should not "fiddle" while Rome burns', *Presidential Studies Quarterly* 40:1 (2010): 38–56.

Eze, Chielozona, 'Nelson Mandela and the politics of empathy: Reflections on the moral conditions for conflict resolutions in Africa', *African Conflict and Peacebuilding Review* 2:1 (2012): 122–135.

Goodwin, Doris Kearns, *Leadership in Turbulent Times*, Simon & Schuster, 2019.

Goodwin, Doris Kearns, *Team of Rivals: The Political Genius of Abraham Lincoln*, Simon & Schuster, 2006.

Kissinger, Henry, *Leadership: Six Studies in World Strategy*, Penguin, 2022.

Mandela, Nelson, *Long Walk to Freedom: The Autobiography of Nelson Mandela*, Hachette, 2008.

Merkel, Angela, *Freedom: Memoirs 1954–2021*, St Martin's Press, 2024.

Morrell, Michael E., 'Empathy and democratic education', *Public Affairs Quarterly* 21:4 (2007): 381–403, http://www.jstor.org/stable/40441496

Nixon, Richard, *Leaders: Profiles and Reminiscences of Men who Have Shaped the Modern World*, Simon & Schuster, 2013.

Obama, Barack, *Dreams from My Father: A Story of Race and Inheritance*, Canongate Books, 2009.

Santos, Juan Manuel, *The Battle for Peace: The Long Road to Ending a War with the World's Oldest Guerrilla Army*, University Press of Kansas, 2021.

Shogan, Colleen J., 'The contemporary presidency: The political utility of empathy in presidential leadership', *Presidential Studies Quarterly* 39:4 (2009): 859–877.

Tutu, Desmond, *No Future without Forgiveness*, Penguin, 2012.

Politics and Policy

Almond, Gabriel Abraham and Verba, Sidney, *The Civic Culture: Political Attitudes and Democracy in Five Nations*, Princeton University Press, 2015.

Annala, Mikko, Leppänen, Juha, Mersola, Silva, and Sabel, Charles F., *Humble Government: How to Realize Ambitious Reforms Prudently*, Demos, 14 December 2020, https://demoshelsinki.fi/publication/the-more-complex-and-uncertain-a-policy-issue-is-the-more-useful-it-is-to-approach-it-through-humility/

Ansell, Ben, *Why Politics Fails: The Five Traps of the Modern World and How to Escape Them*, Random House, 2023.

Aristotle, *Nicomachean Ethics*, Penguin Classics, 2004.

Bason, Christian, *Leading Public Design: Discovering Human-Centred Governance*, Bristol University Press, 2017, https://doi.org/10.2307/j.ctt1t88xq5

Brint, Michael E., *A Genealogy of Political Culture*, Routledge, 2019.

Collingwood-Richardson, Kit, 'Empathy and the future of policy making', Medium, 14 May 2018, https://medium.com/foreword/empathy-and-the-future-of-policy-making-7d0bf38abc2d

Gorokhovskaia, Yana, Shahbaz, Adrian, and Slipowitz, Amy, 'Marking 50 years in the struggle for democracy', Freedom House, 2023, https://freedomhouse.org/report/freedom-world/2023/marking-50-years

Harbridge-Yong, Laurel, Volden, Craig, and Wiseman, Alan E., 'The bipartisan path to effective lawmaking', *Journal of Politics* 85:3 (2023): 1048–1063, https://www.journals.uchicago.edu/doi/10.1086/723805

Hardman, Isabel, *Why We Get the Wrong Politicians*, Atlantic Books, 2018.

Leftwich, Adrian, *What is Politics? The Activity and Its Study*, John Wiley & Sons, 2015.

Love Politics, https://www.lovepolitics.net

Lupia, Arthur, *Uninformed: Why People Know So Little About Politics and What We Can Do About It*, Oxford University Press, 2016.

McDonald, Jared, 'Who cares? Explaining perceptions of compassion in candidates for office', *Political Behaviour* 43 (2021): 1371–1394, https://doi.org/10.1007/s11109-020-09592-8

Naím, Moisés, *The End of Power: From Boardrooms to Battlefields and Churches to States: Why Being in Charge Isn't What It Used to Be*, Hachette, 2014.

Norman, Jesse and Ganesh, Janan, *Compassionate Conservatism: What It Is, Why We Need It*, Policy Exchange, 2006, https://www.policyexchange.org.uk/wp-content/uploads/2016/09/compassionate-conservatism-june-06.pdf

Paxman, Jeremy, *The Political Animal*, Penguin UK, 2007.

Project 2025: Presidential Transition Project, https://www.project2025.org

Renstrom, R.A. and Ottati, V.C., ' "I feel your pain": The effect of displaying empathy on political candidate evaluation', *Journal of Social and Political Psychology* 8:2 (2020): 767–787, https://doi.org/10.5964/jspp.v8i2.1292

Robert Bosch Foundation, https://www.bosch-stiftung.de/en/project/programs-political-decision-makers/details

FURTHER READING

Street, John, 'Political culture: From civic culture to mass culture', *British Journal of Political Science* 24:1 (1994): 95–113.

Tilly, Charles, *Stories, Identities, and Political Change*, Rowman & Littlefield, 2002.

Addressing Populism, Divisions, and Conflict

Allport, Gordon W., *The Nature of Prejudice*, Addison-Wesley, 1954.

America in One Room, https://helena.org/projects/america-in-one-room

Anderson, Benedict, *Imagined Communities: Reflections on the Origins and Spread of Nationalism*, Verso, 2016.

Bai, Xuechunzi, Ramos, Miguel R., and Fiske, Susan T., 'As diversity increases, people paradoxically perceive social groups as more similar', *Proceedings of the National Academy of Sciences* 117:23 (2020): 12741–12749.

Boxell, Levi, Gentzkow, Matthew, and Shapiro, Jesse M., 'Cross-country trends in affective polarization', *Review of Economics and Statistics* 106:2 (2022): 557–565, https://doi.org/10.1162/rest_a_01160

Braver Angels, https://braverangels.org

BridgeUSA, https://bridgeusa.org

Coleman, Peter, *The Five Percent: Finding Solutions to Seemingly Impossible Conflicts*, Public Affairs, 2011.

Fukuyama, Francis, *Identity: The Demand for Dignity and the Politics of Resentment*, Farrar, Straus & Giroux, 2018.

Giridharadas, Anand, *The Persuaders: Winning Hearts and Minds in a Divided Age*, Random House, 2022.

Goldsworthy, A., Osborne, L., and Chesterfield, A., *Poles Apart: Why People Turn Against Each Other, and How to Bring Them Together*, Penguin, 2022.

Iyengar, Shanto, Lelkes, Yphtach, Levendusky, Matthew, Malhotra, Neil, and Westwood, Sean J., 'The origins and consequences of affective polarization in the United States', *Annual Review of Political Science* 22 (2019): 129–146.

Martelli, J.-T. and Jaffrelot, C., 'Do populist leaders mimic the language of ordinary citizens? Evidence from India', *Political Psychology* 44 (2023): 1141–1160, https://doi.org/10.1111/pops.12881

More in Common, https://www.moreincommon.org.uk

Morris, Stephen G., 'Empathy and the liberal-conservative political divide in the US', *Journal of Social and Political Psychology* 8:1 (2020): 8–24.

Petersen, Michael Bang, Rasmussen, Magnus Storm, Lindholt, Marie Fly, and Jørgensen, Frederik Juhl, 'Pandemic fatigue and populism: The development of pandemic fatigue during the Covid-19 pandemic and how it fuels political discontent across eight Western democracies', *PsyArXiv*, 2021, psyarxiv.com/y6wm4

Santos, L.A., Voelkel, J.G., Willer, R., and Zaki, J., 'Belief in the utility of cross-partisan empathy reduces partisan animosity and facilitates political persuasion', *Psychological Science* 33:9 (2022): 1557–1573, https://doi.org/10.1177/09567976221098594

Simas, Elizabeth N., Clifford, Scott, and Kirkland, Justin H., 'How empathic concern fuels political polarization', *American Political Science Review* 1141 (2020): 258–269.

Van Bavel, Jay J. and Packer, Dominic J., *The Power of Us: Harnessing Our Shared Identities to Improve Performance, Increase Cooperation, and Promote Social Harmony*, Little, Brown, 2021.

The 'Good' Society

Arendt, Hannah, *The Human Condition*, University of Chicago Press, 1998.

Berardi, M. Kate, White, Annie M., Winters, Dana, Thorn, Kaila, Brennan, Mark, and Dolan, Pat, 'Rebuilding communities with empathy', *Local Development & Society* 1:1 (2020): 57–67, https://doi.org/10.1080/26883597.2020.1794761

Berlant, Lauren, *Cruel Optimism*, Duke University Press, 2011.

Bregman, Rutger, *Humankind: A Hopeful History*, Bloomsbury, 2020.

Chandler, Daniel, *Free and Equal: What Would a Fair Society Look Like?*, Penguin, 2023.

Christakis, Nicholas A., *Blueprint: The Evolutionary Origins of a Good Society*, Little, Brown Spark, 2019.

Clarkson, Linda, Morrissette, Vern, and Régallet, Gabriel, *Our Responsibility to the Seventh Generation: Indigenous Peoples and Sustainable Development*, International Institute for Sustainable Development, 1992, https://www.iisd.org/system/files/publications/seventh_gen.pdf

Lamont, Michèle, *Seeing Others: How Recognition Works – And How It Can Heal a Divided World*, Simon & Schuster, 2023.

Maslow, A.H., 'A theory of human motivation', *Psychological Review* 50:4 (1943): 370–396, https://doi.org/10.1037/h0054346

Mills, C. Wright, *The Sociological Imagination*, Oxford University Press, 2000.

New Zealand Treasury, 'The Wellbeing Budget', May 2019, https://www.treasury.govt.nz/sites/default/files/2019-06/b19-wellbeing-budget.pdf

Putnam, Robert D., *Bowling Alone: The Collapse and Revival of American Community*, Simon & Schuster, 2000.

Raworth, Kate, *Doughnut Economics: Seven Ways to Think Like a 21st-Century Economist*, Penguin, 2018.

Shafik, Minouche, *What We Owe Each Other: A New Social Contract for a Better Society*, Princeton University Press, 2021.

Singer, Peter, *The Expanding Circle: Ethics, Evolution, and Moral Progress*, Princeton University Press, 2011.

The Media

Bruneau, E., Casas, A., Hameiri, B., et al., 'Exposure to a media intervention helps promote support for peace in Colombia', *Nature Human Behaviour* 6 (2022): 847–857, https://doi.org/10.1038/s41562-022-01330-w

Cohen, Bernard Cecil, *Press and Foreign Policy*, Princeton University Press, 2015.

Egab, https://www.egab.co

Gowing, Nik, *'Skyful of Lies' and Black Swans*, Reuters Institute for the Study of Journalism, Department of Politics and International Relations, University of Oxford, 2009.

Hacked Off: Campaign for a Free and Accountable Press, https://hackinginquiry.org

Iyengar, Shanto and Kinder, Donald R., *News That Matters: Television and American Opinion*, University of Chicago Press, 2010.

Martingano, A.J., Konrath, S., Zarins, S., and Okaomee, A.A., 'Empathy, narcissism, alexithymia, and social media use', *Psychology of Popular Media* 11:4 (2022): 413–422, https://doi.org/10.1037/ppm0000419

Report for the World, https://reportfortheworld.org
Schudson, Michael, *Why Democracies Need an Unlovable Press*, Polity, 2008.
Sontag, Susan, *Regarding the Pain of Others*, Penguin, 2004.

Gender

Alderman, Naomi, *The Power*, Hachette UK, 2017.
Criado Perez, Caroline, *Invisible Women*, Random House, 2019.
Geppert, Dominik, 'Emotions and gender in Margaret Thatcher and Helmut Kohl's Cold War', *Diplomacy & Statecraft* 32:4 (2021): 766–788, https://doi.org/10.1080/09592296.2021.1996719
Gillard, Julia and Okonjo-Iweala, Ngozi, *Women and Leadership: Real Lives, Real Lessons*, MIT Press, 2022.
He for She, https://www.heforshe.org/en
National Democratic Institute, 'Men, power and politics', https://www.ndi.org/men-power-and-politics
Reeves, Richard V., *Of Boys and Men: Why the Modern Male is Struggling, Why It Matters, and What to Do About It*, Brookings Institution Press, 2022.
Traister, Rebecca, *Good and Mad: The Revolutionary Power of Women's Anger*, Simon & Schuster, 2018.
World Economic Forum, *Gender Gap Report 2022*, 13 July 2022, https://www.weforum.org/reports/global-gender-gap-report-2022/in-full

Participatory Democracy and Citizens' Assemblies

DemocracyNext, https://demnext.org
Global Assembly Report 2021, https://globalassembly.org/report
The National Dialogues Module: Finland, https://kansallisetdialogit.fi/en/about-national-dialogues/the-national-dialogues-model/

Technology

Han, Byung-Chul, *In the Swarm: Digital Prospects*, MIT Press, 2017.
Haidt, Jonathan, *The Anxious Generation: How the Great Rewiring of Childhood is Causing an Epidemic of Mental Illness*, Random House, 2024.
Phillips, Kaitlin Ugolik, *The Future of Feeling: Building Empathy in a Tech-Obsessed World*, Little A, 2020.
Schneider, Philipp J. and Rizoiu, Marian-Andrei, 'The effectiveness of moderating harmful online content', *Proceedings of the National Academy of Sciences* 120:34 (2023): e2307360120.
Tessler, Michael Henry, Bakker, Michiel A., Jarrett, Daniel, Sheahan, Hannah, Chadwick, Martin J., Koster, Raphael, et al., 'AI can help humans find common ground in democratic deliberation', *Science* 386 (2024): eadq2852, https://doi.org/10.1126/science.adq2852
Turkle, Sherry, *Alone Together: Why We Expect More from Technology and Less from Each Other*, Hachette, 2017.
Turkle, Sherry, *Reclaiming Conversation: The Power of Talk in a Digital Age*, Penguin, 2016.

Weber, W., Dingerkus, F., Fabrikant, S.I., Zampa, M., West, M., and Yildirim, O., 'Virtual reality as a tool for political decision-making? An empirical study on the power of immersive images on voting behavior', *Frontiers in Communication* 77:842186 (2022), https://doi.org/10.3389/fcomm.2022.842186

Weyl, E. Glen, Tang, Audrey, and the Plurality Community, *Plurality: The Future of Collaborative Technology and Democracy*, GitHub, 2023.

To Be a More Active Citizen

Alexander, Jon, with Conrad, Ariane, *Citizens: Why the Key to Fixing Everything is All of Us*, Canbury Press, 2022.

BridgeUSA, https://www.bridgeusa.org/about-us/

DemocracyNext, https://www.demnext.org

Empathy Action, https://www.empathyaction.org

Empathy Studios, https://www.empathystudios.com

Human Library, https://humanlibrary.org

Kasriel, Emily, *Deep Listening: Transform Your Relationships with Family, Friends, and Foes*, eBook, Thorson's, 2025.

Parker, Priya, *The Art of Gathering*, Riverhead Books, 2018.

Russell, Cormac, *Rekindling Democracy: A Professional's Guide to Working in Citizen Space*, Wipf and Stock Publishers, 2020.

Sager der Samler, http://sagerdersamler.dk/sager/

School of International Futures, https://soif.org.uk

Thurston, Baratunde, *How to Citizen* podcast, https://www.howtocitizen.com//

UNDP (United Nations Development Programme), 'Youth Parliament Toolkit', https://www.undp.org/asia-pacific/publications/youth-parliament-toolkit-effective-platforms-future-leaders

United Nations Climate Action, 'The Second Youth Advisory Group on Climate Change', 2023, https://www.un.org/en/climatechange/youth-in-action/youth-advisory-group

Index

Page spans in bold signify particularly in-depth explorations of the entry.

INDEX

INDEX

INDEX

INDEX

INDEX

World Health Organization (WHO)
232
worthiness 2, 88, 238

xenophobia 109
Xi Jinping (People's Republic of China)
158

Yemen 177, 182, 197
Yoon Suk Yeol (Republic of Korea)
159
YouGov 33, 80

young people 93–4, 145–9, 204–5,
246–9, 262
Yousafzai, Malala 48
youth
activism 93–4, 246–9
engagement 246–9
parliaments 249

Zelenskyy, Volodymyr (Ukraine) 7,
46–7, 229
zero-sum (approaches to power) 20, 29,
94